POPULATION STUDIES FROM PARISH REGISTERS

A Selection of Readings from
Local Population Studies

**Edited by Michael Drake
at the Open University**

The cover illustration is from W. H. Pyne **Encyclopaedia of illustration of
the Arts, Agriculture, Manufacture, &c of Great Britain,** 1845

i

First published 1982

by **Local Population Studies**

Tawney House, Matlock, Derbyshire, DE4 3BT

Printed and bound in Great Britain by G. C. Brittain & Sons Ltd., Church Street, Ripley, Derby.

Selection and editorial material

ISBN 0 9503951 7 X

CONTENTS

Introduction: Local Population Studies

Interest in historical demography has grown enormously over the last twenty-five years. It is an interest that is to be found in primary and secondary schools, in colleges and universities. Many an evening class now spends its time poring over parish registers or census enumerators' returns. Historical demography has also brought together professional and amateur scholars; witness **Local Population Studies,** [1] a journal whose editors, contributors and readers are drawn from both. This co-operation, which had its first notable expression in the work sponsored by the **Cambridge Group for the History of Population and Social Structure,** [2] has more recently found a further vehicle in the **Local Population Studies Society** [3] which through its day and weekend schools and its book club fosters the work of individuals and groups throughout the country.

The fruits of some of that work appear in the pages which follow. Not all of it by any means. Indeed the selection of articles has been restricted to work carried out on parish registers. There is thus nothing on household size or structure. Nor are pre-census listings or the census enumerators' returns of the second half of the nineteenth century, which have revealed much about our demographic past, to be found in this volume. There is nothing in this volume on literacy, the study of which has depended very heavily on parish registers. The technique of family reconstitution, by which the various entries in the registers are linked together, rather in the manner used by genealogists, is also not represented in these pages. In some ways this is a pity as the technique allows one to calculate sophisticated measures of population change. The procedures of family reconstitution are, however, extremely arduous and as only a few registers are sufficiently comprehensive to allow a successful family reconstitution to be carried out, the exercise is not one to be embarked upon lightly. Indeed at the time of writing only sixteen such studies are known to have been carried out in England, though France, which pioneered the technique, can show rather more.

Readers of this volume should not then make the mistake of believing it to be fully representative of the work that has appeared in the pages of **Local Population Studies.** Nor should they run away with the idea that **Local Population Studies** is but a journal of the traditional type publishing articles and nothing more. Rather it is a forum for all interested in local population studies and like a true forum it exhibits a variety of activities. Much correspondence is published: there is a Miscellany column, a section for Notes and Queries, as well as brief notices of recent publications and work in progress. Through its editorials **Local Population Studies** attempts to alert its readers and the powers-that-be (the Registrar General, the Lord Chancellor, the Anglican authorities etc) to matters of current concern. Above all the journal tries to encourage individuals and groups to try their hand at the study of the population history of the localities in which they live and work.

The twenty one articles reprinted have been organised into five sections: marriage, baptism, burial, migration and area studies. The first three of these section titles have been chosen quite deliberately in order to emphasise a major feature of parish register demography, namely its reliance upon a source that is ecclesiastical rather than demographic in origin. It is a feature which is referred to again and again by the contributors to this volume, especially those whose work appears in the section headed **baptism.** The section on **migration** is a good illustration of the way in which parish registers can be made to reveal information on events that are only indirectly related to the purpose for which the registers were kept. Finally, the section headed **area studies** reminds us that demographic experience, lying, as it does at the core of local social and economic history can provide an excellent organizational framework.

Characteristic of all the articles is their practical, down-to-earth quality. Indeed much of their strength lies in the care with which their authors describe the strengths and weaknesses of their sources; the possibilities and pitfalls of their techniques; the tentative nature of their findings and their proposals for alternative avenues of enquiry. It is hoped that readers of this volume will wish to carry out their own studies, perhaps replicating some of the work presented here or taking up some of the suggestions made. Newcomers to the field should — to avoid disappointment and to maintain the high academic standard of studies in historical demography — take to heart the warning made time and again in these pages: **make sure of your sources.** Whatever parish register you choose to work on, it must be put through a rigorous testing procedure. One way of going about this takes up the remainder of this introduction.

The history of parish registers

It was Thomas Cromwell, one of Henry VIII's chief advisers who first ordered the Anglican clergy to keep registers of baptisms, marriages and burials. The year was 1538. Some parishes have an unbroken series of registers from that date to this, but they are few in number. In fact only 500 or so date back to the 1530s and many of them fail to maintain an unbroken record of registration. Many more registers began with the accession of Elizabeth I in 1558 and from that date on the coverage rapidly extends across the country; though, as we shall see, few registers are complete. Anglican parishes remain, however, the single most important source for historical demographers for 300 years, up until 1837 when civil registration began in England. After that date their value diminishes as more and more births, marriages and deaths come to be registered by the State rather than the Church. [4]

The content of parish registers

Before we determine how we can use the information in these registers we must first attempt to discover what was registered and, equally important, what was not. The various steps in this process have been set out in the form of an algorithm. [5] How seriously one takes this must remain a matter for individual decision. I have, perhaps, been rather too cautious especially where at various points I have suggested a particular line of enquiry be reconsidered. For the historical record is a rich one and there are many instances where my 'playing safe' advice would lead to the neglect of potentially valuable data. However, only the student on the spot can decide in such instances.

Figure 1: Analysing a parish register

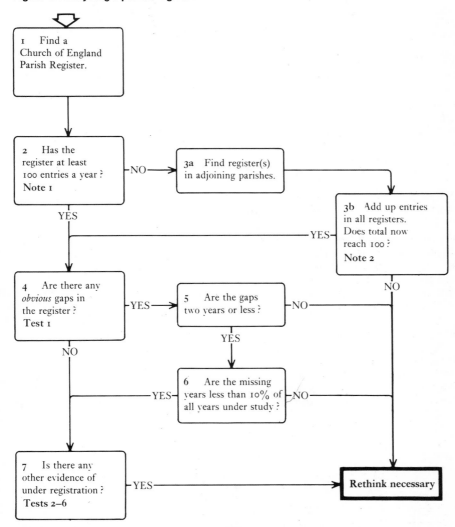

Note: I would like to acknowledge the help of Michael Macdonald-Ross, Institute of Educational Technology at the Open University, in the design of this algorithm.

You will note that at various stages in the algorithm, the words **Note** or **Test** appear. These indicate various steps in the exercise. I will go through each of these as they occur.

Find a Church of England Parish Register.

In the period 1538-1837 the Church of England maintained between 10,000 and 11,000 parishes. The number varied from time to time as new ones were created or existing ones amalgamated. The obvious place to look for registers covering this period would appear to be the parish church, since the responsibility for them has rested with the parish clergy and their church wardens. Very recently, however, a major change has occurred. Largely because the Church of England has become aware of the parlous state of the repositories available for storing its registers, more and more have been put into the care of local record offices and libraries. If then you wish to work on original registers you should enquire at your local library, county or municipal record office. Should you want a broader view of what is available you should consult the invaluable guides published by **Local Population Studies.** The first of these — **Original parish registers in record offices and libraries** — appeared in 1974. Since then there have been four supplements. These were necessary partly because of the number of new deposits by the Church and partly because local government changes have led to many registers being transferred. [6]

It is not necessary to work with original registers. Because of their interest to genealogists, many have been transcribed. These transcripts are to be found, in manuscript form, in local libraries, county record offices or the headquarters of archaeological and historial societies. Such transcripts are usually easier to work with than the original registers, though one should always bear in mind the possibility of their being copied inaccurately. Easier still, of course, are printed transcripts. Again there are many of these and usually they are to be found in the same places as the manuscript transcripts. [7]

Note 1 Has the register a mean of at least 100 entries per year?

A register with 100 entries annually might, in the period 1538-1837, be expected to show a burial total of from twenty five to sixty five, a baptism total in the same range, and a marriage total varying from five to ten. The figure of 100 is an arbitrary one. Much of value can undoubtedly be learned from registers with fewer entries. Just how much is indicated by some of the chapters in this present volume.

There are, however, two main reasons for being chary about using registers whose entries total much below this figure. One is that if the mean number of entries per year falls below 100, it is often difficult to tell whether below average entries in any particular year are due to under-registration, or to actual changes in the number of events (baptisms, marriages and burials) being recorded. Deciding on this particular question is always difficult, as we shall see in a moment. Wherever possible, then, it seems sensible not to make the task more problematical. The second reason for sticking with the figure of 100 is that often, even if only for relatively short periods of time, a register will specify such matters as whether a baptism is of an illegitimate child or not, what the presumed cause of death is, or what the ages of brides and bridegrooms are. Much can be made of such information *if* there is enough of it. This is more likely to be the case when the mean number of entries is at least 100, than when it is under this figure.

Note 2 Are there registers in adjoining parishes which together with the original register produce 100 entries a year?

One may have little choice here, since the registers of at least some adjoining parishes are likely to have either disappeared or be inaccessible. If a choice is possible, however, it is worth taking some care over it. The reason for this goes back to what one always hopes the registers will provide, namely a reliable picture of population change in the *area.* One reason why they may not is because inhabitants of the parish they supposedly serve may have some of their vital events recorded in neighbouring parishes. For instance, a man may marry a woman in an adjoining parish. The ceremony may well take place there even though the couple return to settle in the husband's parish. Again, it may be that families living further from their own parish church than from that of a neighbouring parish would baptize their children and bury their dead in the latter, for the sake of convenience. Sometimes too the main settlement of a parish may be close to one of its boundaries. When this occurs there is invariably some seepage across it, so far as the recording of baptisms, marriages and burials is concerned. It is worthwhile, therefore, getting a map showing the parish boundaries (e.g. the Tithe Map; or the early nineteenth century Greenwood series of maps; or even a modern one-inch ordnance survey), and then trying to find out where the main settlements appear to be and how far they are from the parish church. [8]Some indication of this may be obtained from a contemporary map, or the various listings described in Appendix 1 and on the cassette tape by Barry Stapleton, **Sources for the demographic study of a local community.** [9]

Another clue may be obtained from entries in what we will call the 'home' register, ie the first one looked at. Dr. Roger Schofield of the Cambridge Group for the History of Population and Social Structure has noted that a good indication of the likely direction of extra-parochial registration can be gained from the addresses of brides and bridegrooms given in the marriage register. This, incidentally, is very useful information in its own right. Schofield has discovered that if, say, ten per cent of brides and bridegrooms married in Parish A, come from Parish B and, say, three per cent from Parish C, then it is likely that roughly three times as many baptisms and three times as many burials of Parish A inhabitants will be registered in Parish B than in Parish C. Of course, there will be a certain compensation mechanism working here. That is to say, a higher proportion of Parish B than of Parish C inhabitants will appear in the registers of Parish A. It is, therefore, worth taking a quick one-in-five sample of the entries in the marriage register to get some indication of the *de facto* registration area as opposed to the *de jure* one. One should then choose one's area of study accordingly.

Test 1 Are there any obvious gaps in the register(s)?

There are few parish registers which do not exhibit quite clear breaks in the registration process. Their extent varies from register to register and from period to period. How one deals with such gaps will vary, depending upon their duration (both absolutely, and relatively to the total number of years under study) as well as upon the aims of the enquiry. Some years ago I went through a number of the registers of the parishes marked on Figure 2 from their first entries up to 1700. Since they revealed much of the promise, and the problems, of the registers you are likely to deal with, should you choose to do a project in historical demography, I think it is worthwhile looking at each of them here. The years listed below are those in which no baptisms, marriages or burials were registered. In passing you might note the wide variety of places where I obtained this information.

Batley (1559)[10] Source: Sheard, M. (1894) **Records of Batley** pp 37-38.

Sheard had done my work for me, having gone through the register and totalled the baptisms, marriages and burials for each year. According to him the gaps were as follows:

Baptisms:	1596-1604; 1606-7; 1610-13; 1642; 1645; 1647.
Marriages:	1568-9; 1596-1604; 1606-7; 1610-13; 1626-27; 1631-33; 1636; 1639-42; 1645-52.
Burials:	1595-1604; 1606-7; 1609-13; 1631-33; 1636; 1641-42; 1645-52.

Bingley (1578) Source: Yorkshire Parish Register Society, Vol ix.
Marriages:	1654-62; 1687-1700.
Burials:	1654-62; 1687-1700.

Birstall (1559) Source: Manuscript registers in Birstall Parish Church.
Marriages:	1578-80; 1654-5.
Burials	1578-80

Bradford (1596) Source: Manuscript transcript in Bradford Free Library. Burials and marriages from a transcript printed in the **Bradford Antiquarian Journal** Vols 5 and 6.
Baptisms:	1596-7.

Calverley (1574) Source: From a transcript made by Samuel Margerison and published privately by him in three volumes.
Baptisms:	1644-8.
Marriages:	1574-96; 1608-26; 1645-8.
Burials:	1574-96; 1608-26; 1645-8.

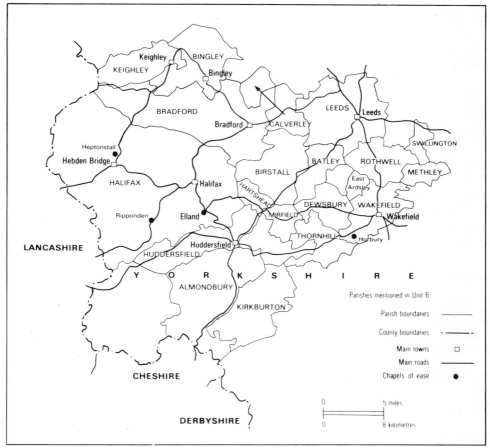

Figure 2: Location of Yorkshire parishes discussed.

Dewsbury (1538) Source: For the years 1538-1653 a transcript made and published privately in 1898 by S. J. Chadwick; for the years 1653-98, a manuscript transcript in the library of the Yorkshire Archaeological Society at Leeds; for the years 1699-1700, the Bishop's Transcripts[11] in the Borthwick Institute, York.

Baptisms:	1554-5; 1559; 1568-70; 1581.
Marriages:	1554-5; 1559; 1568-70; 1581.
Burials:	1554-5; 1559; 1568-70; 1581.

East Ardsley (1598) Source: Manuscript transcript in the library of the Yorkshire Archaeological Society at Leeds.

Baptisms:	1599-1601; 1605-6; 1612-62.
Marriages:	1599-1601; 1605-6; 1612-53; 1657; 1659; 1676; 1680; 1682-3; 1687.
Burials:	1599-1601; 1605-6; 1612-53; 1674; 1677; 1686.

Elland (1559) Source: For the years 1559-1639 transcribed and published privately by J. W. Clay; for the years 1640-1700 by H. Ormerod.
Baptisms: 1642; 1648.
Marriages: 1642; 1648.
Burials: 1642; 1648.

Halifax (1540) Source: For the years 1540-93, a published transcript by the **Yorkshire Parish Register Society** Vol xxxvii; for the years 1594-1700 the manuscript Register in Halifax Parish Church.
Marriages: 1647-52.

Hartshead (1612) Source: **Yorkshire Parish Register Society** Vol xvii.
Marriages: 1622; 1654.

Heptonstall (1594) Source: For the years 1594-1652, **Yorkshire Parish Register Society** Vol lxxviii; for the years 1653-1700 from the manuscript Register in Heptonstall Parish Church.
Baptisms: 1594-98; 1686-7
Marriages: 1686
Burials: 1686-7

Horbury (1598) Source: **Yorkshire Parish Register Society** Vol iii
Baptisms: 1613
Burials: 1613
Marriages: 1613

Huddersfield (1606) Source: Microfilm of the register in Huddersfield Public Library.
No gaps

Keighley (1562) Source: **Yorkshire Parish Register Society** Vol lxxvii
Marriages: 1587; 1651; 1653.

Kirkburton (1540) Source: Transcribed and published privately by F. A. Collins (1887)
Baptisms: 1555; 1576; 1611-12; 1614; 1617-26; 1630-2; 1636
Marriages: 1555; 1576; 1611-12; 1614; 1617-26; 1630-2; 1636
Burials: 1555; 1576; 1611-12; 1614; 1617-26; 1630-2; 1636

Leeds (1572) Source: **Thoresby Society Publications** Vols i, iii, vii, x, xiii
Marriages: 1592

Methley (1559) Source: **Thoresby Society Publications** Vol xii
Marriages: 1677

Mirfield (1560) Source: **Yorkshire Parish Register Society** Vol lxiv.
No gaps

Table 1. Mean annual number of entries in twenty-two Yorkshire parish registers in the years 1600-4[1] and 1690-4.

Parish	1600-4	1690-4
Batley	49 (1590-94)	49
Bingley	98	131 (1680-4)
Birstall	159	208
Bradford	321	297
Calverley	83	137
Dewsbury	91	143
East Ardsley	17 (1607-11)	18
Elland[2]	293 (1604-08)	297
Halifax	891	601
Hartshead	30 (1612-6)	38
Heptonstall[2]	178	250
Horbury[2]	27	51
Huddersfield	214 (1606-10)	279
Keighley	71	80
Kirkburton	148	185
Leeds	573	686
Methley	39	46
Mirfield	40	65
Rothwell	114	115 (1685-9)
Swillington	16	18
Thornhill	71	81
Wakefield	325 (1613-17)	297

[1] Except where gaps in the register have caused other years to be chosen.

[2] Elland and Heptonstall were chapels within Halifax parish; Horbury, a chapel within Wakefield parish.

Table 2. Number of one-year gaps in twenty-two Yorkshire parish registers, by decade, 1540-1699.

Parish	1540-9	1550-9	1560-9	1570-9	1580-9	1590-9	1600-9	1610-9	1620-9	1630-9	1640-9	1650-9	1660-9	1670-9	1680-9	1690-9	1540-1699
Batley			2	0	0	4	7	4	2	5	8	2	0	0	0	0	34
Bingley					0	0	0	0	0	0	0	6	3	0	3	10	22
Birstall			0	2	0	0	0	0	0	0	0	2	0	0	0	0	4
Bradford					2	0	0	0	0	0	0	0	0	0	0	0	2
Calverley			6	10	7	2	10	9	0	4	0	0	0	0	0	0	48
Dewsbury	0	3	2	1	1	0	0	0	0	0	0	0	0	0	0	0	7
East Ardsley						1	4	8	10	10	10	10	3	3	5	0	64
Elland			0	0	0	0	0	0	0	0	2	0	0	0	0	0	2
Halifax	0	0	0	0	0	0	0	0	0	0	3	3	0	0	0	0	6
Hartshead								0	1	0	0	1	0	0	0	0	2
Heptonstall					5	0	0	0	0	0	0	0	0	0	2	0	7
Horbury							0	1	0	0	0	0	0	0	0	0	1
Huddersfield							0	0	0	0	0	0	0	0	0	0	0
Keighley			0	0	1	0	0	0	0	0	0	2	0	0	0	0	3
Kirkburton	0	1	0	1	0	0	0	6	7	4	0	0	0	0	0	0	19
Leeds				0	0	1	0	0	0	0	0	0	0	0	0	0	1
Methley				0	0	0	0	0	0	0	0	0	0	1	0	0	1
Mirfield				0	0	0	0	0	0	0	0	0	0	0	0	0	0
Rothwell	3	4	4	2	0	2	0	1	0	0	0	0	0	0	0	0	16
Swillington	3	3	3	1	1	7	0	1	2	1	7	6	2	0	1	1	39
Thornhill				3	5	0	0	0	0	0	0	0	0	0	0	0	8
Wakefield							0	0	0	0	1	0	0	0	0	0	1
All Parishes	6	11	11	13	16	34	13	31	31	20	34	33	8	4	11	11	287

Rothwell (1540) Source: For the years 1540-1689, **Yorkshire Parish Register Society** Vol xxvii, for the years 1691-1700, the **Bishop's Transcripts in the Borthwick Institute, York.**

Baptisms: 1545-6; 1551; 1556-8; 1563-4; 1568-9; 1676; 1690; 1693.
Marriages: 1545-6; 1556-8; 1563-4; 1568-9; 1676; 1690; 1693.
Burials: 1540; 1545-6; 1551; 1556-8; 1563-4; 1568-9; 1676-7; 1690; 1693.

Swillington (1543) Source: **Yorkshire Parish Register Society** Vol cxv.

Baptisms: 1545; 1554-5; 1560-1; 1643-50; 1657-61; 1663.
Marriages: 1544-6; 1553-5; 1560-1; 1575; 1582; 1591-7; 1614; 1629; 1633; 1644-51; 1656-61; 1663; 1669; 1688; 1691.
Burials: 1545-6; 1553-5; 1560; 1562; 1628; 1641; 1644-51; 1657-61; 1663.

Thornhill (1580) Source: **Yorkshire Parish Register Society** Vol xxx.
Baptisms: 1584-6; 1594.
Burials: 1584-6; 1594.
Marriages: 1584-6; 1594.

Wakefield (1613) Source: Manuscript transcript in the library of the Yorkshire Archaeological Society Leeds.
Marriages: 1654

At this point you may care to pause and ask yourself the following question. Suppose you have the information given above on twenty-two Yorkshire registers. Which would you work on? For the purpose of this exercise imagine that you lived in the area; that you had decided not to spend more than 150 hours working on your project and that none of the registers had any special characteristics which the others did not have, e.g. information on the age at marriage, cause of death, birth as well as baptism dates. I suggest you bear in mind the first six steps of the algorithm when tackling the question. For my answer see the end of this introduction.

Having decided upon a register, or registers, we now take step 7 of the algorithm. 'Is there any other evidence of under-registration?' To answer this question we need to run a series of further tests.

Test 2 The first involves going through each register[12] month by month, to see whether there are any suspiciously large gaps. Here again one draws benefit from taking a register with a 100 entries a year, since a gap of, say, a couple of months between entries of any sort would suggest under-registration. If on the other hand, a register had only fifty entries a year, such a gap would quite possibly be due to lack of business, as it were. One should make a preliminary assessment of the situation by taking a sample of years (every fifth would do) and going through them carefully. After that, assuming the gaps are in not more than about ten per cent of the years and do not extend over more than two to three months, one should total each month's events (baptisms, marriages and burials) and enter them on a schedule. The ones shown in Appendix 2, which were designed by the

Cambridge Group for the History of Population and Social Structure, provide a convenient model.

After the preliminary test of the register's fullness noted above, one might decide to abandon it. This could well have happened with what appeared to be a leading contender for my favours after steps one to six of the algorithm, namely Kirkburton. Here are my notes on the breaks, *within* years, in that register.

1545   Register ends on 30 March and begins again on 30 October.
1546   Register ends 10 October
1547   Register begins 9 December 1547
1556   Register begins in August
1558   Register ends 2 November
1566   Burials begin 7 July
1577   Begins 19 April
1581   Ends 8 October
1587   Gap in register 29 July to 7 October
1639   Begins 1 July
1645   No entries in November, February or March
1648   No entries in July: the word 'nothinge' appears instead
1650   Register mutilated: possibly ten entries missing.

One can overcome these deficiencies to some degree by *interpolation*.[13] If a gap appears in a particular month or months one can take the mean number of entries in the same month or months in the five years on either side, and take this to be as near an approximation as one can get to what should have been registered. There is, of course, the possibility that one is going to be wildly out, but if it is a matter of a month or two, the effect on the series as a whole is likely to be slight. If one comes across an entry like that noted for July 1648, interpolation is best avoided. I take it that a 'nothinge' entered in the registers indicated, quite literally, that in that month there were no baptisms, marriages or burials.

The tests we have suggested so far can be carried out on any register. One has merely to locate the gaps and then decide whether they are too many for the purposes of the study one has in mind, and, if not, how to accommodate them. With the other tests I am about to turn to, the problems are not so easily dealt with, for in each case carrying out the test depends upon having ancillary information which, in the case of the parish or parishes of your choice, may simply not exist.

Test 3 The first of this category of tests concerns those who were responsible both for entering items in the register and for preserving the registers themselves. By law the vicar was responsible, though in practice the dual task seems to have fallen on curates and church wardens in many cases. Sometimes a register will, in a marginal note, give an indication of what was happening. Here are some examples from the registers (and the transcripts) listed in Tables 1 and 2 above.

Going through the Methley register I counted the following number of entries:

Year	Baptisms	Marriages	Burials
1683	23	6	31
1684	23	9	30
1685	29	8	36
1686	27	4	12
1687	14	3	16
1688	20	4	17

I also noted a marginal comment in the register to the effect that a new parson was inducted in 1687. Could it be that the quite sharp fall in baptisms in that year (and of burials the previous one) was due to the changeover?

Another example of the same thing comes from the Kirkburton register:

Year	Baptisms	Marriages	Burials
1560	70	15	36
1561	48	15	48
1562	44	19	19
1563	25	3	15
1564	55	10	33

Henry Suthel, the vicar of Kirkburton for fifty-six years, from 1506-1562, died in the latter year. The new vicar also held the living of Methley, fourteen miles away as the crow flies. It is possible that here again the changeover had an adverse effect on the registration. Incidentally, in 1564, a fresh handwriting appears in the register, suggesting the end of an interim period.

From 1653 to 1660 registration was taken out of the hands of the clergy and secular registrars were appointed. In very many parishes this led to a deterioration in the system. Of the twenty-two registers in Table 2 as many as nine had at least a one-year gap in the 1650's. In other parishes both the quality of the registration and the coverage increased during this period. In Halifax for example, from 1654 to 58, the age of bride and bridegroom was given in 564 marriages and from 1654 to 57, the occupation of the bridegroom in 422 out of 465 marriages. Frances Anne Collins, the transcriber of the Kirkburton register, noted that from 1653 to 1660 the sworn registrar was one William Hepworth. He was a layman, and she writes (pp 39—40), 'his fitness for the office as a writer is shown by his handwriting, which is clear and better than any in the Kirkburton registers'.

Sometimes the break in registration caused by the changeover in the registrar, whether civil or secular, was quite dramatic. For instance, on a flyleaf in the Heptonstall register for 1631 is written: 'In the year 1631 the Minister of this place, his wife, his son and the Parish Clerk all died of the plague in August, October and November'. Not surprisingly the totals of baptisms and marriages for that year show a pronounced fall, compared to neighbouring years (see below).

The marriage register in 1631 ends on 8 June; the baptism register on 14 August. The burial register does not show a gap and the number entered in it is higher than for the surrounding years. Nevertheless, here too there may have been under-registration. For the register contains the comment 'theise parsones dead of the plague

Year	Baptisms	Marriages	Burials
1628	110	20	77
1629	81	28	71
1630	109	26	82
1631	48	8	117
1632	114	20	62

or supposed to dy of that disease within the parish of Heptonstall to the number of one hundreth and seven'. Some are said to have been 'buried at home'. Others, one can but surmise, may have been buried in like manner, and not registered.

Whilst the efficiency of any registration system depends a good deal on the conscientiousness of the registrars, one must also keep an eye on the extent of the public's demand for registration. Occasionally one comes upon comments in the registers indicating a very great concern on the part of certain people that they should appear in the register. Note this cry of anguish from the Keighley register:

February 1590 Richard Holmes the son of Francis Holmes was baptised the second day of this moneth above written and was left unsett (ie in the register) to my greatt harts greife but I pray to the O Lord that I be found in the booke of lyfe....

It is, of course, impossible to generalize from individual statements like that. One can, however, narrow the range of probabilities a little more when it comes to considering the number of those who, for one reason or another, were reluctant to use the services of the Church of England, and to the extent that they avoided using them were not registered.

Test 4   The assumption has been made, up to this point, that the register, or registers, under analysis cover the *entire* population of the area, at least officially for the *entire* period under examination. That is to say, it is assumed that the parish (or parishes as the case may be) is not reduced in size and that new registers for different parts of the parish are not begun. In fact, with rising populations, many parishes did set up *chapels*[14] and 'daughter' churches within their boundaries and, sometimes, baptisms, marriages and burials performed at them, were recorded in separate registers. Local enquiries of the vicar, library or County Record Office will normally elicit whether or not such registers were kept, from what date and whether or not they are accessible. An alternative starting point is the return printed in Vol III of the *1831 Population Census*. This says what registers were believed to be in existence at that time and gives the date they began.

Naturally the commencement of new registers within existing parishes varies widely from one part of the country to another. In the area covered by the registers listed in Table 2, the number of new registers was probably atypically high. This was because in the sixteenth and seventeenth centuries, not to speak of the eighteenth, the woollen cloth industry was growing rapidly and there are a number of indications that the population was increasing accordingly.

It should be emphasized that the dates given on pp x-xiv and Table 3 refer to the earliest registers known to have existed in 1831. Others could have been started and lost. What is more, it is known that sometimes items were recorded on separate slips of paper, to be entered in the register at some later date. If a parish were between registers, as it were, it is not unlikely that some of these slips were lost before they could be copied into the new register. When one notes what happened to some registers, the misplacing of such odd slips of paper appears even more likely.[15] The smaller the parish or chapel, the fewer the number of entries, the greater the likelihood that such *ad hoc* methods operated. Larger parishes probably had a more efficient system.

Table 3. Dates and places at which registers of baptisms, marriages and burials were begun in parts of twenty-two Yorkshire Parishes up to 1700.

Parish	Chapelry	Register commenced
Birstall	Tong	1550
Bradford	Haworth	1645
	Thornton	1678
	Wibsey	1640
Halifax	Elland	1559
	Heptonstall	1593
	Cross Stone	1640
	Todmorden	1666
	Ripponden	1684
	Rastrick	1614
	Luddenden	1653
	Illingworth	1695
	Sowerby	1643
Huddersfield	Slaithwaite	1684
	Armley	1665
Leeds	Hunslet	1686
Wakefield	Horbury	1598

Source: Population Census 1831.

The setting up of a chapel subordinate to a church did not necessarily mean that a new register was begun. Nor did it follow that such a chapel performed the full range of rites. For example, we learn from a note at the end of the Kirkburton register entries for 1695 that it was 'a true register of all baptisms, marriages and burials in the church and churchyard of Kirkburton and of *all the baptisms* in the chappell of Holmfirth'. A similar note appeared after the 1699 entries, though note the cautionary last phrase 'a true register of all baptisms, burials and marriages which have happened in the parish church of Kirkburton and in the chappell of Holmfirth *to our best knowledge'.*

One of the problems with chapels within a parish is knowing when they were, and when they were not, supposed to record whatever rites they performed, in the register of the mother church. So far as Halifax is concerned, it seems that the chapelries of Heptonstall and Elland probably kept registers from 1538-58 and 1538-93 respectively, but that the earlier volumes have not survived. Certainly there is no reduction in the number of entries in the Halifax register at the time the registers we do have for Heptonstall and Elland begin.[16] In the course of the seventeenth century other chapels were opened in Halifax and appear to have started their own registers (Table 3). Sometimes these were under Elland or Heptonstall and, it appears, should have reported whatever baptisms, etc. they performed to these more ancient chapels. Thus, to take an example, the chapel of Cross Stone has a register (or had in 1831) dating from 1640. Yet in the Heptonstall register for 1685, at the end of the marriage entries, there is a letter from the then Archbishop of York complaining that the 'curate or chappell wardens of the Chappell of Crosstone have carelessly and wilfully omitted and neglected to make returns of the names of all such persons as have been married baptised and buried as aforesaid to the curate and clerke of Heptonstall'. He goes on to point out that this has meant a financial loss to the said curate and clerke as the appropriate fees had not been handed over. It does not follow, of course, that because baptisms etc. should have been returned to Heptonstall, they were supposed to be registered there too. We have already noted that Cross Stone was under Heptonstall, not Halifax: a chapel under the jurisdiction, apparently, of another chapel. This same phenomenon was repeated in the case of the chapel of Ripponden which reported to Elland. From 1687, the Elland register lists the entries from Ripponden separately, suggesting that in this case there was a dual registration for Ripponden appears to have its own register from 1684 (Table 3).

Leeds Parish Church registration seems to have suffered increasingly, from the 1630s to the end of the seventeenth century, as a result of baptisms and marriages being conducted in chapels and private houses, within the parish, which were not reported to the mother church. Notes complaining of this appear again and again. This one made at the end of the December 1631 entries is typical: 'There were divers children for these 2 or 3 yeares last past, baptized at severall chappels within this Parish whose names were not made knowne to us and therefore if you find them not registered according to your expectation, blame not the clarke'.

The importance of these developments for the use of parish registers for demographic analysis is twofold. First it may lead one to believe erroneously that a decline in the number of entries in a parish register, or even a slowing down in the rate of increase of such entries, is due to demographic changes, when it may be a product of jurisdictional ones. And, of course, it may happen that the entries of baptisms, marriages and burials are affected differentially. It seems more likely, for instance, that baptisms failed to be recorded, even though burials were, as the chapelries were perhaps less likely to have their own burial grounds, at least in the sixteenth and seventeenth centuries. Certainly I would imagine that some part at least of the excess of burials over baptisms recorded in the Leeds parish register, in all but four of the years, 1660-99 was due to this cause. The second important matter raised by this kind of situation concerns the decision whether or not to analyse a particular register. Unfortunately, it seems likely that the bigger parishes, whose registers we believe offer the best opportunities for demographic analysis for reasons given above, are likely to be just the ones which may suffer from the development of chapels, either nonconformist or Anglican, with the consequent problems we have outlined. One should, therefore, make as sure as possible, in any *particular case,* that one understands what is happening at any *particular* time to the church-chapel relationship so far as the registration of baptisms, marriages or burials is concerned.

Test 5 One of the reasons commonly put forward for under-registration is that nonconformists boycotted Church of England services, particularly baptisms. After checking on the arrival and departure dates of incumbents (Test 3), it is then worthwhile finding out what one can of the existence of nonconformity in a parish. Much attention has been paid to this, so far as the late eighteenth and early nineteenth century registers are concerned.[17] It is possible that earlier registers were similarly affected. For instance, in the registers listed above (Table 2), notes to the effect that nonconformists are not entering their baptisms, marriages and burials in the Church of England parish registers are particularly noticeable after 1660. One example is a note in the Leeds baptism register for 31 January 1694 which reads, 'Mr Mawde, curat at the Old Church hath baptised children in many men's houses, and neither he nor ye parents acquainted me therewith, and likewise many children att the severall Chappels, and as for Presbiterian children not one ingrost because of their obstinacy and let others blame them that are blameworthy'.

One way in which some indication of the extent of nonconformity (though not necessarily of its impact on the registration system) can be obtained from the various ecclesiastical censuses is noted in Appendix 1. For example, Archbishop Herring's Visitation Return made in 1743 includes the parishes listed in Table 2. For each of them it gives the number of families in the parish and the number of dissenting families (indicating of what kind) and also states whether the Church of England incumbent resided in the parish or not. This latter fact is useful for Test 3. It appears that about ten per cent of families in the area were dissenters though this varied from nil in Thornhill ('not a dissenter of any sort in ye parish' according to the

Table 4.   Batley: religious allegiance of 819 families.

In the Township of:	The Church	Presbyterians	Anabaptists	Independents	Quakers	Moravians	Methodists
Batley	224		1	51	1		49
Morley	72	129	4	1		6	47
Gildersome	65	6	60		11	1	23
Churwell	40	22	1		1		4
	401	157	66	52	13	7	123

Source: **Archbishop Drummond's Visitation Returns (1764) Cited in Stephens W.B. (1971) Sources for the Study of Population and their Uses. University of Leeds Institute of Education** p 31.

informant) to over a third (233 out of 622) in Batley. At first sight the difference is somewhat startling, especially as Batley was only about four miles from Thornhill. Two additional pieces of information suggest that at least so far as the Batley figures are concerned they may not be wholly spurious. One is the report that the Church of England chapel in Morley (a township in Batley Parish) was taken over by the Presbyterians during the Civil War and never restored to the Church. Secondly, Archbishop Drummond's Visitation Return of 1764 for the parish of Batley is broadly in line with the 1743 return. Furthermore, the detail of the return suggests it was more than mere guesswork on the part of the informant. The figures given in Table 4 were in answer to the questions: 'What number of families have you in your Parish? Of these, how many are dissenters? And of what sort of denomination are they?'

It does not, of course, follow that because a parish has dissenting families within it, registration of baptisms, marriages and burials by the Church of England was bound to be less than complete. The dissenters could, after all, accept these rites. Sometimes one gets direct evidence of this. For example in the same Visitation Return (Archbishop Drummond's) as provided the information for Table 4 above, the vicar of Birstall remarked 'I cannot tell how many (families) are Dissenters as most of them bring their children to be christened at the Church'. Despite this, however, one must I think assume that, other things being equal, the registers of parishes with a high proportion of dissenters would be less complete than those with a small one. It is, therefore, worthwhile searching local histories (particularly the volumes of the **Victoria County History**) for evidence of dissenting congregations.[18]

Quite apart from what might be termed ideological objections to accepting the rites of the Church of England, it is not unlikely that others objected to their cost and inconvenience. Take the latter point first. If the parish church was five or six miles from one's home, taking a child for baptism could be quite a chore, no matter how committed one was to the Church of England.[19] If the weather was bad, the roads difficult, or if one was sick (a not unlikely occurence just after childbirth) such a journey might well be delayed. Sometimes, too, baptisms were delayed because a custom had developed of conducting them at special times of the year, partly so that one could get one's friends together perhaps, and make it more than just a private event[20]. Whatever the cause of the delay, the effect was to increase the number of children who were buried *unbaptized* and, therefore unentered in the baptism registers. The registers were almost invariably registers of baptisms, not of births though there are exceptions to this.

Test 6 We now need to search the register for any indication that baptisms were delayed. Chambers *op cit* p19 suggests that 'in the marsh parishes of Lincolnshire, for instance, where the Church may be five miles from the outlying farms, the failure to baptize the newly born was a much more common occurence than to bury the dead, and this was reflected in the greater frequency with which burials outstripped baptisms.[21] Here again the quasi-censuses listed in Appendix 1 may give some indication of the settlement pattern within a parish. Sometimes a burial register will indicate whether a child is unbaptized or not. One example of this occurs in the Rothwell register. There, from 1634 to 8, some 135 out of 1, 231 entries in the burial register bear the description 'infants not baptized'. This figure represents eleven per cent of the total registered burials and ten per cent of the total registered baptisms. Among the registers listed in Table 2 one notes the appearance of *unbaptized* children in the burial registers of Kirkburton, Dewsbury, Horbury, Thornhill, Mirfield and Keighley as well as Rothwell. The Kirkburton registers are interesting in this connection because they contain large numbers of burials of so-called 'chrisom' children. One use of the term is to describe a child buried within one month of birth. The actual form of the entry in the Kirkburton register, however, suggests it referred to unbaptized children. For example, the following two entries appeared next to each other:

January 28 1698:   'Martha daughter of William Littlewood of
                          Scholes, a twin, baptized the 28th day'.

January 28 1698:   'A crisom child of the said William Lockwood,
                          another twin, buried the 28th day'.

An earlier entry reads:
January 1655-6:   'A crisom child of George Killner borne and
                          buried the first day'.

If no direct indication is given of the baptismal status of persons appearing in the burial register, one should keep an eye open for entries like this: 'An infant of John Smith buried...' This could mean unbaptized, though it may mean no more than that the person keeping the register had forgotten the name.

It was once supposed that the burial registers reflected the number of deaths more accurately than baptismal registers did the number of births, because disposing of a body was more difficult than neglecting to baptize one. Work by Krause,[22] however, has shown that many private burial grounds existed, particularly in London and the industrialized areas of the North. He does not, however, think that such burial grounds existed on any scale elsewhere, or outside London, much before the last decade of the eighteenth century.

The presumed reason for the existence of these private burial grounds is that burial there was cheaper than in those belonging to the Church of England. Charges varied even within the Church, and this it was alleged led to some people choosing the cheaper ones, even if it meant going out of their home parish. Information on these matters for the early nineteenth century can be obtained from two large folio manuscript volumes in the British Museum (BM Additional Manuscripts 6896 and 6897). One illustration will serve to show the type of entry. It refers to a part of Birstall, one of the parishes in Table 2. The date is 1811.

> *Cleckheaton:* The number of baptisms and burials is unknown. The marriages take place at Birstall, Cleckheaton being a Chapel of Ease under it. At one small village, Lower Wike, in this Chapelry there is a chapel and seminary of United Bretheren. Upper Wike is situated near Wibsey Chapel, which is in the parish of Bradford, to which chapel more, I suppose, are taken than to Cleckheaton Chapel; the dues are also less, our dues being double, one half is passed to Birstall, namely 10d each baptism and 10d each burial.

When considering the inadequacy of registration, one should bear in mind that it affected different events (ie baptisms, marriages and burials) at different times.

The impact of dissent on baptismal registers was probably increasing in the mid-seventeenth century and in the second half of the eighteenth century. The impact of the inconvenience of travelling long distances to the church, which in rural parishes may have been constant, probably increased in industrializing areas in the north and in Wales during the late eighteenth and early nineteenth centuries. This was because new areas were settled (eg around coal mines and water-driven spinning mills) which were not well served by churches built in earlier centuries for different settlement patterns, though some industrialists, like Richard Arkwright, built churches or chapels. So, too, the patronage of private (ie non Church of England) burial grounds was probably greater in industrializing areas in the late eighteenth and early nineteenth centuries than at any other time.

So far as marriages are concerned one can distinguish between the period prior to 1753 and the period after it. In that year Hardwicke's Marriage Act was passed. This made it virtually impossible to contract a valid marriage unless it were carried out in a church according to an Anglican ceremony. The act was passed because it was alleged that many clandestine marriages were being contracted which, of course, was a source both of scandal and of loss of income for the Church. There is certainly evidence of these marriages. Sometimes it is explicit and can be quantified. Wrigley, for instance,[23] has analysed a marriage register from the Gloucestershire parish of Tetbury. Here the vicar differentiated between marriages which were contracted in his parish according to the proper form and those that were not. Of the sixty-eight marriages occuring there in the years 1696-9, some thirty-three were irregular and of these, fourteen were termed 'clandestine'. Though it is rare to find such evidence, a test can be carried out which would indicate under-registration of marriages. This consists of totalling the number of baptisms, in, say, a five-year period and dividing it by the number of marriages in the same period, or in the immediately preceding five years. The ratio should be about 1:4 or 1:5. If it is as high as 1:7 or 1:8 (in other words if there are eight baptisms for every marriage) then the registration of marriages is almost certain to be defective. The reason for this is that to have a ratio as high as 1:7 or 1:8 would mean a rate of marital fertility far higher than any other evidence we have would suggest was possible.

Answer to the question posed on p xiv

The first factor to be considered is that of time — your time that is! As this is limited to 150 hours, one should avoid the really large registers such as Halifax and Leeds and possibly even Elland, Bradford and Wakefield. One should also avoid registers or transcripts which are to be found in different places. For instance, the Dewsbury register has many admirable qualities. It is a convenient size; it covers the maximum time span (1538-1700); it has few gaps. Assuming, however, that it is accessible only in the places I found it, then a lot of time will have to be spent on travelling: ie Dewsbury Public Library for the published transcript covering the years 1538-1653; the Library of the Yorkshire Archaeological Society at Leeds for the manuscript transcript of the years 1653-98 and (if you must be a perfectionist!) a trip to the Borthwick Institute at York for the Bishop's Transcripts covering the yeras 1699-1700. Remember too that many Record Offices are closed on Saturdays!

It may be, of course, that the amount of time spent travelling is less than the time it takes to decipher the sixteenth and seventeenth-century script of an original register, even though it is on your very doorstep. In an ideal world one would obviously work with the original register, since one can never be sure that a transcriber has done his job well. But in doing research one is not operating in an ideal world. There is a *Concorde* quality about it; the time needed shows a strong tendency to escalate. For this reason I would hesitate about the Birstall register and the Heptonstall one.

Having narrowed the field a bit, we move on to the second step of the algorithm. 'Has the register at least 100 entries a year?' Quite a number of the registers do not: Batley, East Ardsley, Hartshead, Horbury, Keighley, Methley, Mirfield, Swillington and Thornhill. If you turn to pp x-xiv you will notice that a number of these have years with no entries of either baptisms, marriages and burials, or indeed of all three. In some cases, of course, this was probably because the population served by the register was so small, that it produced no one to be baptized, married or buried. But with a small register there is no way of telling the difference between under registration and nothing to the registered.

One could adopt the strategy suggested in step three of the algorithm to overcome the problem of small registers. Here the neighbouring parishes of Horbury and Thornhill would make a good pair. Together they cover the whole of the seventeenth century with only a one year gap. Another possible combination would be Mirfield and Hartshead. Each of these four parishes appears in a published transcript which reduces the workload, though there is still the problem of bring together the entries from two registers.

Of the remaining registers I would not use Calverley because of the large number of missing years (see Table 2), nor Bingley for the same reason. My argument is weaker in the latter case. We are left with Rothwell, Huddersfield and Kirkburton. Of these I would exclude Rothwell because, although it covers almost the entire period (1540-1700) it has a number of gaps in the early decades and may entail a trip to York to complete the last ten years. I say *may* because the original register could be accessible in the parish church. Huddersfield has an unbroken register, but it begins only in 1606; has rather a large number of entries and is on microfilm. Seventeenth-century script is often difficult to read; on microfilm, deciphering it can be a very trying task indeed, but for an aggregative study, this is not a major problem.

We are left with Kirkburton. It is in the form of a printed transcript; it covers almost the whole period (1540-1700); it is not too big. Unfortunately it has some rather large gaps in the 1620s. In fact, if we pick Kirkburton we must do so after consciously rejecting the advice in steps 5 and 6 of the algorithm; that is after going through the 'rethink necessary' step. Perhaps we should go back again over the ones we have rejected because of their size. Perhaps Elland would be a better bet. In the last analysis we must make a value judgement. All our algorithm can do it to help us ask the right questions.

As noted earlier many original parish registers are no longer to be found in the church vestries, having been deposited in record offices and libraries. Of the registers mentioned above those for Batley, Birstall, Elland, Halifax, Hartshead, Heptonstall, Horbury, Huddersfield, Mirfield, Thornhill, and Wakefield are now in the West Yorkshire and Diocese of Wakefield Record Office at Wakefield. Those for Swillington are to be found in the Archives Department of Leeds City Libraries. To conclude, three points need to be emphasized. First, in using parish registers one is dealing with fallible data. Second, although deficiencies in the registers can occur at any time, the really serious problems of under-registreation are not likely to appear before the 1780s. After that the registers deteriorated rapidly. Indeed Wrigley and Schofield (**op cit,** p 77) conclude that 'at its worst point in the 1810s only sixty-eight per cent of all live born children received Anglican baptism. Anglican burial registers contain the names of barely two thirds of those who died during the decade'. By contrast in the last decade of the seventeeth century, ninety-seven per cent of all deaths are believed to have been recorded in Anglican burial registers and ninety-two per cent of all births in Anglican baptism registers. Third, one should not despair of using Anglican parish registers. Much interesting demographic work has been done on them, as the following chapters will show, and much remains to be done.

Notes

1. For subscription details write to: Local Population Studies, Tawney House, Matlock, Derbyshire, DE4 3BT.

2. The Cambridge Group for the History of Population and Social Structure was founded in 1964. Its directors — Dr. Peter Laslett, Dr. R. S. Schofield and Professor E. A. Wrigley — maintained from the start close links with local demographic historians, over four hundred of whom have made returns to them of monthly totals of baptisms, marriages and burials from registers in their areas. These returns form the main source of data for the Group's most important publication to date: E. A. Wrigley and R. S. Schofield, **The population history of England 1541-1871: a reconstruction,** Edward Arnold, 1981. The returns are to be made available shortly in a series of regional collections under the general title **Parish Register Data** to be published by **Local Population Studies** with financial assistance from the Ernest Cook Trust. The Group, which is now financed by the Social Science Research Council continues to collaborate with local historians and welcomes contact with amateurs and professionals alike. It's address is: 27, Trumpington Street, Cambridge, CB2 1QA.

3. For membership details write to: Mrs. Helen Forde, The Honorary Secretary, The Local Population Studies Society, 10 Holmbush Road, London SW15 3LE.

4. For more details on the history of English parish registers see Roger Finlay, **Parish registers: an introduction,** Historical Geography Series No. 7, Geo. Abstracts, 1981, pp 6-10.

5. An algorithm is 'a means of reaching a decision by considering only those factors which are relevant to that particular decision' (D. M. Wheatley and A. W. Unwin, **The Algorithm Writer's Guide,** Longmans, 1972, p 10) An algorithm is often presented in the form of a flow chart. Followed step by step, the desired result will be achieved.

6. The guides are: **Original parish registers in record offices and libraries,** 1974: **The first supplement to original parish registers,** 1976: **The second supplement to original parish registers,** 1978: **The third supplement to original parish registers,** 1980: **The fourth supplement to original parish registers,** 1982. These titles are available from booksellers or Local Population Studies, Tawney House, Matlock, Derbyshire DE4 3BT.

7. **According to Lynda Ovenall the principal series of printed parish register transcripts are as follows:**
   Bedfordshire Parish Registers (Bedford 1931—   )
   Cumberland and Westmorland Antiquarian and Archaeological Society: Parish Register Section (1912—   )
   Devon and Cornwall Record Society (Exeter 1910—   )
   Durham and Northumberland Parish Register Society (Sunderland, Newcastle-upon-Tyne 1898-1926)
   Dwelly's Parish Records (Herne Bay 1913-26)
   Harleian Society — Registers of London Parishes (London 1877—   )
   Lancashire Parish Register Society (Rochdale, etc. 1898—   )
   Lincoln Record Society — Parish Register Section (Lincoln 1914-25)
   Parish Register Society (London 1896—   )
   Shropshire Parish Register Society (1900—   )
   Staffordshire Parish Register Society (London 1902—   )
   Sussex Record Society (Lewes 1911—   )
   Worcestershire Parish Register Society (Worcester 1913—   )
   Yorkshire Parish Register Society (Leeds 1899—   )
   Phillimore Series of Marriage Registers (ed. successively by Phillmore, W. P. W., Blagg, T. M. and Ridge, C. H. from 1897) for the counties of Berkshire, Buckingham, Cambridge, Chester, Cornwall, Cumberland, Derby, Dorset, Essex, Gloucester, Hampshire, Hertford, Huntingdon, Kent, Leicester, Lincoln, Middlesex, Norfolk, Northampton, Nottingham, Oxford, Somerset, Suffolk, Warwick, Wiltshire, Worcester and Yorkshire. In addition there are a number of registers printed privately, often by their transcribers. See also D. J. Steel, **National Index of Parish Registers,** 1968, Society of Genealogists.

8. For an excellent guide to maps as sources of historial data see J. B. Harley, **The historian's guide to ordnance survey maps,** National Council of Social Service, 1964 and J. B. Harley, **Maps for the local historian: a guide to British sources,** National Council of Social Service, 1972.

9. This audio tape in cassette form is available from Open University Educational Enterprises, 12 Cofferidge Close, Stony Stratford, Milton Keynes, MK11 1BY.

10. The date in brackets marks the beginning of the earliest surviving register I found.

11. The Bishop's Transcripts are copies of the registers made by the incumbent and sent by him to the Bishop's Registry at stated intervals. The procedure appears to have started towards the end of the sixteenth century. Although there are often discrepancies between them and the registers and they sometimes lack the detail of the parish version of the registers there are instances in which they are more detailed and frequently they are useful for filling gaps. The late Professor J. D. Chambers used them extensively in his 1957 study 'The Vale of Trent 1670-1800: a regional study of economic change', **The Economic History Review, Supplement 3,** Economic History Society, and spoke highly of them. They are usually to be found in diocesan or county record offices.

12. The Church year in this period ran from 25 March to 24 March. Since most registers used it, there was an obvious advantage in my doing so (though in many recent studies the old calendar has been converted to the new). It was also useful because it meant that all the winter months were included in the one year. Burial peaks in any one winter could thus be more easily spotted than if they were split between two calendar years. The Church year has also been used by the late Professor J. D. Chambers (1957) and so to make comparison with his work easier, the same periodization has been followed here. Since then other writers have used the 'harvest year' (Michaelmas — 29 September — to Michaelmas, or 1 August to 31 July) as well as the calendar year. Recently Wrigley and Schofield (**op cit,** p 156) have used a year running from 1 July to 30 June in connection with their work on demographic crises.

13. Interpolation is most dangerous in the case of burials, because a gap can easily occur at the time of a major crisis. It is particularly difficult to keep corrections standard, and ideally one would like two versions of each return, one before and one after correction.

14. See Institute of Heraldic and Genealogical Studies (nd) for maps showing the chapelries, as well as the parishes, specifying for all the date that the registers commence. See also J. D. Steel, **National Index of Parish Registers,** 1968, Society of Genealogists.

15. For example, in 1859 Mr. John Nowell transcribed the register of Almondbury parish (near Huddersfield). After completing this task he noted:
Thus ends the labour of reading and collecting these ancient papers, all tattered, torn and mutilated, covered with dirt, defaced and the writing in many cases illegible and the contractions in the words made after a manner now quite obsolete . . . the mutilated register comprised in all about 350 detached leaves which evidently once formed a book — the back gone and the margins frittered away by time, bad usage or both. They have been tramped under feet of careless churchwardens, soiled perhaps in their imputed orgies and certainly the succession of vicars have 'set no store upon them' or their mutilation at least would have been prevented.
Referring to another register Nowell writes: 'I have seen the entries of half a century cut away in shreds from a register by a parish clerk to subserve the purposes of his trade as a tailor'. (The transcript by Nowell is in the church chest of Almondbury Parish Church.) The editors of the Richmond (Surrey) parish register transcript write in a similar vein:
. . . Richmond's parish clerks were for about two centuries members of one family who passed on, each generation to the next, a tradition of slovenliness and neglect in regard to their duty. The 'method' adopted during the whole of the period mentioned would seem to have been to compile the Register at intervals of many years from such memoranda and notes as had not been mislaid or lost. There are some hundreds of instances in which Christian names or surnames or both are unrecorded . . .
C. Challenor and J. Smith (eds) **The parish register of Richmond Surrey,** Surrey Parish Register Society, Vol 1.

16. The transcriber of the Halifax register notes in his introduction that 'the ancient parish of Halifax covered a wide area, and in addition to the mother church was served by two chapels, Elland and Heptonstall, which though dependent upon it had certain parochial rights and **registers of their own** (my emphasis 7). He then lists separately the townships under the mother church and the two chapels and remarks that other pre-Reformation chapels were gradually resuscitated but if weddings, baptisms and burials took place there the events were noted in the Halifax register until 1812. E. W. Crossley (ed) **The Parish Register of Halifax 1540-1593,** 1910, Yorkshire Parish Register Society, Vol xxxvii.

17. For the most recent — and most comprehensive — discussion of this see E. A. Wrigley

and R. S. Schofield, **The population of England 1541-1871: a reconstruction,** 1981, Edward Arnold.

18. In addition to the **Victoria County History,** a useful source is the list of non-parochial registers published by the Registrar General in 1859. Also in Dr. Williams' Library in London, there are two lists of dissenting congregations at two dates — 1751 and 1772. The only realistic test of whether dissenters were registered is to take one of the early registers or a list of those deposited by the church for absenting themselves from communion, and see exactly how many of them turn up in the Anglican registers. See V. T. J. Arkell 'An enquiry into the frequency of the parochial registration of Catholics in a seventeenth century Warwickshire parish', **Local Population Studies,** 9, pp 23-32 for an example of such a study.

19. See below, pp 77-78

20. See below, pp 44-45

21. Also see below, pp 77-78

22. J. T. Krause 'Changes in English fertility and mortality 1781-1850' **Economic History Review,** second series 1958 vol 11, 1, pp 52-70.

23. E. A. Wrigley 'Clandestine marriage in Tetbury in the late seventeenth century', **Local Population Studies,** 10, pp 15-21.

References for Appendix 1

BAKER, D (1973) **The Inhabitants of Cardington in 1782,** Bedfordshire Historical Record Society, Vol 52.

BOND, David (1973) 'The Compton Census-Peterborough', **Local Population Studies** No 10, pp 71-4.

BOYNTON, L. (1967) **The Elizabethan Militia 1558-1638,** David and Co, London.

CHALKIN, C. W. (1960) 'The Compton Census of 1676: the dioceses of Canterbury and Rochester', **Kent Records** Vol 17, pp 173-83.

CORNWALL, J. E. (1959) 'An Elizabethan Census', **The Records of Buckinghamshire** Vol 16, No 4, pp 258-73.

CORNWALL, J. E. (1970) 'English population in the early sixteenth century', **Economic History Review,** Second series, Vol 23, No 1, pp 32-44.

DALRYMPLE, Sir John (1771-3) **Memoirs of Great Britain and Ireland. From the Dissolution of the Last Parliament of Charles II until the Sea-Battle of La Hague,** Edinburgh and London, Vol 11, pp 11-15.

FORSTER, G. C. C. (1961) 'York in the seventeenth century' in Tillot, P. M. (ed) **The Victoria History of the County of York: The City of York,** Oxford University Press, pp 162-5.

FORSTER, G. C. C. (1967) in Beresford, M. W. and Jones, G. R. J., **Leeds and its Region,** British Association, Leeds.

FORSTER, G. C. C. (1969) 'Hull in the sixteenth and seventeenth century' in Allison, K. J. (ed) **Victoria History of the Counties of England: York East Riding,** Vol 1, Oxford University Press.

GLASS, D. V. (1965) 'Two papers on Gregory King' in Glass, D. V. and Eversley, D. E. C. (eds) **Population in History,** Edward Arnold, London.

GUILFORD, E. L. (1924) 'Nottinghamshire in 1676', **Transactions of the Thoroton Society,** Vol 28, pp 106-13.

HOLLINGSWORTH, T. H. (1969) **Historical Demography,** Cambridge University Press.

JAMES, F. G. (1952) 'The population of the diocese of Carlisle in 1676', **Transactions of the Cumberland and Westmorland Antiquarian Society,** Vol 52, pp 137-41.

KYD, J. G. (1952) **Scottish Population Statistics including Webster's Analysis of Population 1755,** Scottish History Series, Third series, Vol 43, Edinburgh.

LASLETT, Peter (1969) 'The household in England over three centuries', **Population Studies** Vol 23, pp 199-223.

Appendix 1   Sources for estimating total population size

Population Count	Content	Areal coverage	Location of documents
1547 Chantry Certificates	'Housling' people. Assumed to be totals of communicants.	English parishes	Public Record Office, London
1563 Ecclesiastical Census	Of families, or households.	English parishes in certain dioceses (11 in all)	British Museum: Harleian Manuscript 594, 595,618
1603 Ecclesiastical census	Communicants and recusants	English parishes	British Museum: Harleian Manuscripts 280,594,595 Diocesan record offices.
1641-7 Protestation Return	Involved an oath to defend, among other things the 'true reformed Protestant religion'. Oath administered to all males over 18. Those refusing the oath to be listed separately.	English parishes	House of Lords Record Office
1676 Compton Ecclesiastical Census	Communicants - assumed to be 16 + years old - and non-conformists	English parishes	Manuscript in Salt Library Stafford for dioceses in Province of Canterbury: Tanner Ms 150 No. 7 fol 27 seq. Bodleian, Oxford for Province of York.
1688/1690 Communicants list	Communicants, non-conformists, catholics	Dioceses in Province of Canterbury	Dalrymple (1771-3)
Bishops Visitation Returns. Sixteenth to Eighteenth Centuries.	Visits by Bishop's representatives to discover state of church buildings + of religious life. Often included number of families in the parish and of what, denomination.	Parishes throughout England	Diocesan and County Record Offices.
Muster Rolls Early sixteenth to mid seventeenth centuries.	Lists of able bodied men, assumed to be aged 15-60	Parishes throughout England	Public Record Office.
Hearth Tax Returns 1660-89	Lists of houses paying the tax (+ sometimes those not paying).	Parishes throughout England	Public Record Office
Poll Tax Late seventeenth century	All over 16 listed	Parishes throughout England	County Record Office.
1695 Marriage Duty Act	Complete listing of all inhabitants	English Parishes	County Record offices, parish chests; private collections
Local censuses	Varied: usually carried out by individuals	Limited coverage of parishes, villages and towns	County Record Offices

Appendix 1 Sources for estimating total population size

Shortcomings	Bibliography	Multiplier to get total population
Doubt as to whether covered people aged 14 + or 16 + : possibly much lower (see Cornwall 1970 p 32)	Thirsk (1959); Hollingsworth (1969); Cornwall (1970)	1¾
Doubt as to whether families or householders	Thirsk (1959): Hollingsworth 1969: Cornwall (1959)	5 or 4
Doubt as to age of communicants	Thirsk (1959): Hollingsworth 1969: Turner (1911) Stapleton (1982)	1 ¾
In some places administered to those over 15 year of age	Thirsk (1959): Hollingsworth 1969: Oxfordshire Record Society (1955)	2 (to include women) + 40% to include under 18 year olds.
Some incumbants returned number of inhabitants, some, the numbers of families and some the number of communicants. Did not always specify which: Nonconformists on occasion deliberately understated.	Thirsk(1959): Hollingsworth (1969) Guilford (1924): Marshall (1934), James (1952): Chalkin (1960): Bond (1973): Stephens (1958 and 1971): Forster (1961, 1967, 1969): Stapleton (1982)	1¾
	Dalrymple (1771-3) Hollingsworth (1969)	1¾
Sometimes families given, sometimes householders or individuals.	Ollard and Walker (1928-31) Stephens (1971) Stapleton (1982)	4 or 5
'Able' is a dubious definition: payment of a 'muster bounty' may have inflated lists.	Hollingsworth (1969): Rich (1950): Boynton (1967)	4 - 7
Unless charged and uncharged houses given are of little use.	Hollingsworth (1969)Marshall (1936); Patten(1971) Owen(1959); Thirsk (1959) Meekings (1940) Stapleton (1982)	4 - 5
Certain people exempted on grounds of poverty. No indication how many.		1¾
Few listings appear to have survived	Glass (1965) Laslett (1969) Wrigley (1966)	1
Unique , one-off events.	.Law (1969): Tranter (1967) Laslett (1969): Youngson (1961) Kyd (1952): Percival (1774-1776) Baker (1973); Stapleton (1982)	

Appendix 2. Forms used for 'Aggregative Analysis'

BAPTISMS

P.E.F. 1

County:

YEARS:

YEAR	MONTH OF CONCEPTION												Baptisms by Civil Year (totals)			Concep- tions by Harvest Year (totals)	Bastards	Comments
	Apr.	May	June	July	Aug.	Sept.	Oct.	Nov.	Dec.	Jan.	Feb.	Mar.						
	MONTH OF BAPTISM													Jan.-Apr.	May-Dec.			
	Jan.	Feb.	Mar.	Apr.	May	June	July	Aug.	Sept.	Oct.	Nov.	Dec.						
TOTAL																		

PARISH:

MARRIAGES

P.E.F. III

County:

YEARS:

YEAR	Jan.	Feb.	Mar.	Apr.	May	June	July	Aug.	Sept.	Oct.	Nov.	Dec.	Civil Year (totals)	Jan.-July	Aug.-Dec.	Harvest Year (totals)	Comments
TOTAL																	

LAW, C. M. (1969) 'Local censuses in the eighteenth century', **Population Studies** Vol 23, pp 87-100.

MARSHALL, L. M. (1934) **The rural population of Bedfordshire 1671-1921,** Bedfordshire Historical Record Society, Vol 16, Aspley Guise.

MARSHALL, L. M. (1936) 'The levying of the hearth tax, 1622-88', **English Historical Review** Vol 51, pp 628-46.

MEEKINGS, C. A. F. (ed) (1940) **Surrey Hearth Tax** 1664, Surrey Record Society, Vol 17, London.

OLLARD, S. L. and WALKER, P. C. (eds) (1923-31) **Archbishop Herring's Visitation Returns 1743,** Yorkshire Archaeological Society Record Series, Vols 71, 72, 75, 77, 79.

OWEN, L. (1959) 'The population of Wales in the sixteenth and seventeenth centuries', **Transactions of the Honourable Society of Cymmrodorion,** 99-113

OXFORDSHIRE RECORD SOCIETY (1955) XXXVI, **Oxfordshire Protestation Returns.**

PATTEN, J. (1971) 'The hearth taxes 1662-89' **Local Population Studies,** 7, pp 14-27.

PERCIVAL, T. (1774-76) 'Observations on the state of population in Manchester and other adjacent places', **Philosophical Transactions of the Royal Society,** Vol 64, pp 54-66: Vol 65, pp 322-35; Vol 66, pp 160-7.

STAPLETON, B. (1982) **'Some sources for the demographic study of a local community'** D301, cassette one and Media Booklet, Open University Press.

STEPHENS, W. B. (1958) 'A seventeenth-century census', **Devon and Cornwall Notes and Queries** Vol 29.

STEPHENS, W. B. (1971) **Sources for the History of Population and their Uses,** Institute of Education, University of Leeds.

THIRSK, J. (1959) 'Sources of information on population, 1500-1760', **Amateur Historian** (now called **Local Historian)** Vol 4, Nos 4 and 5, pp 129-33 and 182-5.

TRANTER, N. L. (1967) 'Population and social structure in a Bedfordshire parish — the Cardington listing 1792' **Population Studies** Vol 21, pp 261-82.

TURNER, G. Lyon (1911) **Original Records of Early Non-conformity under Persecution and Indulgence,** T Fisher Unwin, London.

WRIGLEY, E. A. (1966) 'Family limitation in pre-industrial England', **Economic History Review,** Second series, Vol 19. Reprinted in DRAKE, Michael (ed) **Population in Industrialization,** Methuen, London, pp 157-94.

YOUNGSON, A. (1961) 'Alexander Webster and his Account of the Number of People in Scotland in the Year 1755', **Population Studies,** Vol 15, pp 198-200.

Appendix 2. The Cambridge Group for the History of Population and Social Structure.

Instructions for use of aggregative analysis forms; Baptisms (PEF$_I$); Burials (PEF$_{II}$); Marriages (PEF$_{III}$)

1 Each form should begin with the first year of an even number decade (for example, 1601, 1621, 1681, not 1611, 1671, etc.) If the first entry in the register is in, say, 1596, begin the form with the year 1581, even though this means that only the last five lines on the first form are used. This is important because it makes the comparison of forms from different parishes easy. If there is a gap in the register, leave the corresponding period on the form blank. If the gap is, say, from 1564-71, the entries for 1571 should be seven lines lower than those for 1564.

2 Where possible, carry the analysis down from the earliest date in the register to 1837, the year in which civil registration of births, deaths and marriages began.

3 The modern calendar year begins on 1 January. This is the year used on the forms. Until 1752, however, the year began on 25 March (in the sixteenth century some registers begin a new year on still other days). This means that dates in the early part of the year must be converted to conform with modern practice — thus the baptisms occuring in February 1679 in the register will be recorded on the form in February 1680. The period from 1 January to 24 March is moved forward by one year.

BURIALS

YEAR	Jan.	Feb.	Mar.	Apr.	May	June	July	Aug.	Sept.	Oct.	Nov.	Dec.	Civil Year (totals)	Jan.-July	Aug.-Dec.	Harvest Year (totals)	Wanderers	Comments
TOTAL																		

4. In some parishes separate registers of baptisms, burials and marriages were kept. In others all entries were made in a single register. Where the latter was the case, go through the register three times dealing with each type of entry separately.

5. Note that it is not always the case that one entry in the register deals with only one event. The baptism of twins is usually recorded in a single entry, and sometimes the burial of a mother and young baby is also recorded by a single entry. Check each page in the register, therefore to make sure you have not missed an event in this way.

6. There is a column on the Baptisms Form for bastards, and on the Burials Form there is a column for wanderers. Not all registers record these sub-classes of event. Where they are recorded only sporadically the column should be left blank. If information about them is given with apparent consistency over a long period (say, fifty years or more), it is desirable to have them listed. The Comments column is provided to make it possible to note unusual entries of importance or changes in the character of the register (eg 'here the register makes it clear that the heavy mortality was due to smallpox'; or 'here the register becomes unusually detailed and records the mother's maiden name at the birth of each child'; or 'here the incumbent began to add notes of the character of some of the deceased'; or 'for several years there are occasional comments on the weather'; and so on).

7. If you are working from the original register and it is still in the parish, you should always approach the incumbent in the first instance to seek permission to make use of the register. He and the churchwardens are jointly responsible for its safety.

	January / July	August / December	Harvest year (total)
1576	33	(28)	48
1577	(20)	19	

8 Calculations. The forms provide for addition by line and column to give totals for the calendar year and the month, and also make it possible to calculate the number of events by harvest year. These calculations yield much of interest, but they are laborious if done without the assistance of a machine.

If you do wish to do the work, the following points should be borne in mind in calculating totals for the harvest year.

(i) The year runs from the beginning of August in any one year to the end of July in the following year.

(ii) On the Marriages and Burials Forms the total for the harvest year is obtained by adding the total for August-December of one year, say 1576, to the total for January-July of the next, 1577.

Thus:

(iii) On the Baptisms Form the procedure is different. We wish to know about the number of conceptions rather than the number of baptisms. The number of conceptions is related to the number of baptisms nine months later. Therefore to derive a figure for conceptions by harvest year one must calculate the number of baptisms nine months later. The number of conceptions in the harvest year August 1576-July 1577 is taken to be equal to the number of baptisms, May 1577-April 1578. Thus:

	January / April	May / December	Harvest year (total)
1576	21	36	56
1577	18	31	
1578	25	37	

AN ENQUIRY INTO SEASONALITY IN BAPTISMS, MARRIAGES AND BURIALS

Part One: Introduction Methodology and Marriages

L. Bradley

When parish registers are used for local population studies, attention is usually concentrated upon <u>annual</u> totals of baptisms, marriages and burials, and on the calculations which can be made from them and which have obvious implications for population change. It is not always realised that there is a great deal to be learned from a study of seasonality, that is of the fluctuations from month to month within the year. We might ask, for example, how the monthly distribution of marriages was affected by the seasonal nature of employment; how far the 'prohibited periods' for marriage, which the canons of the church still imposed in the 16th century, were actually effective and when they fell into disuse; whether the long hours of winter darkness affected the distribution of conceptions, and so of baptisms; whether a comparison of the distribution of marriages and of baptisms suggests that a high proportion of brides were pregnant; whether the seasonal distribution of burials throws any light on the main causes of death. These and many other such questions can be attacked, though not necessarily answered, by an investigation into seasonality.

As a first hypothesis we might suppose that seasonal factors affecting baptism, marriage and burial fell into three groups.

(a) The fundamental factors, persistent over considerable periods and common to the whole nation, or at any rate to large regions. These would include church law, such as prohibited periods for marriage; widespread and lasting occupational factors such as the long hours of work in harvest in rural areas; possibly

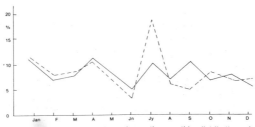

FIGURE 1. The dotted line shows the monthly distribution of baptisms for ASHOVER: 1781-90. The full line shows the distribution of the **total** baptisms for **five** parishes, including Ashover, for the same decade. Note how this has elminiated the significant July peak in Ashover.

TABLE 1

BAPTISMS

PARISH: **WIRKSWORTH**
County: **DERBYSHIRE**
YEARS: **1621–40**

Conceptions

YEAR	MONTH OF CONCEPTION												Baptisms by Civil Year (totals)	Conceptions by Harvest Year			Bastards	Comments
	Apr.	May	June	July	Aug.	Sept.	Oct.	Nov.	Dec.	Jan.	Feb.	Mar.		Jan.–Apr.	May–Dec.	(totals)		
	MONTH OF BAPTISM																	
	Jan.	Feb.	Mar.	Apr.	May	June	July	Aug.	Sept.	Oct.	Nov.	Dec.						
1621	13	11	9	7	6	6	5	8	2	4	4	3	78					
2	4	6	8	7	5	7	4	2	12	3	6	9	72					
3	3	5	7	9	5	9	4	6	6	5	3	5	64					
4	11	11	15	8	4	5	6	6	12	7	7	5	91					
5	9	4	11	8	7	8	7	8	4	7	5	6	81					
6	9	6	11	14	11	4	5	5	7	5	10	5	92					
7	7	7	10	2	7	6	6	7	9	8	5	9	80					
8	2	5	10	12	9	6	3	8	6	4	9	8	90					
9	6	6	8	13	1	9	6	0	4	7	4	8	78					
1630	11	8	9	9	9	6	3	8	10	10	4	11	98					
1	8	6	6	7	11	4	2	5	7	5	9	2	69					
2	7	5	7	6	13	2	4	3	9	5	9	8	78					
3	13	7	8	11	9	5	6	6	9	8	8	3	94					
4	8	11	11	6	6	8	6	11	5	8	7	12	99					
5	9	12	9	10	10	4	2	6	9	4	13	3	91					
6	11	9	11	11	5	6	7	6	7	6	3	12	94					
7	12	8	12	8	8	5	5	4	1	7	4	5	79					
8	8	10	7	9	4	8	5	7	6	6	8	12	90					
9	15	7	8	9	1	5	5	13	12	5	6	10	96					
1640	8	5	16	8	8	5	6	6	12	7	7	8	96					
TOTAL	174	146	202	161	139	118	97	131	149	118	131	147	1710					

2

97, 118, 118, 131, 131, 139, 144, 146, 149, 149, 174, 202

142.5

biological factors which may conceivably affect human mating and reproduction as they do those of animals.

(b) More localised, but still fairly persistent factors such as might be expected to cause significant local modifications of the fundamental pattern. In hill sheep-farming areas, for example, lambing might have a local effect similar to the more usual harvest effect in arable areas. Local customs, too, as will be seen later, can affect seasonality.

(c) Almost accidental factors. A 'slump' in marriages in May and June in the 1770s in Much Binding may mean no more than that the incumbent of the time habitually spent those months away from his parish. [1] The local historian will be interested in identifying and explaining these anomalies, but they will usually have little or no demographic significance.

The professional demographers have, until recently, concerned themselves almost entirely with the first group, which they have investigated by lumping together the statistics from a large number of parishes, often averaged over quite lengthy periods. This procedure is necessary if local and short-term factors are to be eliminated (Figure 1), but it has serious dangers if the investigation stops at this point. It may be obscuring some of the very factors which actually determine the pattern of demographic events and which are important if we wish to understand the detailed mechanism of population change. Recent work has shown considerable regional differences in demographic pattern which it is important to understand, and there are similar differences even within the regions. Even in a large-scale enquiry, then, there is a place for local studies. Those of us whose main interest is in local history or local demography must, of course be concerned with the fundamental factors, but we are especially concerned with the local modifications and with unravelling the interactions between local seasonality and local historical, social and economic circumstances.

What follows, then, is an attempt to see how far a quite simple method can be used to investigate and compare seasonality in individual parishes and to uncover the difficulties which such an enquiry will meet. It is in no sense a complete investigation, even for a single parish, and it will raise, rather than answer, questions - questions which, perhaps, other readers of L.P.S. will help to answer.

METHOD

I had available, on the Cambridge Group aggregation forms (Table 1), the monthly figures of baptisms, marriages and burials taken from the registers of six Derbyshire and six Nottinghamshire parishes (2). The parishes are varied in character, including a small market town, rural parishes of different sizes and parishes which, by the end of the 18th century, were becoming industrialised. The period covered is 1570 to 1840, though not all parishes provided figures for the entire period.

It was first necessary to decide on a time unit. The significant patterns for which we are looking are subject, in any year, to quite accidental variations which tend to obscure the pattern. We can reduce the effect of these accidental variations if we work in units of several years. But the time-unit must not be too long. Just as averaging the figures for several parishes may, as shown above, eliminate significant local differences, so averaging for too long a period may eliminate significant differences within the period. In the parish of GEDLING, for example, a significant feature of the marriage pattern is that December is an unpopular month for marriage until 1740, after which it becomes a popular month. If we average the results over two hundred years, 1630-1830 as is shown in figure 2, this feature is lost.

After some experiment, the decade appeared to be a suitable unit.

The following procedure was carried out for each separate parish:

(1) From the aggregation forms, decadal totals of baptisms were calculated for each month of the year, and each month's total was reduced to a percentage of the total number of baptisms for the decade (Table 2). In subsequent pages I have called each square of the decadal table a 'cell' - e.g. the March cell for 1631-40.

(2) Most people find it easier to appreciate statistical relationships from a graph than from a lengthy table of figures. Accordingly, the monthly percentages were displayed in two series of graphs:

Series A. A separate graph was drawn for each decade, showing how the baptisms for that decade were distributed over the calendar months (Figure 3). The number at the right of each graph is the total number of baptisms for that decade.

4

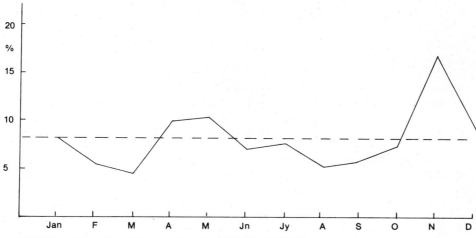

FIGURE 2. Distribution of **total** marriages for GEDLING: 1631-1830.

<u>TABLE 2</u>

<u>Wirksworth - Baptisms</u>

	Jan	Feb	Mar	Apl	May	June	July	Aug	Sept	Oct	Nov	Dec	Total
1621-30													
Number	75	66	106	79	64	66	49	64	72	57	57	69	824
%	9.1	8.0	12.9	9.6	7.8	8.0	6.0	7.8	8.7	6.9	6.9	8.4	
1631-40													
Number	99	80	96	82	75	52	48	67	77	61	74	75	886
%	11.2	9.1	10.8	9.3	8.5	5.9	5.5	7.6	8.7	6.9	8.4	8.5	
1641-50													
Number	69	64	84	76	54	72	53	53	56	64	56	57	758
%	9.1	8.5	11.1	10.1	7.2	9.6	7.0	7.0	7.4	8.5	7.4	7.6	

etc.

5

Series B. A separate graph was drawn for each calendar
month, showing how the percentage of baptisms attributable
to that calendar month varied with the passage of the
decades (Figure 4).   The numbers at the left and right
are the total number of baptisms in the initial and final
decades.

The dotted line on each graph represents the <u>average</u> monthly
percentage of baptisms, i.e. 100/12, or 8.1/3 %.

Although these two series of graphs convey essentially the same
information, it was found useful to have both available.

(3) The process was repeated for marriages and for burials.

An expected difficulty soon emerged.   The distribution of vital events
over the month is, in any decade, the total result of both the seasonal
factors discussed in the introduction and of pure chance.   There will,
for example, in any decade be marriages whose timing is dictated by
the seasonal factors, but there are likely to be some few whose
timing is a matter of purely personal and unpredictable choice.
The fewer the total number of marriages in the decade, the greater
is likely to be the effect of the purely personal element and the more
difficult it will be to disentangle the seasonal elements.   In the
parish of BRADBOURNE, the 22 marriages in the decade 1711-20 were
distributed as follows:

Month	J	F	M	A	M	Jn	Jy	A	S	O	N	D
Number	2	3	0	1	3	2	2	1	1	1	3	3
%	9.1	13.6	0	4.5	13.6	9.1	9.1	4.5	4.5	4.5	13.6	13.6

Had one marriage taken place in March instead of February, one in
April instead of May and one in October instead of November, the
distribution would have been:

Month	J	F	M	A	M	Jn	Jy	A	S	O	N	D
Number	2	2	1	2	2	2	2	1	1	2	2	3
%	9.1	9.1	4.5	9.1	9.1	9.1	9.1	4.5	4.5	9.1	9.1	13.6

Which, as Figure 5 shows, is a substantially different pattern.
But if the same shift of marriages had happened in WIRKSWORTH
(1721-30), where the actual distribution of 114 marriages was:

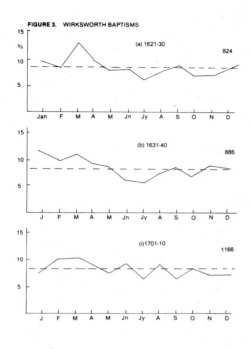

FIGURE 3. WIRKSWORTH BAPTISMS

(a) 1621-30   824

(b) 1631-40   886

(i)1701-10   1166

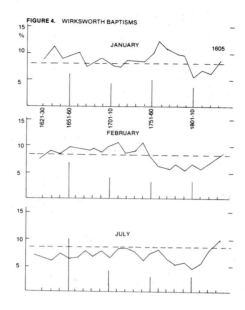

FIGURE 4. WIRKSWORTH BAPTISMS

JANUARY   1605

FEBRUARY

JULY

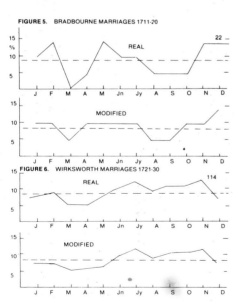

FIGURE 5. BRADBOURNE MARRIAGES 1711-20

REAL   22

MODIFIED

FIGURE 6. WIRKSWORTH MARRIAGES 1721-30

REAL   114

MODIFIED

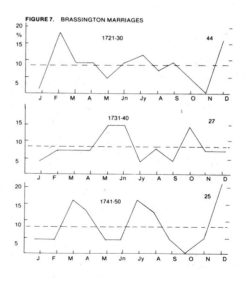

FIGURE 7. BRASSINGTON MARRIAGES

1721-30   44

1731-40   27

1741-50   25

7

Month	J	F	M	A	M	Jn	Jy	A	S	O	N	D
Number	8	9	5	5	8	11	13	10	12	11	14	8
%	7.0	7.9	4.4	4.4	7.0	9.7	11.4	8.8	10.5	9.7	12.3	7.0

we would have arrived at:

Month	J	F	M	A	M	Jn	Jy	A	S	O	N	D
Number	8	8	6	6	7	11	13	10	12	12	13	8
%	7.0	7.0	5.3	5.3	6.1	9.7	11.4	8.8	10.5	10.5	11.4	7.0

which makes little difference to the pattern (Figure 6).

Where the number of events is small, then, the element of chance may distort the whole picture. Figure 7 shows the marriage graphs for BRASSINGTON (1721-30). It is difficult to see any consistent pattern. This may either be because seasonal factors did not operate in this village, or it may be due to the effect of chance on the small decadal totals. Since the baptism graphs for the same village in the same period do not show this erratic behaviour, and the decadal totals of baptisms are much larger (of the order of 170), the likelihood is that the cause is the small number of marriages per decade.

This lack of consistent pattern from decade to decade is, then, common where the decadal totals are small, though there are parishes where the seasonal pattern is so dominant that even small numbers give consistent patterns. It follows that great care must be taken in interpreting the seasonal graphs whenever the decadal totals are small. This is especially likely to affect the marriage graphs, since marriage totals tend to be of the order of a quarter of the baptisms or burial totals. This is, of course, the reason for indicating the decadal totals on the graphs. _Author's observation_

As a rough, but purely empirical rule, I have found it necessary to exercise great care in interpretation when decadal totals are less than 60, and I feel much happier if they are over 100.

MARRIAGE SEASONALITY

The marriage graphs of two parishes were, for reasons discussed above, so irregular as to defy analysis. The following discussion is, therefore, based on the graphs of the remaining ten parishes.

The only 'fundamental' factor for the existence of which there is concrete evidence is the ecclesiastical 'prohibited periods'. If the effect of this factor is considered first, we shall then be able to look for further seasonal marriage phenomena and, possibly, make hypotheses about the underlying factors.

The 'prohibited periods' - though one gathers that the church discouraged, rather than prohibited, marriage in these periods - were:

> Septuagesima to Low Sunday
> Rogation to Trinity
> Advent to Hilary

How far were they observed and what was their effect?

Although the date of Easter can vary by about a month, the addition of data by decades gives the effect of Easter varying by only about a week in the course of the decades (3), so that the timing of the prohibited periods is not, for our purpose, seriously affected.

The first prohibited period would affect marriages in roughly three weeks in February, the whole of March and two weeks of April. The graphs show that March marriages fell well below the average in every parish but one (See Figure 8 for an example). March was, indeed, by far the least popular month for marriages in the whole year throughout the period. Of a possible 234 March 'cells' over the ten parishes, the March percentage reached the average of 8.1/3% in only 32. Of these 32, 12 came in the 19th century, right at the end of the period. Of the 20 cells in the 17th and 18th centuries, 6 were barely above average. Of the remaining 14, 4 lie between 1641 and 1670, and 6 between 1731 and 1770. February marriages are distinctly below average in 6 parishes and above average in only one. April marriages are much more variable, being above average in five parishes and below in two. In both February and April, the percentage of marriages rose towards the end of the period.

It is impossible, in a short article, to present all the evidence, but I am left with the impression that this prohibited period was shortened at both ends, but that a reduced period, possibly from the beginning of Lent until Easter, was observed in most of the parishes, though with decreasing fidelity, until at any rate the second decade of the 19th century.

The second prohibited period would affect about two weeks in May. May marriages were above average in five parishes and oscillated about the average in five more. May, indeed, ranked high in popularity, and it seems clear that this second prohibited period was not extensively observed in these parishes.

The third period would cover almost the whole of December and about two weeks of January. In the 17th and early 18th century, December marriages were distinctly below average in all ten parishes, but rose to the average at some date between 1720 and 1770 (varying from parish to parish) and then exceeded the average, sometimes by a considerable amount (Figure 8). There were only 10 'cells' in the 17th century out of 79 when the December percentage rose above the average, 8 of them between 1630 and 1660. December was, in fact, the second least popular month for marriage in the 17th century, but was amongst the most popular months by the end of the 18th century. January marriages showed great variation, but oscillated about the average, and certainly did not show the deficit which would arise from two weeks prohibition. The impression left is that the Advent prohibition was observed, though decreasingly, in most parishes until varying dates in the 18th century, except for lapses in the Common-wealth period which are discussed below. The extension to Hilary does not appear to have been regularly observed.

The persistence of the effect of prohibited periods until at least the early part of the 18th century and, in the case of Lent, until the early 19th century is in contrast to Miss Cowgill's suggestion (4) that their effect declined from the early 17th century. Unfortunately Miss Cowgill's graphs are in terms of the monthly number of marriages in successive periods of 50 years, whereas only a comparison of percentages will enable us to compare periods adequately.

It is interesting to note that there were distinct peaks in the marriage graphs in several parishes both in March and December in the Commonwealth period when, of course, the canons of the Anglican church were not officially observed. Peaks of this nature are indicated by the arrows in Figure 9. In most parishes the peak was for one decade only. but not the same decade for every parish. the peak sometimes occurring in 1641-50, sometimes in 1651-60, some-times even in 1661-70. It would be interesting to discuss the size and dating of these peaks in the light of what is known of the religious history of each parish in the Commonwealth period, and especially of the shade of opinion of the incumbent and his patron. In parishes for which figures for the late 16th century are available, similar peaks are noticeable at that time when, according to Tate (5), unsuccessful attempts were made to have the prohibited periods abolished.

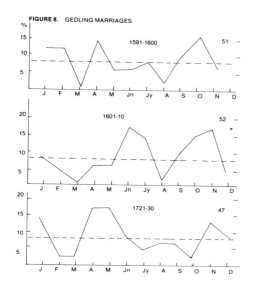

FIGURE 8. GEDLING MARRIAGES

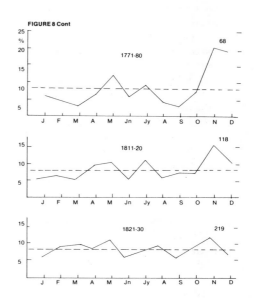

FIGURE 8 Cont

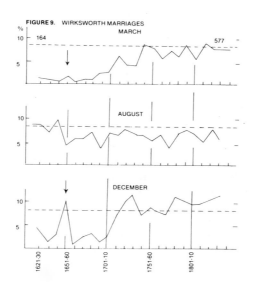

FIGURE 9. WIRKSWORTH MARRIAGES

11

Throughout the period, the graphs show a summer trough which has no connection with the prohibited periods. In every one of the ten parishes, August is an unpopular month for marriage, exceeded in unpopularity only by March and December in the 17th century, and by March only in the 18th. September marriages are below average in every parish in the 17th century and in every parish except MATLOCK and WIRKSWORTH (for which see below) in the 18th. In the 17th century the trough included July in three parishes and October in five others. In the 18th century the trough was wider, sometimes covering four or five months. This may in part be due to the decreasing effect of the prohibited periods, for if the percentags of marriages are increasing in some months, they must be decreasing in others.

It is usually assumed that the factor underlying the summer marriage trough is occupational and connected with the harvest, the suggestion being that long hours of harvest work left no time for planning marriage. This sounds feasible - but is there any direct evidence? It is noticeable that August, at any rate, is just as unpopular in the less rural parishes.

Far and away the most popular month for marriage in these ten parishes (and, according to Cowgill, for York) was November. It is true that most other months are affected to some extent by either the prohibited periods or the summer trough, but was there any more direct factor operating in favour of November?

There do not appear to be any other marriage phenomena which are both common to all parishes and persistent over very long periods - what I have earlier called fundamental phenomena. We can now look for examples of the second group, prominent and fairly persistent, but peculiar to a specific parish. The graphs show a number of these, and I shall take one as an example. The WIRKSWORTH marriage graphs show a peak for September commencing in the 1731-40 decade and persisting throughout the rest of the century, September marriages sometimes rising as high as 16% of the decadal total. MATLOCK shows a similar September peak. As this phenomenon is even more strikingly visible on the baptisms graphs, further discussion will be left until part two of this article.

Finally, there is a marked tendency for the graphs to flatten out (i.e. for marriages to be distributed more evenly throughout the year) in the early 19th century (Figure 8). This means that the seasonal influences of all kinds were losing their influence towards the end of our period.

NOTES

1.   See, for example 'Parson Woodforde's Diary'

2.   I am indebted for my statistics to the following:-
Derbyshire parishes
        For Ashover, Brassington and Bradbourne to
        Mr. David Hool.
        For Brailsford to Mr. Christopher Charlton.
        For Matlock and Wirksworth to the Matlock
        Population Study Group.

        Nottinghamshire parishes
        For Arnold, Cropwell Bishop, Edwinstowe,
        Gedling and Oxton to Mrs. Janet Young.
        For Burton Joyce to the Burton Joyce
        Population Study Group.

3.   Cheney: Handbook of Historical Dates

4.   'The People of York: 1538-1812' by U.M. Cowgill
        in Scientific American, January 1970.

5.   W.E. Tate: The Parish Chest - C.U.P. - Chapter 1.

MARRIAGE SEASONALITY 1761-1810: AN ASSESSMENT OF PATTERNS IN SEVENTEEN SHROPSHIRE PARISHES

W. J. Edwards

In an earlier article Leslie Bradley has argued that marriage seasonality appears to reflect three factors — fundamental, local and accidental.[1] The first of these factors includes elements such as ecclesiastical discouragement of marriage in certain months or economic constraints and produces consistent regional or national patterns, while 'local' and 'accidental' factors introduce variations. Most of the published studies have emphasised the more 'fundamental' seasonal features arising from ecclesiastical and economic control, but obviously other factors, such as the size and social cohesiveness of the community concerned, or the level of extra parochial marriage, may modify the seasonal pattern. However, before these local factors can be assessed, more detailed studies of the extent to which periods of ecclesiastical prohibition were observed in all parts of the country are necessary.

The present study uses data drawn from seventeen published registers of parishes of different sizes in central Shropshire over the period 1761-1810.[2] The parishes lie in a discontinuous north-south belt, ranging from the market town of Wem on the north Shropshire plain, with a population of 3,121 in 1811 to a group of small parishes, all with populations below 300 in 1811, situated on the southern bank of the Severn floodplain south of Shrewsbury. To avoid the problem of small samples, the seventeen parishes have been divided into five groups, based on their population size in the 1811 census, as shown in Table 1. For each group of parishes the information on marriage seasonality is presented in the form of a standard index, in which the figure 100 represents the number of events that would occur in a month if the annual total of marriages occurred evenly taking account of the different number of days in each month.[3]

Table 1. Parishes grouped by size of population in 1811.

Size-group	Parish	1811 Population	Size-group	Parish	1811 Population
2000+	Wem	3121	300-599	Berrington	575
				Stokesay	489
1000-1999	Condover	1289		Hopesay	484
	Bitterley	1083		Onibury	415
	Stanton Lacy	1026		Smethcote	359
600-999	Stretton	944	200-299	Acton Burnell	290
	Wistanstow	659		Pitchford	255
	Bromfield	610		Stapleton	234
				Longnor	231
				Leebotwood	208

Source: Population Enumeration Census Volume 1811.

The first panel of Table 2 presents a seasonal marriage index for each parish size group over the whole period, while the second panel combines the parishes and presents a seasonal index for individual decades. The immediate impression gained from the aggregate figures is the similarity in patterns of marriage seasonality between these Shropshire examples and those presented in **LPS** for other areas. This reinforces the idea of fundamental ecclesiastical constraints having a national impact.

The church discouraged marriage during three periods of the year. The first of these from Septuagesima to Low Sunday, covering three weeks of February, the whole of March and two weeks in April, is clearly evident in these data. March is consistently the lowest month in all parish size-groups and for the bulk of the period; only ceasing to be so from 1801-10 when August replaces it. There is some indication that marriages were also infrequent in April and February in certain decades, but the levels of marriage in February vary in parishes of different size. It appears that the main impact of ecclesiastical prohibtion is concentrated in March, but its impact is noticeably weaker in the case of the large market town of Wem. These data also suggest that the observance of this prohibition weakened during the early nineteenth century, with an increase in the proportions of marriages solemnised in March, but earlier the discouraged period was widely recognised. This corresponds well with Bradley's findings for Nottinghamshire and Derbyshire parishes[1] and with Massey's findings in Burton Joyce[5]. Similar findings also occur in the data for Oswaldkirk (North Riding, Yorkshire)[6] and in the Ardèche[7]. It therefore seems fair to conclude that in general throughout the latter half of the eighteenth century Lent was still avoided for weddings and that only in the early years of the nineteenth century did the situation change, but the strength of observance depended very much on the size of parish, which in turn may well reflect the control of social convention and more specifically that of the incumbent.

These data also raise questions concerning the relative performances of February and April. If March marriages were discouraged, is the February peak simply a response to this constraint, an attempt to beat the ban which Lent imposed? But if this were so, why is April which comes after the end of Lent such a quiet month?

Table 2. Marriage seasonality in seventeen Shropshire parishes 1761-1810 by size of parish.

	Total No. of marriages	Index values/month											
		J	F	M	A	M	J	J	A	S	O	N	D
c.3000 (Wem)	891	143	130	73	96	110	88	81	68	76	76	69	183
1000-1999	992	80	100	52	96	217	136	65	94	72	92	95	95
600-999	599	70	107	45	85	268	138	84	64	52	106	89	86
300-599	590	73	78	35	93	304	113	101	80	53	73	97	97
200-299	283	75	114	53	98	246…120		100	62	64	62	112	88
All parishes	3355	93	107	53	94	215	118	82	77	66	84	89	116

By decade

	Total No. of marriages	Index values/month											
		J	F	M	A	M	J	J	A	S	O	N	D
1761-1770	660	98	112	54	87	242	98	81	77	61	89	85	116
1771-1780	734	89	121	35	94	262	117	76	75	58	76	89	107
1781-1790	639	94	87	40	97	194	137	94	60	66	107	91	131
1791-1800	659	95	88	48	101	186	120	70	98	76	82	87	121
1801-1810	663	89	122	82	95	194	120	71	73	69	89	92	103

(100 = annual total/365 x number of days in a month)

The second period when marriages were discouraged was from Rogation to Trinity, covering two weeks in May; here the published evidence is more equivocal, but the results are plain. For the total sample May is easily the most popular month, rising in importance until 1780 and falling slightly thereafter. In the villages May dominates the marriage pattern, with index values double and treble those that might be expected with an even monthly distribution. In the market town of Wem however, while May always features as a popular month, it is December which dominates the registers. Thus the second period appears to have less impact than the first, confirming Bradley's findings[8]; refuting the notion that 'marriages in May were unlucky'[9], and suggesting a possible regional contrast between Shropshire and Yorkshire, as May never features as a peak month in the Oswaldkirk data[10]. Indeed this may be an example of local, economic or customary factors shaping patterns of marriage seasonality. For example, May festivities and fairs seem to have been common in Shropshire[11]. Two contemporary **Directories** list May Day fairs in a majority of market centres in the county, but whether these together with the spring time season encouraged marriage is an open question[12].

The final prohibited period, from Advent to Hilary, covering December and two weeks in January does not appear to have been observed at all. In the villages the index numbers for December and January are at about the same level as in November and several other months in the year, while Wem records both December and January as peak months over the whole period. Bradley has noted that from 1720-70 any discouragement on marriage in these months appears to have been relaxed, so that by the end of the eighteenth century December was frequently the most popular month[13]. Certainly there is evidence of December peaks in other areas, but their incidence is infrequent.

A number of other features can be noted from these aggregate tables. It has been suggested that a summer trough in marriage is a fairly general phenomenon, with August recording low monthly totals; this has been connected with the labour demands of harvest time, but Bradley has noted that the same pattern recurs in less rural parishes, in part refuting such an occupational explanation[14]. In these data, while levels of marriage in July, August and September are low, there is considerable variation through time and between groups. Generally September is the lowest of these three months followed by August and then July: indeed July seems to be one of the more popular months in the smaller parishes. Overall, marriages appear to be concentrated in May, June and July, with the summer period of above - average numbers increasing in length as parish size decreases. In many other studies November stands out as a popular month, possibly reflecting an easing of the farming year and a time of surplus, but here a November peak only occurs amongst the smallest parishes[15].

The broad pattern that stands out in these aggregate data confirms the importance of Lent as a control on monthly seasonality, but indicates that more diverse factors, probably highly local in nature, influence the degree of observance of the other two discouraged periods. These data also suggest that certain of the contrasts that exist may well be a function of the size of the parishes concerned, reflecting the degree of economic diversity. In particular the monthly pattern of Wem, the small market town differs from that of the rural parishes, suggesting that size and degree of urbanisation may influence seasonal characteristics, producing contrasts between town and countryside. Moreover in the smaller parishes the incumbent or chief landowner played a dominant role. This was particularly true in 'estate parishes' where the influx of new employees was closely controlled from year to year[16]. In such circumstances, marriage may well have been associated with certain constraints and customary months of solemnisation. Similarly, in such parishes a devout incumbent might have been particularly effective in maintaining the ecclesiastical periods of discouragement free of marriages, particularly in December when Christmas services and festivities may well have taken precedence.

Finally, there are a number of ways in which marriage seasonality could be investigated further with profit. Firstly, marriages could be divided into those between local people and those where spouses come from outside the parish. If there are differences in the seasonality of the marriages of the two groups then both mobility and employment may be influential in shaping the aggregate seasonal pattern. Secondly, greater attention needs to be given to the precise role of economy in shaping seasonal trends. Chambers has indicated the close relationship between nuptiality and the economy over longer time periods[17], and there is no reason why comparable associations should not hold good on an annual and seasonal basis. As Ogden found among the silk-growers of the Ardèche[18], annual and seasonal hiring, the contractual terms of service, and the regional and temporal emphasis on 'living in' and 'cottage labour' may be important[19].

Where possible it would also be useful to identify 'local' customs and the role they play. It has been suggested that the Shropshire May fairs may have contributed to the higher frequencies of that month, but other local customs may equally sway the pattern and determine the tempo of this aspect of vital events.

These issues and their interconnection form one route to the explanation of marriage seasonality, and by so doing, illustrate the internal connectivity of 'the world we have lost' and the need that exists for further research on this topic.

NOTES

1. L. Bradley, 'An enquiry into seasonality in baptisms, marriages and burials', Part one, **LPS** No. 4, 1970, pp. 21-40.

2. The seventeen registers used have all been published by the Shropshire Parish Register Society. The volumes consulted were: Wem, (Lichfield [L], vols 9 &10, 1583-1812); Condover (L, vol. 6, 1570-1812); Bitterley, (Hereford [H], vol. 4, 1658-1812); Stanton Lacy, (H, vol. 4, 1561-1812); Stretton, H, vol. 8, 1661-1812; Stretton, H, vol. 8, 1661-1812; Wistanstow, (H, vol. 17, 1 1661-1812); Bromfield, (H, vol. 5, 1559-1812); Berrington, (L, vol. 14, 1559-1812); Stokesay, (H, vol. 17, 1559-1812); Hopesay, (H, vol. 18, 1660-1812); Onibury, (H, vol. 18, 1577-1812); Smethcote, (L, vol. 1, 1609-1812); Acton Burnell, (L, vol. 19, 1568-1812); Pitchford, (L, vol. 1, 1558-1812); Stapleton, (L, vol. 1, 1658-1812); Longnor, (L, vol. 5, 1586-1812); Leebotwood, (L, vol. 5, 1547-1812).

3. A detailed discussion of the calculation of the marriage index is presented in: M. Fleuri and L. Henry, **Nouveau manuel de dépouillement et d'evploitation de l'état civil ancien,** Paris, 1965, pp. 103-5.

4. L. Bradley, **LPS, No. 4, 1970, p.34.**

5. M. Massey, 'Seasonality, some further thoughts,' **LPS,** No. 8, 1972, pp. 48-54.

6. P. Rowley, 'Seasonality in Oswaldkirk, North Riding, Yorkshire,' **LPS,** No. 11, 1973, pp. 44-47.

7. P. E. Ogden, 'Patterns of marriage seasonality in rural France,' **LPS,** No. 10, 1973, pp. 53-64.

8. L. Bradley, 'Marriage seasonality — May marriages,' **LPS,** No. 3, 1969, p.54.

9. A. W. Smith, 'Marriage seasonality,' **LPS,** No. 2, 1969, p.67.

10. P. Rowley, **LPS,** No. 11, 1973, p.45.

11. B. Trinder, **The Industrial Revolution in Shropshire,** 1973, p.364.

12. Barfoot and Wilkes, **Universal British Directory,** 1797, and Tibnam and Co. **The Salop Directory,** 1828.

13. L. Bradley, **LPS,** No. 4, 1970, p.37.

14. L. Bradley, **LPS,** No. 4, 1970, p.39.

15. L. Bradley, **LPS,** 4, 1970, p.39. H. Palli, 'Seasonality of marriage in Estonia', **LPS,** No. 14, 1975, pp. 50-52.

16. D. Mills, 'English villages in the eighteenth and nineteenth centuries: a sociological approach,' Part one, **Amateur Historian,** vol. 6, No. 8, 1965, pp. 271-8.

17. J. D. Chambers, **Population, economy and society in pre-industrial England,** 1972, Chapter 6, pp. 128-151.

18. P. E. Ogden, **LPS,** No. 10, 1973, p.63.

19. R. E. Prothero, **English farming past and present,** 1912, pp. 53-4, 86-9, specifies some of the characteristics of hiring fairs and the conditions of service that governed annual hirings. An introduction to the role of fairs and markets is given in the **Report on Markets and Fairs in England and Wales,** vol. 1, HMSO 1927, No. 13.

Seasonality, some further thoughts

Margaret Massey

Having read again Mr. Bradley's articles on Seasonality (L.P.S. 4, 5 and 6) I wondered what pattern might appear for my own parish, Burton Joyce, if I examined the peak months per decade.

When dealing with a very small parish in isolation the very smallness of the numbers involved can cause difficulty. Percentages can be most misleading. For example, in dealing with, say, baptism numbers one might say that 22% of the baptisms for a given year took place in February and 55% in June. It sounds an enormous increase, but if the total number of baptisms for the year is only 9, then the 22% is 2 and the 55% is 5. Of course using percentages is essential if comparing one parish with another. Or is it? There is a much less laborious way of examining trends in a variety of parishes. I am not sure that it would be statistically acceptable, but it certainly gives a picture, a pattern, which may be all one wants.

For any parish for which there is an aggregative analysis it is comparatively easy to find the number of events, baptisms, burials or marriages in each month for a decade at a time. These, of course are the figures that Mr. Bradley has used for his work on seasonality. Instead of working out and drawing graphs for every month or every decade, marking on a chart the peak months for each decade quickly and clearly shows a pattern, if there is one.

The accompanying diagrams for the years 1581-1830 in the Parish of Burton Joyce shows these patterns very clearly. Of course these patterns give an incomplete picture. They take no account of the events which took place in the other months of the year, and they give no hint at all of variations in the numbers of events between one decade and another. Nevertheless I think they give a reasonable picture of seasonality. It would be quite quick to do this for a large number of parishes and the results might be illuminating.

Marriage

If we look at the Marriage diagram there is no difficulty in deciding which month wins, but it indicates other things too. We notice that

Peak months for Marriages in decades

J	F	M	A	M	J	J	A	S	O	N	D	Decade
						X						1581–90
										X		91–1600
										X		1601–10
					X				X			11–20
										X		21–30
					X				X			31–40
			X	X								41–50
						X						51–60
			X									61–70
X					X					X		71–80
						X		X				81–90
										X		91–1700
										X		1701–10
						X				X		11–20
										X		21–30
										X		31–40
										X		41–50
									X			51–60
										X		61–70
											X	71–80
				X						X		81–90
								X				91–1800
										X		1801–10
		X										11–20
				X								21–30

never in the whole 250 years did March top the poll.   March is
always largely if not completely in Lent.   August, perhaps surprisingly,
was never a peak month.   Too busy in harvest?   December features
only once, and that late in the period under consideration.
December is always Advent.   Do March and December reflect Church
prohibitions? Probably.   But what is the explanation of January and
February? Is this in fact the result of drawing a diagram showing
only the peak months? Well, as some check here is a table showing
the number of years in which marriages took place in each month.
For example, in no less than 99 of the 250 years marriages occurred
in November.   There appears to be no local social custom which
might account for this.

Table showing the number of years in which marriages
took place in each month.   (Table covers 250 years)

November	99
July	62
May	61
April and June	57
October	54
December	48
January	47
February	41
August	34
September	28
March	26

It has to be remembered all the time that these diagrams and Tables
take no account of the number of marriages, only of when they took
place.

AN ENQUIRY INTO SEASONALITY IN
BAPTISMS, MARRIAGES AND BURIALS

L. Bradley

Part 2. Baptism Seasonality

In the first part of this article (L.P.S. No. 4, page 21) it was
suggested that a study of seasonality, that is of the fluctuations in
the numbers of baptisms, marriages and burials from month to
month within the year, provides useful material not only, as is
obvious, for the general demographer, but also for the local historian.
It was suggested, as a first hypothesis, that the factors underlying
seasonal variations would be of three kinds:

(a)   those which were common to the whole nation, or at any rate
        to large regions and which persisted over considerable periods.
        These would include church law (such as prohibited periods
        for marriage), widespread occupational factors (such as the
        long hours of work in harvest in rural areas) and possibly
        biological factors associated with the seasons.

(b)   more localised factors, but still fairly persistent and not
        confined to single parishes, such as might be expected to
        produce significant local variations of a general pattern.
        Lambing might, for example, have a local effect in sheep-
        farming districts similar to the more widespread harvest
        effect, but at a different season.   Regional customs, too,
        would be included here.

(c)   very localised and short-term factors, often almost accidental
        in nature, reflecting happenings in a parish or small region.
        An example would be that the incumbent habitually spent
        certain months of the year away from his parish.

The method suggested for the investigation of seasonality in a single
parish or group of parishes starts by calculating the decadal totals
of baptisms (or marriages, or burials) for each month of the year
and expressing the total for each month as a percentage of the total
of all baptisms for the decade.   These monthly percentages are then
exhibited in two series of graphs:

(i)   a separate graph for each decade, showing how the baptisms
        for that decade are distributed through the calendar months.

(ii)   a separate graph for each calendar month, showing how the
percentage of baptisms attributable to that month varies
with the passage of the decades.

The choice of the decade as the time unit was discussed, and also
the advantages and _disadvantages_ of aggregating the figures for several
neighbouring parishes (to eliminate very local effects) and of using, in
addition to the decadal graphs, some graphs for 50-year periods (to
eliminate further short-term effects).

The method was then applied to a study of the seasonality of marriage
in six Derbyshire and six Nottinghamshire parishes.   This article
similarly studies baptism seasonality, and it will be followed by a
final article on burial seasonality.

When the two series of graphs are drawn for the baptism distributions
in the twelve parishes, they suggest a marked seasonal pattern with a
peak of baptisms in spring, a summer trough and a second peak,
usually smaller, in autumn.   This pattern is, as would be expected,
modified by local variations.   Figure 1 shows how the pattern
emerges for WIRKSWORTH.

Averaging parish by parish over 50-year periods, to reduce the short-
term variations, the peak of baptisms almost always comes in
February, March or April, with March as the most favoured month.
The autumn peak comes most frequently in October or November.
The summer trough is most often at its deepest in August in the
Nottinghamshire parishes, taken separately, and in July in the
Derbyshire parishes.   Figure 2 shows the distribution in successive
50-year periods for the _combined_ Nottinghamshire parishes.

The variations which disturb the long-term pattern rarely last, in any
parish, more than two decades, but they are distinctly more pronounced
than were the variations on the general marriage pattern.   Figure 3,
for example, shows how August, normally a very unpopular month for
marriages, shows in OXTON very marked peaks in some decades.
Nevertheless, the general pattern persists in the Nottinghamshire
parishes throughout the period (1600-1840), and in the Derbyshire
parishes until 1750.

In 1750, a striking phenomenon emerges in all the Derbyshire parishes
examined - the concentration into one particular month of the year of
a very high percentage of the total baptisms for the decade.
Figures 4 and 5 show how, in WIRKSWORTH, a September peak of

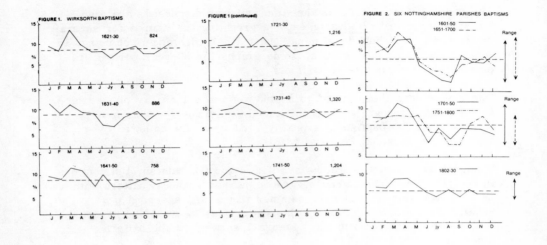

FIGURE 1. WIRKSORTH BAPTISMS

FIGURE 1 (continued)

FIGURE 2. SIX NOTTINGHAMSHIRE PARISHES BAPTISMS

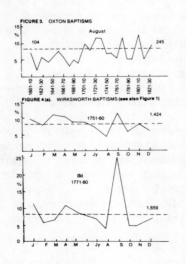

FICURE 3. OXTON BAPTISMS

FIGURE 4 (a). WIRKSWORTH BAPTISMS (see also Figure 1)

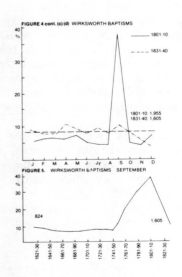

FIGURE 4 cont. (c) (d) WIRKSWORTH BAPTISMS

FIGURE 5. WIRKSWORTH BAPTISMS SEPTEMBER

baptisms began to appear in 1751–60, rose to a maximum in 1801–10, when it comprised 38% of the decadal baptisms, and then subsided until, by 1831–40, it had amost disappeared.   The other Derbyshire parishes showed a similar pattern, but with different peak months:

Parish	Peak month	Decade when phenomenon commenced	Decade when peak reached maximum	Peak percentage
Ashover	July	1751–60	1781–90	19
Bradbourne	November	*	1801–10	32
Brailsford	October	1791–1800	1801–10	23
Brassington	August	1761–70	1801–10	51**
Matlock	September	1751–60	1801–10	25
Wirksworth	September	1751–60	1801–10	38

* Baptism figures for 1751–60 are missing in Bradbourne, but the peak was well established in 1761–70.

** The exceptionally high peak of 51% in Brassington was followed by a decade in which August baptisms were 10.2%, little above average.

Amongst the Nottinghamshire parishes, EDWINSTOWE shows the phenomenon clearly, with an October peak of 21.5% in 1781–90, and Gedling a much modified November peak, barely perceptible in 1761–70, rising to 17% in 1781–90, after which it vanishes.

Finally, the graphs for every parish but one show a flattening in the early 19th century.   Figure 2 shows this flattening for the combined Nottinghamshire parishes, for which the <u>range</u> (the difference between the highest and lowest monthly percentages for the period concerned) in the successive periods diminished thus:

Period	1601–50	1651–1700	1701–50	1751–1800	1801–40
Range	4.4%	4.2%	4.1%	3.0%	2.0%

In other words, the seasonal influences diminish as we approach the end of the period.

How can we interpret these observations?   The fundamental natural events preceding baptism are conception and birth.   We have to disentangle a complex of factors, some of which operate directly on the choice of the date of baptism, others of which act indirectly on baptism by determining the seasonal pattern of conception.   Clearly, if conceptions follow a seasonal pattern, this will <u>influence</u> the baptism pattern, but will not completely determine it, since as a rule the actual date of baptism is a matter of choice.

The factors acting directly on baptisms might include, for example, canonical law on baptism, such as we have seen operating on marriage; local customs, such as the saving up of baptisms for the patronal festival of the parish; or superstitions regarding favourable or unfavourable months for baptism.   I have not been able to find any canonical law on baptism which would affect its seasonality, but possibly readers of L. P. S. may be able to enlighten me.   What can explain the Derbyshire 'peak month' phenomenon described above?   It is surely inconceivable that it can be due to a conception pattern; that, for example, the 51% of the total decadal baptisms (1801-10) occurring in August in BRASSINGTON could mean that 51% of conceptions occurred in November - or in any other one month.   Baptisms were obviously being saved up for some special occasion.   The first possibility seemed to be the patronal festival, but some parish peaks were not in the right month for this.   Was the occasion religious or secular?   Why did it arise at this time in this group of parishes? I hope that other readers of L. P. S. who have come across similar phenomena may help towards an explanation.   Clearly any such significant local deviation from a generally established regional pattern will interest the local historian, who will wish to establish the reasons for it.   It will be of importance, too, to the local population student, for, as will be shown below, it can be a source of error in reconstitution studies.

Turning now to factors which operate on conception and birth rather than directly on baptism, and which might determine a seasonal pattern, some possibilities come readily to mind.   There may be a biological rhythm, as there is in plants and animals.   There might be ecclesiastical influences, such as the discouragement of indulgence in intercourse during Lent.   There might be occupational factors; it has been suggested that long hours of hard work in harvest time in a predominantly agricultural community left little time or energy for intercourse.   It has been suggested, too, that long hours of winter darkness encouraged intercourse - it was reported that a period of power cuts in a New York winter produced a peak of births nine months later!   And, of course, it might be suggested that there should be some relationship between the known seasonal pattern of marriage at any period and the pattern of conception.   But one has to be very cautious in linking these possible factors to the known baptism pattern. We need to keep clear the distinction between birth and baptism.   An example may help to reveal the difficulties.

U.M. Cowgill has written three articles (1) in which she discusses, amongst other issues, birth seasonality in York between 1538 and 1812, using the printed parish register transcripts. Dividing the period into five parts, 1538-1601, 1602-1651, 1652-1701, 1702-1751 and 1752-1812, she aggregates the baptisms over each of these periods and obtains baptism patterns very similar to those which I have established for my Derbyshire and Nottinghamshire parishes. She then treats these as birth patterns, counting nine months backwards, for example, to obtain conception patterns, and drawing inferences about seasonal influences on conception. The registers, of course, give the dates of baptism, but the date of birth is given in only a few years in any parish. Miss Cowgill justifies her assumption by the following statement in the Nature article: "In the limited number of cases for which data for both events are given prior to 1750, the average waiting time is about three days. After 1750, with the exception of adults who are being admitted to the Established Church, the waiting time is five days. In most cases the difference is so small that, for the purposes of this study, the baptism and the birth date can be considered to be essentially the same". Miss Cowgill is not alone, of course, in making this assumption; it is frequently made in reconstitution studies. I suggest that the evidence offered is often missing or entirely inadequate.

Under what circumstances can we establish a credible relationship between the baptism pattern and the birth pattern for a specific parish – in other words, establish a birth-baptism interval which can be taken as reasonably representative? I suggest that there are two essentials:

    i.   The proportion of cases in which both dates are given must be high enough to make it clear that they constitute the general rule and are not exceptions. If, for example, only one birth date were given for every twenty baptisms, there would be a strong probability that they were given for some special reason and were not representative. Such a high proportion is only likely to occur in a few years in any parish.

    ii.   Even if we find a period in which every baptism has its birth date recorded, this is still not enough to establish a representative birth-baptism interval. The following table shows the distribution of the birth-baptism intervals for two imaginary parishes.

Interval(days)	0-7	8-14	15-21	22-28	29-35	36-42	43-49	50-56	57-63
Distribution									
Parish A	12	36	22	2	1	0	0	1	2
Parish B	3	7	8	8	9	6	8	2	4

For Parish A we could fairly assume a birth-baptism interval of
about 12 days (the median has been used as it is usually a better
guide than the average).   For Parish B, the spread is so wide and
so even, that it seems to me to be quite unrealistic to assume any
representative interval.   So that not only must there be a high
proportion of cases in which both dates are given, but there must be
a high degree of concentration of the intervals about the chosen
representative interval.

There is a further difficulty.   Since there are few parishes in which
birth dates are given over a long period of time it is, as a rule, only
possible to establish a representative birth-baptism interval, if at all,
for isolated and comparatively short periods?   Can we assume that
such an interval is valid for other periods in the same parish.   Or
for other parishes?   There can undoubtedly be considerable variations
in the same parish between one period and another.   In the
Derbyshire parish of WINSTER, for example, I have found an abrupt
change in the interval within five years due, so far as one can tell,
to the arrival of a new incumbent.   Dr. R.S. Schofield tells me that
he has found considerable variation from one parish to another, the
range of the median interval for the parishes which he has surveyed
varying from around 18 days in the late 17th century to 111 days in
the late 18th century.   It is clear, then, that one must be very
cautious in transferring a known birth-baptism interval from one
period to another or from one parish to another unless further
evidence becomes available.   It would be most useful to have a
comprehensive survey of all the evidence which parish registers
provide on this important matter.   Until this is done, and unless a
recognisable pattern emerges, much work which involves a knowledge
of the birth-baptism interval in a given parish at a given time is
bound to be speculative.

Let us consider how far the York figures satisfy these requirements.
Printed transcripts are available for eleven parishes (2), though not
all of them are complete.   Analysing the baptism entries produces
the following table, in which the period covered by the transcript is
shown under the name of the parish, the columns headed (a) give the
total numbers of baptisms in each period, and the columns headed (b)
the number for which birth dates are given.   Figures are, of course,
approximate, owing to obscurities in a few entries.

It would seem that there is no evidence from the transcripts adequate
to establish a representative birth-baptism interval for the periods
1538-1601 and 1602-1651.

	1538–1601 (a)	1538–1601 (b)	1602–1651 (a)	1602–1651 (b)	1652–1701 (a)	1652–1701 (b)	1702–1751 (a)	1702–1751 (b)	1752–1812 (a)	1752–1812 (b)
St. Michael le Belfry 1565–1778	1,311	0	2,458	0	2,330	178	2,128	44	1,085	166
St. Olave 1538–1644	852	1	923	2						
St. Martin, Coney St. 1557–1812	506	0	644	1	778	25	611	13	693	522
St. Crux 1540–1716	911	0	1,189	0	1,245	0	320	0		
All Saints, Pavement 1554–1738	517	0	914	0	1,128	0	947	1		
Holy Trinity, Goodramgate 1573–1812	261	0	1,007	0	1,037	189	1,101	39	1,374	1,358
St. Laurence 1606–1812			368	1	253	0	462	7	908	590
St. Mary Bishophill Jnr 1602–1812			427	0	862	4	808	1	1,143	2
Holy Trinity, King's Court 1663–1812					676	1	901	3	465	224
St. Martin cum Gregory 1540–1734	388	0	528	0	608	104	404	0		
Holy Trinity Micklegate 1586–1777	313	0	949	0	793	38	912	0	446	3
TOTAL	5,059	1	9,407	4	9,710	539	8,594	108	6,114	2,865

In the period 1652-1701, five parishes, which had not previously given birth dates, began to do so in 1653, though two of them gave so few as to be of no use in determining a birth-baptism interval.   The following table shows the period for which they continued to give birth dates, the period for which the proportion of birth dates given was high, and the median and mean interval calculated from these periods of concentration.

	Period for which birth dates given	Period of concent-ration	Number of baptisms	Number of birth dates	Median (days)	Mean (days)
St. Michael le Belfry	1653-1656	1653-1656	171*	167	6	6
St. Martin, Coney St.	1653-1654		(24)	(10)		
Holy Trinity Goodramgate	1653-1664	1653-1662	202	181	5	5
St. Martin cum Gregory	1653-1662	1653-1662	131	104	6	7
Holy Trinity Micklegate	1653 Only		(11)	(3)		

* There were a further 20 baptisms in 1653
before the giving of birth dates commenced.

There is a case for inferring a birth-baptism interval of 5 or 6 days for three parishes in the years immediately following 1653.   Its extension to the other parishes would rest entirely on analogy, and there is no evidence for years subsequent to 1662.   One doubt remains. The commencement in 1653 of the inclusion of birth dates would appear to be related to the transfer, by the Commonwealth Government, of legal registration to civil officials, and, in the three parishes which did change their registration style, there may have been associated circumstances promoting early baptism in these years.   It would be interesting to know why only the minority of parishes changed their style and why two of them maintained it until after the Restoration. It may be worth noting that, averaging the numbers of baptisms for 1648-52 and for 1653-57, there is a drop of about 5% for the whole city, but rises of 10% and 15% for Holy Trinity, Goodramgate, and St. Martin-cum-Gregory respectively, though St. Michael-le-Belfry shows a drop of 6%.

Turning to the period 1701-1752, only one parish, Holy Trinity, Goodramgate, shows more than scattered birth dates.   In this one parish, between 1726 and 1734, out of 186 baptisms, 39 have some reference to birth, but not in the form of a birth date.   In 31 of them, baptism is recorded as following one month after birth, which can hardly be intended as a precise interval.   The other 8 are recorded as 1, 3, 5, 6, 6 and 11 weeks, 2 months and 3 years.   In no parish, then, is there adequate evidence to establish a birth-baptism interval.

The situation between 1752 and 1812 is more complicated.   Five of the seven parishes for which the transcripts extend into this period show substantial numbers of birth dates.   In St. Michael-le-Belfry, there is no year in which as many as half of the birth dates are given, and they reach a quarter in only 7 out of the 27 years.   It is noticeable that, of the 166 birth-baptism intervals given, all but 16 are over a month, which may mean that only those over a month are normally recorded.   For the other four parishes, I have analysed the figures by decades, and I have calculated the median and the mean intervals (in days) for decades in which there is a high proportion of birth dates. The figures in brackets in the following table show the total number of baptisms, followed by the number of recorded birth dates, in the appropriate decades.

		1762-1771		1772-1781		1782-1791		1792-1801		1802-1812	
		Med	Mean	Med	Mean	Med	Mean	Med	Mean	Med	Mean
St. Martin Coney St.	1762-1812	9	13	4	12	3	9	3	10	7	20
		(134- 92)		(136-125)		(125-111)		(90-83)		(114-107)	
Holy Tnty Good/gate	1782-1812					5	12½	25	48	57	70
		(177- 1)		(246- 4)		(246-242)		(207-207)		(285-285)	
St. Laurence	1779-1812					8	15	7	12	7	11
		(123- 0)		(130- 41)		(148-135)		(172-170)		(246-244)	
Holy Tnty Kings Ct.										4½	12
		(179- 6)		(220- 53)		(193- 93)		(207- 34)		(258-190)	

The considerably greater difference between the median and the mean in this period, as compared with the years following 1653, shows that the spread of birth-baptism intervals is wider.   In St. Michael-le-Belfry and Holy Trinity, Goodramgate, it is very wide indeed, so that in the former no reasonable representative birth-baptism interval can, in my opinion, be inferred, and in the latter (where the spread is clearly increasing towards the end of the period) no reasonable interval can be inferred, at any rate after 1791.   There remain, then, three parishes out of the seven for which transcripts extend into this period, for which a short birth-baptism interval of between 3 and 9 days can reasonably be inferred.   Do the remaining eight parishes follow this pattern, or do they follow that of Holy Trinity, Goodramgate, or do they diverge even further?   There is no evidence in the registers to determine this.

If I have discussed the York figures at, perhaps, inordinate length, it is because they provide an excellent example of the great care which must be taken in making any pronouncement about the relation between baptism and birth or baptism and conception.   It is, of course, possible that Miss Cowgill is right but, in my opinion, she has failed to give the evidence needed to support her main assumption in the discussion of conception seasonality, and this reduces her discussion of seasonality factors to interesting but unsubstantiated speculation.   And clearly the same care needs to be taken in some of the issues arising out of family reconstitution.   Calculations of peri-natal mortality and of the time interval between successive births to the same mother, for example, will be affected of there is no representative birth-baptism interval or if it has been wrongly estimated.

It is, perhaps, of interest that these York parishes are giving such detail in their baptism entries at a time when, according to one authority, Anglican registration had "virtually collapsed".   And is it a coincidence that this period coincides with the incidence of the Derbyshire baptism peak phenomenon described earlier?

There remain two further points which I would like to discuss.   If a representative birth-baptism interval can be established, the actual length of the interval will obviously be crucial to any discussion of birth or conception seasonality.   The following table shows the months of conception which would correspond to the months of baptism, assuming 0-, 1-, 2- and 3-month intervals

	Jan	Feb	Mar	Apl	May	Jun	Jly	Aug	Sep	Oct	Nov	Dec
Interval					Corresponding month of conception							
0 months	Apl	May	Jun	Jly	Aug	Sep	Oct	Nov	Dec	Jan	Feb	Mar
1 month	Mar	Apl	May	Jun	Jly	Aug	Sept	Oct	Nov	Dec	Jan	Feb
2 months	Feb	Mar	Apl	May	Jun	Jly	Aug	Sep	Oct	Nov	Dec	Jan
3 months	Jan	Feb	Mar	Apl	May	Jun	Jly	Aug	Sep	Oct	Nov	Dec

Month of baptism

It will be seen that a three-month interval will produce quite a different seasonal conception pattern than if we had supposed birth and baptism to coincide. This table can be used to examine some of the suggested possible factors influencing the conception pattern, though it is not possible to do this in detail in this article.

i. Abstinence from intercoure in Lent would reduce March conceptions, and consequently December births, to a low level. The corresponding baptism trough would be in December, January or February with a 0-, 1- or 2 month interval respectively. Figure 2 would suggest that, after 1600, December baptisms in my Nottingham-shire parishes, though not high, could not be said to show a trough. Looking at all twelve Derbyshire and Nottinghamshire parishes, out of 254 December baptisms 'cells' (3), 61 or 24% showed less than 6% of the decadal baptisms, and only 34, or 13%, less than 5%. January and February have above-average baptisms throughout. It seems fair to conclude that, in these twelve parishes, there was no consistent and pronounced avoidance of intercourse in Lent after 1600, unless the birth-baptism intervals were unexpectedly long. Miss Cowgill's graphs for York do show a marked December trough in the first period (1538-1601) and a small deficiency in her second period. If she is right in assuming a short birth-baptism interval, this would be consistent with Lent abstinence though, since other factors may be operating, it would not prove it.

ii. A reduction in intercourse at harvest would result in low baptisms in May to August, according to the length of the birth-baptism interval. May does not appear to show any marked deficiency, but June, July and August certainly do.

It has been suggested, as noted above that there might be some connection between the known seasonality pattern of marriage at a given period and the corresponding conception pattern. The attempt to trace such a relationship meets a further difficulty. Assuming that intercourse and conception follow shortly after marriage, one might expect a relationship between the marriage distribution and the distribution of _first_ births. The two marked marriage troughs of the earlier periods, March and December, would then give rise to troughs in the baptism distribution of first children, and the November peak to a baptism peak, though the positions of these troughs and peak would depend on the length of the birth-baptism interval. Unfortunately, all our distributions are for _all_ children, and there is no way, in an aggregative analysis, of separating out the distribution

33

for first children.   Baptisms of other than first children would not be
linked to the marriage distribution so that, for example, any peak
resulting from the birth of first children would be modified by the
differing pattern for subsequent children, the extent of the modification
depending on the relative numbers of first and subsequent children.
Miss Cowgill writes (4) "The short life-span of the adult would lead
to a disproportionate number of families that bore only one child
conceived at the time of marriage."   This is quite inadequate.   How
disproportionate? Was the life-span so short (5)? Miss Cowgill's
own estimate for York is that the average family size between 1538
and 1751 was 3.56 (6).   Other writers have suggested, for various
parishes, averages of between 3½ and 6 (7).   If only a quarter of
the births were first births, the 'first-birth' effect would be very
severely modified, and this modification would be increased by both
extra-marital and pre-marital conceptions.   My own impression is
that it is hardly worth while to investigate this marriage-baptism
relationship by aggregative analysis, though the more laborious family
reconstitution approach may be more effective.

In this article I have given an account of the seasonal pattern of
baptisms as it appears in six Derbyshire and six Nottinghamshire
parishes.   I have suggested that such a seasonal pattern will be due
to a combination of factors of two kinds, those operating directly on
the choice of the baptism date, and those operating indirectly through
their effect on the seasonal pattern of conception, and I have discussed
the difficulties which arise in considering the latter group of factors.
The birth-baptism interval has been discussed at length because it is
here that one frequently finds unproved assumptions which may
seriously affect the validity of the conclusions, both in discussions of
seasonality and in calculations from family reconstitution.

I hope that I have not left the impression that the investigation of
baptism seasonality is unprofitable or too difficult.   I am convinced
that it can lead to useful results, especially by the investigation of
local deviations from the general pattern, but only if the underlying
assumptions are clearly stated and supported by adequate evidence.
My article raises more questions than it answers, and I shall be glad
to hear from other readers of L.P.S. who have experience to
contribute.

The concluding article of this series will be devoted to burial
seasonality.

NOTES

(1)   'Historical Study of the Season of Birth in the City of York, England', in <u>Nature,</u> No. 5028, March 12th, 1966.

       'Life and Death in the 16th century in the City of York' in <u>Population Studies,</u> XXI Pt. 1, July 1967.

       'The People of York 1538-1812' in <u>The Scientific American</u> January 1970.

(2)   The first volume of the transcript for St. Mary, Castlegate, has recently been published, but would not be available to Miss Cowgill.

(3)   For the definition of a 'cell', see 'An Enquiry into Seasonality in Baptisms, Marriages and Burials', Part 1, in <u>L.P.S.</u> No. 4, Spring 1970, p. 25.

(4)   <u>Scientific American,</u> January 1970, page 104.

(5)   "It is still quite likely that a man of 21 could have something like 30 years to live. If he married at 30 - not an unlikely age, as we have seen - he could probably expect to live 25 years with his wife" - P. Laslett in <u>The World We Have Lost.</u> p. 94.

(6)   <u>Scientific American,</u> January 1970, page 112. I find it odd that Miss Cowgill should assume that the average family size would remain constant over so long a period.

(7)   See <u>The World We Have Lost</u> - P. Laslett - Methuen, 1965, p. 102. <u>Population in History</u> - ed. Glass and Eversley - Edward Arnold, 1965. p. 48.

The Christening Custom at Melbourn, Cambs.

Dennis R. Mills

Until recently there was a generally accepted convention in English historical demography that children were usually baptised within the month after their birth and often within a few days. This convention has been seriously challenged by Berry and Schofield,[1] not only for the late eighteenth and early nineteenth centuries, when the registers are known to be defective, but also for earlier periods. Moreover a marked seasonality of baptisms, which can only be explained in terms of long intervals between birth and baptism, has been demonstrated for certain Nottinghamshire and Derbyshire parishes by Bradley.[2] The present article offers further evidence on both seasonality and the birth-baptism interval based on the Anglican and Congregational registers of Melbourn, Cambridgeshire.

Using the rubrics of the Prayer Books of 1549, 1552 and 1662, Berry and Schofield summarise the official attitude of the Church of England as follows. It "encouraged universal baptism, with a delay of not more than seven days up to about 1650 and of not more than 14 days after that date".[3] The article then goes on to draw together all the consistent evidence of birth-baptism intervals found in parts of forty-three printed registers.

This is shown in their table 2, where the data are presented in terms of earliest, median and latest baptising parishes in the three periods 1650—1700, 1771—1789 and 1791—1812. In the median parishes the birth-baptism interval was eight days or less for 50 per cent of the children baptised between 1650 and 1700. Comparable figures for the two later periods were 26 and 30 days, thus supporting the very broad generalisation that the birth-baptism interval increased with the passage of time. Much larger increases occurred in the latest baptising parishes, the actual figures being 27, 155 and 444 days, while earliest baptising parishes were still following the forms of the Prayer Book. The overall impression gained from the evidence gathered by Berry and Schofield is of very great geographical variation and many changes within individual parishes, quite often "back" to a shorter interval.

Melbourn is a large nucleated village on the arable chalk plain of south Cambridgeshire. In 1801 it contained a total population of 819, rising rapidly to a peak of 1,931 in 1851. Broadly speaking, the number of baptisms kept pace, rising from 297 in 1781—1800 to 534 in 1821—37, but under-registration was probably heavy because nonconformity, including a Baptist following, was well established by the second half of the seventeenth century. However, the registers were well kept and the marriage register shows that the curate was seldom absent from the parish for very long.[4] The data used in this paper, therefore, would seem to be reliable for the Anglican population of the village and can be supplemented for a short period by data from a Congregational register.

The July maximum of baptisms emerges first of all in the decade 1741—50, virtually disappears in 1751—60, but re-appears in the next decade, rises to a peak in 1791—1800 and subsides gently into the nineteenth century, but is still persisting when civil registration of births begins. In addition to the July maximum, sub-maxima in spring and autumn can also often be discerned.

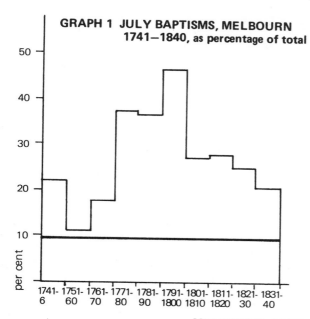

GRAPH 1 JULY BAPTISMS, MELBOURN
1741–1840, as percentage of total

■
LEVEL OF BAPTISMS
IF EVENLY DISTRIBUTED
BETWEEN MONTHS

MELBOURN, CAMBS.

TABLE 1
BAPTISMAL COUNT BY MONTHS 1561–1840

Period	Jan.	Feb.	Mar.	Apr.	May	Jun.	Jul.	Aug.	Sept.	Oct.	Nov.	Dec.
1561–80	42	22	30	33	30	31	37	36	36	39	42	33
1581–1600	42	28	33	43	34	33	38	37	28	39	44	38
1601–1620	39	35	37	40	34	36	22	36	39	39	41	53
1621–1640	47	37	50	38	35	17	19	19	27	37	39	38
1641–1660	29	27	31	28	22	21	17	22	16	19	27	33
1661–1680	25	20	12	13	13	20	21	12	21	35	15	21
1681–1700†	15	9	11	9	12	9	13	8	12	9	15	12
1701–1720	14	18	11	27	26	20	13	16	19	10	12	6
1721–1740	10	5	18	20	21	22	21	9	21	13	17	17
1741–1760	8	18	21	25	24	15	40*	12	18	14	24	13
1761–1780	15	31	20	18	13	5	73*	7	15	22	11	24
1781–1800	24	10	12	18	19	11	124	9	17	19	9	25
1801–1820	31	26	27	41	30	11	124	35	15	57	22	31
1821–1840	24	22	40	40	39	31	118	48	41	52	34	45

* There was a period of gradual emergence of the July maximum, e.g. 1743–4, 1744–6,
1746–10, 1752–4, 1771–1780 only three years less than 3.
† Register could be defective or baptisms not regularly carried out.

TABLE 2

MELBOURN JULY BAPTISMS 1741—1840

Decade	Total Baptisms	July Baptisms No.	Per cent.
1741—1750	139	30	21.6
1751—1760	93	10	10.8
1761—1770	104	18	17.3
1771—1780	150	55	37.6
1781—1790	141	52	37.0
1791—1800	156	72	46.0
1801—1810	243	66	27.2
1811—1820	207	58	28.0
1821—1830	263	63	24.0
1831—1840	271	55	20.2

Comparison with Bradley's parishes is most interesting. There he found a persistence of spring and autumn maxima from 1600 to 1840 in Nottinghamshire and from 1600 to 1750 in Derbyshire. After 1750 in the six parishes studied in the latter county, there occurred a "concentration into one particular month of the year of a very high percentage of the total baptisms for the decade".[5] Although the month varied from July to November, the six parishes shared the common feature of a gradual rise in the phenomenon, a peak decade occurring in 1801—10 in five of the six parishes, and a consequent flattening out by 1840. This is very similar to Melbourn where the peak decade was 1791—1800 (Graph 2). In two Nottinghamshire parishes a peak occurred in the decade 1781—90, rising and falling more rapidly than at Melbourn or in Derbyshire. We must obviously expect to find both long and short-lived christening customs, as the balance between religious and socio-economic circumstances would vary so much from parish to parish.

The lower part of table 3 shows that by comparison with baptisms, on the whole, the births were much more evenly spread throughout the year and, therefore the peaking of baptisms must be largely due to postponement. However, we should not pass over the observation that between 1795—1810 there was a modest peak of births in May, June and July, which could have made some contribution to the July peak of baptisms, when it was at its highest. In the next decade this peak of births had virtually disappeared and between 1821—30 the winter months were showing a maximum but this was not strongly marked.

TABLE 3

MELBOURN CAMBS DATA ON BAPTISMAL POSTPONEMENT

1795 – 1830

DATE AND PERIOD	Jan.	Feb.	Mar.	Apr.	May.	Jun.	Jul.	Aug.	Sept.	Oct.	Nov.	Dec.	Averages	Totals
Median birth-baptism interval, by month of birth.				Figures (rounded) refer to whole months.										
1795–1810	4	5	4	4.5	3.5	2	5	4	4	5	6	7	4.5	
1811–1820	6	5	4	4	2.5	3.5	3	11.5	4.5	2	5	7	4.8	
1821–1830	6	5	5	6	5	9.5	10	10	3	8	8	7	6.8	
Average	5.3	5	4.3	4.8	3.6	5	6	8.5	3.8	5	6.3	7	5.4	
Median interval by month of baptism														
1795–1810	4	4	4	4	6	2	6	7.5	5	3	8	5	5.0	
1811–1820	3	6.5	4	3	5	3	6	6	3	8	2	4	4.4	
1821–1830	7.5	2.5	3	3	7	8	7	7	7.5	7.5	7	3	5.8	
Average	4.8	5	3.6	3.3	6	5	6.3	6.8	5.1	6.1	5.6	4	5.1	
Total children recorded by month of birth														
1795–1810	21	20	29	26	32	34	37	18	22	20	35	30	27.0	324
1811–1820	18	18	19	17	22	20	21	12	14	15	16	22	17.8	214
1821–1830	32	16	29	25	23	18	17	14	12	26	24	24	21.6	260
1795–1830	71	54	77	68	77	72	75	44	48	61	75	76	67.3	808
Total children recorded by month of baptism														
1795–1810	22	16	19	27	21	9	105	22	11	33	14	25	27.0	324
1811–1820	14	10	11	15	20	7	56	17	15	28	9	12	17.8	214
1821–1830	6	2	15	15	22	20	63	27	22	30	23	15	21.6	260
1795–1830	42	28	45	57	63	36	224	66	48	91	46	52	67.3	808

39

TABLE 4

MELBOURN CAMBS.

Marriages

Period	Jan.	Feb.	Mar.	Apr.	May	Jun.	Jul.	Aug.	Sept.	Oct.	Nov.	Dec.
1781—90	0	2	1	2	5	3	6	2	7	17	2	4
1791—1800	3	5	3	4	2	1	2	4	2	25	3	7
1801—1810	1	7	5	5	3	2	6	0	1	24	15	5
1811—1820	7	8	5	7	5	1	5	2	4	19	11	11
1821—1830	5	9	11	12	6	3	3	6	8	17	21	8
1831—1840	4	7	2	1	5	5	10	1	9	14	13	9
1781—1840	20	38	27	31	26	15	32	15	31	116	65	44

One possibility is that the tradition of autumn weddings (table 4) might help to explain the midsummer maximum of births between 1795—1810, but as this tradition continued until 1840 without apparently continuing to produce a corresponding seasonality in births, not much reliance can be placed on its causality between 1795—1810. Although this represents the limit of analysis of birth seasonality, much more can be said about the seasonality of baptisms in Melbourn.

Returning to table 3, the upper half summarises the median values of the birth-baptism interval, in one part by months of birth and in the other by months of baptism. Whichever way the aggregation is calculated, it shows that Melbourn babies could expect to wait rather more than five months after their birth before they were baptised. This was certainly a very high figure, even for this relatively late period.

In Berry and Schofield's data the longest comparable interval occurred at Kempston, Bedfordshire in 1800—03 when 50% of the children were baptised within 114 days or less of birth.[6] This represents a period of just under four months.

In York the highest known median interval between birth and baptism was 57 days in 1802—1812 in the parish of Holy Trinity, Goodramgate[7]. A further comparison can be made with Tranter's data for Bedfordshire, where a delay of over two weeks became about twice as frequent as a delay of less than two weeks in having the child baptised (table 5). Although these data are presented differently from those for Melbourn, the contrast between pre-1750 and post-1750 is supported, especially by Kempston where figures for either end of the period are available for the same parish.[8]

TABLE 5

Data on the birth-baptism interval in Bedfordshire

Source : Tranter, 1966, p. 158—9.

(A)   Median interval in Kempston :

        1740—50   :   13 days.

        1801—12   :   87 days, with none less than 10 days.

(B)

Period and Parish	Length of interval (per cent of baptisms).		
	Less than 2 weeks.	2 weeks— 2 months.	3 months and more
Ampthill			
1695—1705/06	81	19	0
1717	79	17	4
Houghton Conquest			
1760—72	38	53	9
1782—90	30	52	18
1791—1800	33	47	20
Milton Ernest			
1783—90	44	34	22
1791—1800	48	29	23

So we have to attempt to answer two questions relating to the birth-baptism interval at Melbourn. First, why was baptism postponed; and second, why was July such a favourite month. It is important to consider these as separate, even if connected questions since children baptised in *all* months of the year were generally several months old (table 3) and not only those who were baptised in July. The separation of the questions also assists comparisons between parishes which had different favourite months, for they may well have experienced similar general conditions, although asserting some parochial individuality as to the choice of month. Melbourn fortunately has data on births, but much of what follows is still speculative.

For instance, how closely did Melbournians follow the Prayer Book rubric and "Baptise not Children at home in their Houses"? The 1662 Prayer Book covered this eventuality by requiring that private baptisms should be certified publicly.[9]   If what we see in the baptismal register is *only* public baptisms following upon private baptisms, then we do not have to explain a postponement of baptism in centuries characterised by heavy infant mortality. This is not completely beyond the bounds of plausibility, for in the 1740's, when the July peak first appeared, children were baptised privately on a significant number of occasions in Melbourn. We can only speculate as to whether or not the practice ceased or became so common as to be unworthy of note in the register.

It is worth adding that the register of Chester Cathedral notes for each child baptised there between 1697 and 1812 the date of its birth and/or private baptism. Where all three dates are recorded, private baptism can be seen as occurring very soon after birth, generally the next day, while the interval between either birth or private baptism and the public baptism was usually several months and occasionally over a year. Nevertheless, this is a record of a small number of children, mainly of privileged homes and cannot be likened safely to the ordinary parish register.[11]

What advantage might accrue from delaying the baptism of a child? First, there may have been some reluctance to take a new-born child out of the house, especially if it was winter and the church was cold and draughty. This is a very general kind of argument and cannot be tested very easily, perhaps not at all; but it should be put in the balance against the presumed anxiety to have a child baptised before it was too late.

Another general argument, in an age noted for laxness in churchgoing, is that the clergy were unable to impress upon parents sufficiently well their duty to have children baptised soon after birth. The general decline in churchgoing in the eighteenth century, followed by a Victorian revival might have some bearing on the appearance and disappearance of baptismal delay in widely separated parishes at roughly comparable dates.

A further advantage of baptismal postponement arises out of the perception of the christening service as a social, as much as a religious occasion, as is so often the case in our own day. Are we to imagine that relations and godparents might be invited from distant parishes, that there would need to be a christening tea in the child's home, and so on? Winter was not a good time for travelling and entertaining, food would be less plentiful, fuel would be a problem and guests could not be dispersed into the cottage garden in that season. Melbourn had a preference for July and Bradley's parishes all preferred a month in late summer or in autumn, when food would be plentiful. Even if postponement to a winter month occurred, it gave the mother time to recover from her confinement and the father an opportunity to save a little.

TABLE 6

MELBOURN, CAMBS.

Nuclear and extended family baptisms
N = Nuclear E = Extended
(i.e. cousins baptised simultaneously)

	N +	E =	All family baptisms	July N + E	Total baptisms	All family baptisms as % of total	July N + E as % of all family baptisms	All July baptisms No.	All July baptisms % of total
1781–1790	17	0	17	9	141	12.0	53.0	52	37.0
1791–1800	31	10	41	23	156	26.3	56.0	72	6.0
1801–1810	51	23	74	19	243	30.4	25.8	66	27.2
1811–1820	39	12	51	13	207	24.6	25.5	58	28.0
1821–1830	46	11	57	9	263	21.6	15.8	63	24.0
1831–1841	63	25	88	12	271	32.5	13.7	55	20.2

Moreover, if children were christened in batches, we can introduce economies of scale into the argument. Table 6 demonstrates that batches were a feature of Melbourn life between 1781 and 1841, a feature referred to here as family baptisms. A family baptism is defined as (a) when children of the same parents are baptised on the same day; and (b) when presumed cousins are baptised simultaneously. For purposes of this calculation children were presumed cousins if they shared the same surname. Although this assumption will have been false in some cases, on balance the number of cousins baptised simultaneously will have been under-estimated, because there is a theoretical 3 : 1 chance *against* cousins sharing the same surname, but this ratio is unlikely to have applied in practice to a small community.

Thus the estimates of family baptisms, ranging from 12 to 32 per cent of all baptisms, are likely to be a conservative figure. Even so, this is a substantial proportion of the total and although insufficient in itself to explain the July preferences, those family baptisms sustain an argument that baptism was seen as much more than a routine, religious event.

TABLE 7

MELBOURN CONGREGATIONAL REGISTER, 1825–37

Median Birth-Baptism intervals in 176 baptisms.

MONTH OF BIRTH	Jan.	Feb.	Mar.	Apr.	May	Jun.	Jul.	Aug.	Sept.	Oct.	Nov.	Dec.
Median delay (months)	6	7	7	5	5	3.5	3.5	10	3.5	8.5	10	7

Average   6.33

Month-by-month distribution of births and baptisms

MONTH	Jan.	Feb.	Mar.	Apr.	May	Jun.	Jul.	Aug.	Sept.	Oct.	Nov.	Dec.	Total
Baptisms	1	3	4	2	14	47	5	14	34	20	17	15	176
Births	16	17	13	16	16	12	18	17	12	10	13	12	176

Source : PRO : RG4/155.

In the Anglican registers, the highest numbers involved in family baptisms were recorded by the Stockbridges in 1804, the Kings in 1805 and the Bakers in 1809, all with six children in the same nuclear family. A similar bunching is noticeable in the register of the Independent (Congregational) chapel, between 1825 and 1837 (table 7). Out of 176 entries, 49 children (or 28 per cent) were baptised on family occasions, 32 of them in sibling groups. Pairs were the most common number, but William Crole Carver and his wife baptised five offspring in 1828; and this gentleman was almost certainly the son of a former minister of the chapel!

While on the subject of this separate register, it is interesting to notice that the median birth-baptism interval was 6.33 months, a figure very close to that for the parish register at the same period (6.8 months). A significant number of baptisms were of children from neigh-bouring parishes in which there was no Independent Congregation; the necessity to travel would influence the choice of season. Very large numbers of children were baptised on a few dates, perhaps at special services, so it is usual to find that all the baptisms for the year fell in two or three months. Over the period 1825—37 marked peaks occur in June (47) and September—October (54 out of the 176) and the cold months of December to April accounted for only 25 baptisms altogether.

Can we account for the different favourite months in different parishes, and even for different churches in the same parish? As Bradley has suggested one should consider the patronal festival as a suitable occasion, but this does not fit in with the peak for some of his parishes[11]; nor does it suit Melbourn where the festival, being All Saints, falls on November 1st.

TABLE 8

MELBOURN FEAST WEEK BAPTISMS (2nd—10th July inclusive).

DECADE	FEAST WEEK	TOTAL JULY
1781—1790	48	52
1791—1800	46	72
1801—1810	41*	66
1811—1820	12	58
1821—1830	17	66
1831—1840	23	72

* The last year of large numbers of feast week baptisms was 1812.

However, other occasions could be equally significant, such as the Melbourn Feast which fell on "the day after the first Thursday in July"[12]. This may well have been a generally recognised "home coming time", as it came between the hay and corn harvests. (In Lincolnshire some villages, such as Metheringham, still retain the tradition of going home for Feast Week). The earliest possible date is July 2nd and the latest July 8th, but to include all Sundays following feast days takes in the period up to July 10th. The numbers of baptisms falling in the period 2—10th July inclusive are set out in Table 8 and Graph 2. These show that an overwhelming majority of July baptisms occurred in Feast Week between 1781 and 1810, when a sudden falling off occurred.

More precisely, the watershed date was 1812 and it is probably significant that this year marked the end of the long curacy of Claude Carter (1788—1812). There was no change of vicar until 1817, and Carter's successor, John Flockton, served three incumbents between 1813 and 1831. During this time there were relatively few feast week baptisms, but if Flockton broke this tradition, he did not break the tradition of July baptisms as a whole, for they continued on a substantial scale after he had gone. (Alternatively, 1800 could be taken as the turning point in the total number of July baptisms, but whichever date is taken it does not coincide with the comings and goings of clergy). The coming of Jonathan Trebeck as vicar

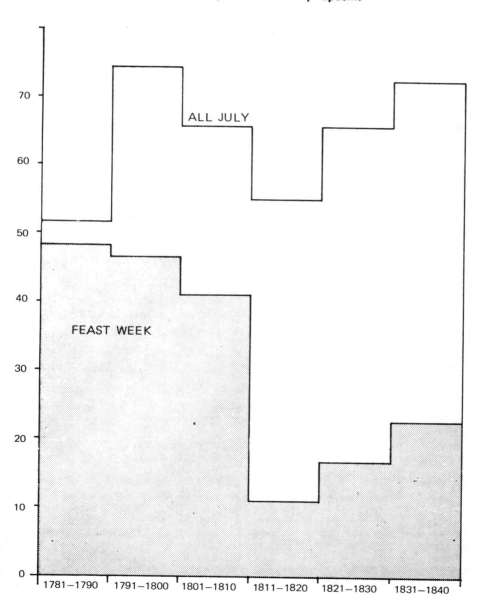

GRAPH 2 MELBOURN FEAST WEEK
BAPTISMS, 1781–1840
as proportion of all July baptisms

ALL JULY

FEAST WEEK

70

60

50

40

30

20

10

0

1781–1790   1791–1800   1801–1810   1811–1820   1821–1830   1831–1840

in 1833, or perhaps the departure of John Flockton, may have been connected with the establishment of Sunday as the regular day of baptism, after a long period in which it was carried out on various days of the week.

In a similar way, the change of minister at the Congregational church may have **modified** a more or less secular or social tradition of christening. When John Medway became minister in 1824 there appears to have been a back-log of baptisms to work through, as the median birth-baptism interval for the first 25 children was 17 months; but by the time he had been in Melbourn for a decade this figure had fallen to 5 months (the median for the last 25 baptisms in the register).

While ministers and vicars may obviously have had a temporary influence on tradition, the same is possibly true of other social leaders. For example, did the village midwives and/or doctors exert any influence on newly confined mothers? For instance, in the church porch at Langton-by-Spilsby, Lincs., there hangs the photograph of an old lady with a baby brought to the church for christening. It was the custom for this lady, and not the mothers of the village, to take babies to be baptised.[13] If she was not the village midwife who was she; and did this custom have parallels elsewhere?

It is obvious that the question of christening customs is eminently suitable for investigation by local students of historical demography, as they will be able to relate data obtained from registers to more general knowledge of their locality. When a bigger picture of the subject emerges what will be revealed? Is it possible to investigate the balance between baptism as a religious rite and christening as a social occasion?

While postponement generally might be found responsive to national or regional changes in the social climate, postponement to a particular month or period may turn out to have been, on balance, more the result of a variety of local factors. These will probably include some of the following:

(a)   Patronal festivals
(b)   Local feasts, fairs, etc.
(c)   The social influence of the clergy and other leaders
(d)   Absence of the clergy from the parish
(e)   Religious leadership of the clergy
(f)   Prayer Book rubrics.
(g)   Local superstitions.

Further research will refine and extend this list. Any reader of this journal who has access to a register that consistently records birth dates should be encouraged to investigate the birth-baptism interval. However, in some parishes the seasonality of baptisms is so marked that it can be investigated to a worthwhile extent without the use of birth dates.

Finally, we might endeavour to relate to our problem the tradition of the churching of women, as newly-confined mothers were theoretically not allowed out of their homes until they had been churched. Consequently a public baptism could not take place with the mother present a few days after the birth, quite apart from the fact of her not being fit enough for the occasion. Is it possible to gather information on godsips (gossips), like the old lady at Langton-by-Spilsby, who took the place of the mother at the baptism? Did the use of godsips vary from time to time and place to place in such a way as to explain shorter and longer intervals between birth and baptism? Did some families use them and others not?.[14]

ACKNOWLEDGEMENTS

I should like to record my thanks to Mr. M. Allsworth, Mr. L. Bradley, Mr. C. Charlton, Prof. M. Drake, Mrs. N. Ogden, Dr. A Rogers, Dr. R.S. Schofield, Dr. N. Tranter and Dr. E.A. Wrigley for help and encouragement in preparing this paper. My thanks are also due to the Rev. and Mrs. D.P. McNiece formerly of Melbourn, for stimulating discussion of the Melbourn christening custom; and to Mr. McNiece and Mrs. D.M. Owen, Ely Diocesan Archivist, for arranging the microfilming of the registers at Cambridge University Library.

NOTES

1. B. M. Berry and R. S. Schofield, "Age at baptism in pre-industrial England", *Population Studies,* 25, 1971, 453—63.

2. L. Bradley, "An enquiry into seasonality in baptisms, marriages and burials: Part Two", *L.P.S.* 5, Autumn 1970, 18—35.

3. Berry and Schofield, *op.cit.,* p. 454.

4. The incumbents, however, appear to have been absent for very long periods.

5. Bradley, *op. cit.,* p. 19—26. The peak percentage of baptisms in the favourite month varied from 17 to 51; while in Melbourn it reached 46.

6. Berry and Schofield, *op.cit.,* p. 457.

7. Bradley, *op.cit.,* p.31. Where very small changes in the birth-baptism interval are sought after, measurement in days is necessary. The measurement was done in months in Melbourn largely because few children were baptised in less than 30 days from birth; these were counted as zeros. While on measurement, the reader should notice that medians have been used throughout this paper, in preference to mean values, as the latter are subject to considerable distortion by the baptism of relatively small numbers of older children, including teenagers and persons of even more mature years.

8. N.L.Tranter, *Demographic change in Bedfordshire, 1670—1800,* unpublished Ph.D thesis, University of Nottingham, 1966, p.158—9.

9. Berry and Schofield, *op.cit,* p. 454.

10. T. and T.C. Hughes, *The Registers of Chester Cathedral,* Parish Register Society, Liverpool, 1904. J.T. Krause also notes that "In some parishes the new-born was baptized privately, and registration was postponed until the later public ceremony was held" in "Changes in English fertility and mortality, 1781—1850", *Econ.Hist.Rev.,* 2nd Series, 11, 1958—59, p. 58.

11. Bradley, *op.cit.,* p.26

12. Edmund Carter, *History of the County of Cambridge,* London, 1753, 1819 ed. p.239. This is still the date of the feast, now marked by the coming of a pleasure fair. When the feast started is, of course, another matter. Did it start before 1740 or did the feast and the christening custom start together?

13. Information from Rev. J. Langton, Tinwell, Rutland and Mr. Terence Leach Dunholme, Lincs.

14. This final paragraph owes its inclusion to information from Mr. C. Charlton.

OF SUCH AS ARE OF RIPER YEARS? A NOTE ON AGE AT BAPTISM
S. Jackson and P. Laxton

'How old be you, Christian?'
'Thirty-one last tatie-digging, Mister Fairway!'
'Not a boy — not a boy. Still there's hope yet.'
'That's my age by baptism, because that's put down
in the great book of the Judgement that they keep
in church vestry; but mother told me I was born some
time afore I was christened.'
'Ah!'
'But she couldn't tell when, to save her life,
except that there was no moon.'[1]

Dr Woodward's recent article on the Commonwealth Act and Yorkshire parish registers reopens some interesting questions about the age at baptism before the 19th century and thus, *inter alia,* about the reliability of Anglican registers as a record of fertility.[2]

I

One of the registers omitted by Berry and Schofield from their study of the birth/baptism interval[3] is that of Liverpool Parish Church (St. Nicholas) which has been published up to 1725.[4] This register would seem to have significance for two reasons. First, it is for a large, rapidly-growing, urban and industrial parish, and thus in its detail a comparative rarity among the records currently being used in studies of demographic history before 1801. Secondly, it records the dates of both birth and baptism for the whole of the eighteenth century. Indeed in common with much of Lancashire all Liverpool's Anglican parishes in the eighteenth century have baptismal registers following this format, the total number of baptisms reaching about 1000 *per annum* by 1750 and about 2000 *per annum* by 1780. Not only does this fill a gap in the evidence for birth/baptism intervals noted by Berry and Schofield[5] but it also helps to overcome the problems of small samples which may be reflected in their results. It provides data comparable to Dr Woodward's splendid figures for Leeds.[6]

Prior to a fuller analysis Table 1 may make a small contribution to this topic. The same percentile divisions (plus the 90 per cent added by Woodward) have been used but the semi-inter-quartile range employed by Berry and Schofield has been omitted since the data are not highly skewed by a few very long intervals (the mean, it will be noticed, is not far from the 50 per cent median value in each period). IE denotes the number of incomplete entries.

Table 1 Interval in days (+ 0.5) by which the stated percentile of births was baptized: four sample periods from Liverpool parish registers.

		25%	50%	75%	90%	N	IE	Mean
St. Nicholas	1697*	3	6	9	11	145	2	
	1698*	4	7	10	14	114	0	
	1699*	4	6	9	13	130	3	
	1700*	4	7	10	14	131	0	
		4	6	10	13	520	5	7.2
St. Nicholas	1720	5	8	12	16	206	25	
	1721	6	9	13	16	196	11	
	1722	6	9	12	17	213	27	
	1723	6	8	12	16	191	19	
		6	9	12	16	806	82	9.6
St. Nicholas	1743	13	17	23	28	268	16	
	1744	13	18	23	28	275	13	
		13	18	23	28	543	29	18.3
St. Nicholas	1765	15	21	27	35	592	5	
St. Peter	1765	14	20	25	29	304	7	
St. Thomas	1765-9	17	21	29	35	285	3	
		15	21	27	33	1181	15	22.3

*denotes old years

Several points can be drawn from this table:

1. The number of incomplete entries (in this case where the date of **birth** is omitted) is small, though higher in 1720 and 1722 than in most of the cases cited in previous studies. Unless one makes the assumption (quite unwarranted by the circumstantial evidence) that many of these were adult baptisms, they may be safely forgotten. In some cases the date was omitted but not the month.

2. Close clustering is clear from the 90 per cent values but is shown even more forcefully in Figure 1 which cumulates the entries up to the 98 per cent level. We would suggest that this kind of graph is the most effective way of describing these data in discrete form.

3 There is little here to support the notion that delayed baptisms were used to hide premarital pregnancies in the record.[7] Possibly such social refinements were not regarded as important in a port city like Liverpool where a low bridal pregnancy rate seems very unlikely. Lack of strictly comparable figures however makes it difficult to tell whether the fear of eternal damnation was causing a mean birth/baptism interval smaller than in other parts of the country in the eighteenth century. The values for the 25 per cent, 50 per cent and

49

75 per cent divisions would seem to fit the general trends outlined by Berry and Schofield (who do not describe the intervals in the remaining 25 per cent of baptisms) and are noticeably similar to those for Culcheth, also in Lancashire.

4. Woodward notes the consistent behaviour of parents especially in Leeds.[8] Our graph illustrates that in the aggregate the lack of random behaviour is also evident through time — in other words that the shape of the graph might reasonably be predicted.

One minor point about the measurement of intervals is worth illustrating by a single example from the Liverpool, St. Nicholas' register: the left side of Table 2 is a transcription of the date columns of part of the register for 1743 in which it seems distinctly possible that there should be five entries for September in the birth column, not one.

Table 2 An extract from the register of St. Nicholas', Liverpool, 1743.

Born	Register Baptised	Recorded interval	Probable interval
August 23	September 4	12 days	12 days
22	5	14	14
18	8	21	21
9	16	38	7
4	18	45	14
7	20	44	13
2	22	51	20
August 30	25	26	26
September 15	September 25	10	10

Such occurrences are not infrequent and might well be edited out in some printed registers where ditto is used indiscriminately.

II

The need to examine baptismal habits geographically has already been implied by Hair and by Berry and Schofield[9] but may be re-emphasized by the following picture being revealed by work in South-west England by one of us (Jackson). It contrasts markedly with what has been described for Liverpool.

Of particular interest in some East Somerset and West Wiltshire parishes is the occurrence of frequent register entries giving the age at baptism of children aged 'one year' or over and adults. Table 3 summarizes the statistics from three Anglican registers in this area. It is noticeable that in all three parishes the proportion of baptisms with a birth/baptism interval exceeding one year (one cannot strictly say 365 days — see note at the bottom of the table) is of the order of 5 per cent or more. This might suggest that baptism as soon as possible after birth was considered to be less important than in most areas for which figures have been published. Indeed it **may** suggest that baptism in general was marginally less universal. In this example the birth/baptism interval is arrived at for children and adults only, not infants which are taken here to be those under 'one year' old: the actual date of birth is rarely stated in this part of the country.

Table 3 Baptisms in Frome, North Bradley and Rode Parishes, 1701-1800.

		<1	1-3	4-6	7-9	-12	-15	-18	-21	-24	-27	-30	<30	IE	Total	>1
						AGE GROUP (years)										
Frome		16234	436	176	95	56	58	47	55	28	21	15	29	1	17255	1017
(Soms.)	%	94.1	2.5	1.0	.6	.3	.3	.3	.3	.2	.1	.1	.2	+	100.0	5.9
N. Bradley		2964	72	37	26	15	12	17	15	7	3	2	8	34	3212	248
(Wilts.)	%	92.3	2.2	1.2	.8	.5	.4	.5	.4	.2	.1	.1	.2	1.0	100.0	7.7
Rode		3054	64	19	10	6	8	10	5	8	2	1	7	8	3202	148
(Soms.)	%	95.4	2.0	.6	.3	.2	.2	.3	.2	.2	.1	+	.2	.2	100.0	4.6
		22256	572	232	131	77	83	69	75	43	26	18	44	43	23669	1413
	%	94.0	2.4	1.0	.6	.3	.4	.3	.3	.2	.1	.1	.2	.2	100.0	6.0

IE = Adults and children over one-year-old but whose precise age is unspecified.

+ = <0.5 per cent.

Note: The division between <1 and 1-3 years (infants and children) is imprecise, depending as it does on a description in the register such as 'one year old'. This further blurs any distinction between the small number of delayed infant baptisms and the even smaller number of child and adult baptisms.

The reasons for delaying baptism in this area are not entirely clear. Table 3 (covering, it should be emphasized, a whole century) describes, as one might expect, a rapid tail-off with over 40 per cent of the non-infant baptisms being of children less than four years. However there is a levelling out of the numbers in the teenage and early 20s groups.

The explanation of these patterns can only be tentative at this stage but four suggestions might be made:

1. A certain degree of laxity on the part of parents bringing infants to be baptized may have been encouraged by remoteness from the parish church, a hypothesis which Woodward was not able to confirm.[10] Frome was an extensive parish without chapelries, but remoteness would certainly not apply to Rode which was small in both area and population.

2. The number of baptisms of young adults may be accounted for by the need for baptism as a prior condition for marriage. This could be verified by simple cross checking with the marriage registers.

3. A number of baptisms, particularly of older persons, may have taken place immediately prior to death. This, incidentally, raises the little explored question of the number of persons who were never baptised at all.[11]

4. The baptism of a child might have led to the baptism of all other eligible members of a family. As in several other districts, instances of whole families being baptized on one day are not uncommonly recorded in the registers of this area, and such cases like all delayed baptisms present problems for aggregative analysis.

5. The probability that a person was born in the parish of his or her baptism must decrease as the birth/baptism interval is enlarged. Family entries, of the kind just referred to, can give interesting

information, in the manner of census enumerators' books, on such movements. The following example from the baptism register of Rode, 1730, will suffice to illustrate this:

September 2 Samuel Withy. Born in the Parish of Westbury 1694

September 21 Mary, d. of Samuel Withy. Born at Rudge in Beckington Parish 1718

September 21 Ann, d. of Samuel Withy. Born at Rudge in Beckington Parish 1722

September 21 Alexander, s. of Samuel Withy. Born in Rode 1725

September 21 Samuel, s. of Samuel Withy. Born in Rode 1730

Obviously where age is known it is necessary to correct entries retrospectively especially where the analysis has a monthly as well as an annual basis, yet it is interesting to note the scanty attention that points 4 and 5 just listed are given in the standard literature on aggregative analysis even where it recognises that these correction procedures may be necessary.[12] A more detailed analysis currently being undertaken of the Bishop's transcripts for the parish of Westbury, Wiltshire, (where either date of birth or age at baptism is recorded in nearly all cases from 1785 till the end of the century) has so far revealed that of the 309 baptisms performed in the years 1785-9 only 80.6 per cent took place within a year of birth, 73.8 per cent within six months, and 60.8 per cent within three months. Nearly 10 per cent of all baptisms were of persons aged three years and over. The ages of those baptized were greater still in the 1790s reducing even further the chances that those being baptized in Westbury were born there, as would normally have to be assumed for most practical analytical work in aggregative studies.

A related feature of the registers of this Somerset/Wiltshire area is a concentration of baptisms on particular days and years which cannot result from real trends in fertility: several baptisms on a single day seem to have taken place at a single ceremony. Examples can be found at Frome in 1711 and 1809, with high proportions of non-infant baptisms (37 per cent in 1711). In 1779 when North Bradley experienced a threefold increase in the number of baptisms over the previous five years' average, 56 per cent of the candidates were baptized on two consecutive Sundays — May 30th and June 6th (twenty-nine and thirty-one respectively out of an annual total of 107 of which forty-four were over one year old). Similarly in Bradford on Avon in 1754 the register records that thirteen children were baptized together on Shrove Tuesday. This phenomenon is not quite the same as that observed by Krause in Bedfordshire, where baptisms were postponed until the saint's day of the particular church:[13] in the Somerset/Wiltshire area it was not generally an annual event (though in Bradford on Avon there was a concentration of baptisms on Christmas Day in many years) and, in addition, large numbers of children and adults were involved as well as infants. The character of these 'mass baptisms' is more suggestive of zealous activity on the part of the incumbent possibly following a period of relative neglect of infant baptisms. No certain connection with the influence of John and Charles Wesley in this district, especially in the 1750s and 1760s, can be established.

III

We are well aware that none of this is very conclusive: it does no more than suggest (and not for the first time) that regional variations in baptismal habits may be important. Several questions remain, for example:

1. was the normal practice in a given locality sufficiently consistent to allow us to talk of 'late baptism' and 'early baptism' regions?
2. if so how large were these regions?
3. do they coincide with dioceses or archdeaconries, or are we simply dealing with the relative activity of parochial clergy as Hair has sug-suggested?[14]
4. what part did the growing strength of nonconformist allegiancies play where these are known to have varied from region to region?
5. is there a regular continuum between late baptism of infants, child baptism and adult baptism?
6. what overall effect will delayed baptism have on aggregative analysis in any region, or if considered seasonally?[15]

So far the birth/baptism interval has been studied chiefly from printed registers with a consequent lack of evidence for the crucial period of the eighteenth century. Answers to questions such as those posed here will be partly answered only through further research with unpublished registers. Before this is undertaken could we make a plea for standardization of statistical procedures and graphical presentation. For example it is important when using discrete scales (as with the percentiles in our tables or graph) to have standard procedures to deal with real numbers since x per cent of a sample will usually possess a decimal point: where, let us say, 40 per cent of a sample of 523 baptisms equals 209.2, then this must be taken as **more than** 209 so that if the total number of baptisms completed within, say eight days is 209, the 40 per cent level falls at nine days **not** eight days. Not only will attention to such details allow for a more precise description of the data so that the true importance of a few long intervals may be more clearly seen, but it will also permit sensible comparative use of statistical significance tests both for sample and non-sample data.

ACKNOWLEDGEMENTS

The authors are grateful to Miss Harriet Richards for extracting the data for the Liverpool parishes 1765-9.

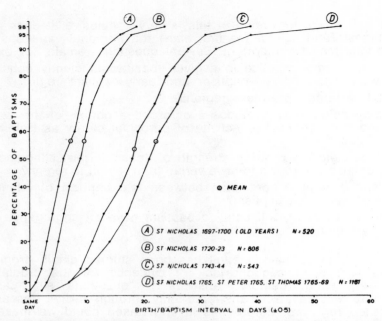

Fig 1 — Birth/baptism intervals in Liverpool, St. Nicholas' Parish for 4 selected periods with additional data from Liverpool St. Peter in 1765 and Liverpool St. Thomas 1765-1769, showing the cumulative proportion of baptisms achieved by a given interval in days.

NOTES

1. A conversation between the ineligible bachelor Christian Cantle and Timothy Fairway, the turf cutter, in Thomas Hardy, **The Return of the Native,** 1878, New Wessex edition 1974, p.53.

2. D. Woodward, 'The impact of the Commonwealth Act on Yorkshire parish registers,' **Local Population Studies,** 14, 1975, pp. 15-31.

3. B. Midi Berry and R. S. Schofield, 'Age at baptism in pre-industrial England,' **Population Studies,** 25, 1971, pp. 453-63.

4. **Lancashire Parish Register Society,** 35, 1909 and 101, 1963.

5. Berry and Schofield, p. 455.

6. Woodward, p.20.

7. P. E. H. Hair, 'Bridal pregnancy in rural England in earlier centuries,' **Population Studies,** 20, 1966, pp.234-5.

8. Woodward, p.20.

9. Hair, pp.235-6; Berry and Schofield, p.460.

10. Woodward, p.22.

11. Hair, p.236.

12. E. A. Wrigley (ed.), **An Introduction to English Historical Demography,** 1966, p.62.

13. J. T. Krause, 'The changing adequacy of English registration,' in D. V. Glass and D. E. C. Eversley (eds.), **Population in History,** 1965, pp.384-5.

14. Hair, p.236.

15. Since this note was written R. E. Jones has estimated that, since christian burial was denied to the unbaptized, delayed baptism caused the 'loss of between one-third and one-half of all infant deaths from English demographic records before 1837.' 'Infant omrtality in rural North Shropshire, 1561-1810,' **Population Studies,** 30, 1976, p.316.

AGE AT BAPTISM IN THE LONDON PARISH OF ST. OLAVE, OLD JEWRY, 1645-1667

Ronald W. Herlan

Several studies have demonstrated the significance of determining the length of the interval which separated the vital event of birth from the ecclesiastical ceremony of baptism recorded in English parish registers.[1] Demographic patterns, statistics, and techniques, social customs, religious conformity and the like, are reflected in, and influenced by, the establishment of this interval.[2] Part of the difficulty in arriving at the length of this interval, especially for the period prior to 1650, is the rarity of baptismal registers which also include dates of birth. One such set of registers which records this vital information from 1645 to 1667 survives from the central London parish of St. Olave, Old Jewry.[3]

Did this London parish begin to record both birth and baptism dates on April 1, 1645 by accident? Was this practice directly associated with the famous enactment of the Nominated Parliament usually referred to as the Marriage Act of 1653 as the recent studies of P. E. H. Hair, B. M. Berry and R. S.Schofield imply?[4] Berry and Schofield also reported that the London parishes of St. Thomas the Apostle and St. Vedast both have printed registers containing birth dates for the 1640's, though they do not attempt to explain what seems to be an otherwise exceptional practice.

Registration of births in the baptismal registers of these two London parishes as well as that of St. Olave, Old Jewry can probably be attributed to the following provisions in the parliamentary Ordinance of 4 January 1644/45 which had as its main purpose the abolition of the Book of Common Prayer and the introduction of 'the Directory for the publique worship of God:'

> And it is further Ordained by the Authority aforesaid, That there shall be provided at the charge of every Parish or Chappelry in this Realm of England, and Dominion of Wales, a fair Register Book of Velim, to be kept by the Minister and other Officers of the Church; and that the Names of all Children Baptized, and of their Parents and of the time of their Birth and Baptizing, shall be written and set down by the Minister therein; and also the Names of all Persons Married there, and the time of their marriage; and also the Names of all Persons Buried in that Parish, and the time of their Death and Burial: And that the said Book shall be shewed by such as keep the same, to all persons reasonably desiring to search for the Birth, Baptizing, Marriage, or Burial of any person therein Registered, and to take a copy, or procure a Certificate thereof.[5]

While the Ordinance does refer to writing down the time of death as well as burial, the last clause seems to indicate that registered dates of birth, baptism, marriage, and burial, but not of death, interestingly enough, were considered to be more critical for determinations of legal or other types of proof.[6] In any case, much to the regret of the historian, demographer, genealogist, or student of local history, dates of death were not included in the burial registers.

Perhaps the inclusion of birth information in the baptismal registers of City parishes such as St. Olave, Old Jewry reflects, in part, a parochial leadership which not only feared God and obeyed the law but also supported Presbyterian-inspired religious and administrative reforms. In 1643 for example the parish promptly replaced their sequestered vicar, Thomas Tuke, with a Puritan minister by the name of William Hignell.[7] A little later that same year a substantial proportion of the adult parishioners signed the Solemn League and Covenant.[8] Similarly, in the summer of 1646, a general parish assembly selected four ruling elders of their congregation by general consent according to a parliamentary ordinance fashioned after Presbyterian practice.[9]

Whatever combination of political or religious scruples moved St. Olave's officials to begin recording both births and baptisms in the parish register in 1645, it is known that universal baptism of infants in public church services within seven days of birth was strongly recommended by the Church of England prior to the Prayer Book of 1662 which extended the interval to fourteen days.[10] In order to determine how closely the parish of St. Olave, Old Jewry, followed these requirements its entries for the period 1645-67 were measured according to the criteria which Berry and Schofield used in their sample. There were at least eighty entries during the period for which both dates of birth and baptism were given and less than 10 per cent of them lacked either of the two dates.[11] Likewise, the percentile values and the semi-inter quartile range which they calculated for their parishes have been employed in making tabulations for St. Olave, Old Jewry.[12] For comparative purposes Table 1 includes the sections of Berry and Schofield's findings for those English parishes recording birth and baptism dates between 1645 and 1670.

Table 1 Interval in days (+-0.5) by which the stated percentile of births had been baptised.

	Parish London	25%	50%	75%	Semi-inter quartile range	% of incomplete entries
1647-1658	St. Olave, Old Jewry	1	7	12	6	4
1647-1648	St. Thomas the Apostle	4	7	11	4	0
1645-1648	St. Vedast	2	6	10	4	8
1645-1656	Allhallows	0	10	15	8	5
1654	St. James, Clerkenwell	2	3	4	1	2
1653-1657	St. Mary Aldermary	0	1	6	3	5
1654-1657	St. Mary Aldermanbury	6	10	13	4	5
1653-1656	St. Michael Cornhill	1	7	12	6	2
1655-1656	St. Peter's Cornhill	6	8	14	4	2
1655-1658	St. Thomas the Apostle	0	4	13	7	10
1665-1670	St. Vedast	1	8	11	5	0
1660-1667	St. Olave, Old Jewry	0	5	12	6	0
1663-1666	Aldenham, Herts.	12	18	27	8	9
1656-1659	Chester, Holy Trinity	13	18	22	4	4
1653-1655	Gisburn, Yorks W.R.	2	4	7	2	0
1653-1657	Horbury, Yorks W.R.	7	12	15	4	0
1661-1662	Ottery St. Mary, Devon	12	17	24	6	0
1653-1654	York, St. Michael le Belfry	4	6	8	2	1

Baptismal practices in St. Olave, Old Jewry for the periods 1645-58 and 1660-67, resemble those of the other London parishes to a remarkable degree. Baptisms generally took place soon after birth. One-half of the baptisms occurred within one week or less of birth and three-fourths of them were completed in less than two weeks. In the interval immediately following the Restoration the evidence shows that children were being baptised somewhat earlier than previously, although an annual break-down of these figures for the period does not reveal a uniform trend.[13] Moreover, percentile values of the birth/baptism intervals for St. Olave, Old Jewry during the years 1645-58 were identical to those reported in St. Michael Cornhill parish for the period 1653-56.

London's parochial baptismal practice remained unusually uniform in the quarter century between 1645 and 1670. Birth/baptism intervals were also noticeably shorter than most of the non-London parochial sample in-cluded in Table 1. These variations are illustrated in Table 2 which pro-vides the 25 per cent, 50 per cent, and 75 per cent birth/baptism inter-vals in days as well as the semi-inter quartile range for the parish with the shortest, the median, and the longest intervals among the London and non-London parishes.

Table 2   Birth/baptism intervals in days (+-0.5) of earliest, median and latest baptising London and non-London parishes.

Period	Area		25%	50%	75%	Semi-inter quartile range
1645-70	London	Earliest parish	0	1	6	3
		Median parish	1	7	12	6
		Latest parish	6	10	15	5
1653-66	Outside London	Earliest parish	2	4	7	2
		Median parish	10	15	19	5
		Latest parish	13	18	27	7

During the twenty-five years reported in the sample, the number of days between birth and baptism in the parishes which baptised earliest and latest both within and without the English Capital were moderate in length.[14] Three-fourths of the children in London's earliest baptising parish were baptised within six days, while in its analogue outside the City, seven days elapsed for the comparable group. Three-fourths of the baptisms in the latest baptising parish outside London by comparison occurred within twenty-seven days. The intervals calculated for the London parishes parallel Hair's findings for six English parishes in the period 1646-66.[15] Likewise, no child in St. Olave, Old Jewry remained unbaptised a month after birth between 1645 and 1667, a phenomenon which Hair also reported for three Lancashire parishes between 1646 and 1654[16] Clearly, the evidence collected from St. Olave, Old Jewry's baptismal records confirms Berry and Schofield's conclusion that London parishes baptised early and that the range of birth/baptism intervals both within and between parishes was small.[17]

Berry and Schofield also maintained that the custom of Sunday baptism which was also prevalent in the late sixteenth century 'seems to have disappeared' by the mid-seventeenth century.[18] Similarly, Mary F. and

T. H. Hollingsworth had called attention to the high frequency of Sunday baptism in the late Elizabethan period in their study of plague mortality rates in the London parish of St. Botolph's without Bishopsgate.[19] They found that between 1600-02 over 70 per cent of the parish's children were baptised on Sundays, though in plague times, such as the year 1603, the figure fell below 60 per cent.[20] The Hollingsworths went on to suggest that frailty and higher social status could be positively correlated to increases in weekday baptisms.[21]

Examination of the registers of St. Olave, Old Jewry furnishes evidence which both confirms and modifies some of these generalisations. Table 3 includes a summary of the day of the week on which infants were baptised in the parish for the period 1645-1658.

Table 3   Day of the week of baptism in St. Olave, Old Jewry, 1645-58.

| Year | Day of Week | | | | | | |
	Sunday	Monday	Tuesday	Wednesday	Thursday	Friday	Saturday
1645	5	2	2	2	6	3	—
1646	5	—	4	2	1	3	—
1647	4	1	5	1	2	2	—
1648	3	2	3	2	5	2	1
1649	1	4	5	4	1	—	1
1650	2	1	5	—	4	1	1
1651	5	1	2	3	1	2	—
1652	1	—	—	1	5	2	2
1653	3	2	3	—	2	1	—
1654	5	1	1	1	3	1	—
1655	1	2	2	3	2	2	2
1656	3	—	2	2	2	1	1
1657	3	—	1	5	2	1	—
1658	2	1	3	2	—	1	1
N = 193							
Totals	43	17	38	28	36	22	9
% of total	22.28	8.81	19.69	14.51	18.65	11.4	4.66

Sunday baptisms did not disappear during the mid-seventeenth century in St. Olave, Old Jewry, although they diminished to a proportion of all baptisms which was only slightly higher than those for Tuesdays and Thursdays. Baptisms were solemnised least frequently on Saturdays during that period. After the Restoration through 1667 the number of Sunday baptisms increased by approximately 75 per cent in the parish.[22] Perhaps this turnabout signalled a renewed emphasis on this time-honoured custom. In thirteen instances between 1645-58 where the high social status of the parents could be documented with reasonable certainty, only two of their children were baptised on Sunday which attests to the correlation which the Hollingsworths established between social distinction and the greater frequency of weekday baptisms. Among those children who were buried in their first year of life the percentage of Sunday baptisms was only half that of the entire period, suggesting that infant frailty did, in fact, lead to more frequent weekday baptisms.[23]

Briefly stated, this investigation has uncovered new evidence on age at baptism in London during the mid-seventeenth century. The practice of registering both births and baptisms beginning in the mid-1640's resulted from parochial adherence to a hitherto unnoticed regulation in the parliamentary ordinance which established the Presbyterian Directory for Public Worship. St. Olave's pattern of baptising three-fourths of its infants within a fortnight and the remainder within a month of their birth generally confirms the London baptismal practices first established by B. M. Berry and R. S. Schofield. Contrary to their suggestion, however, that Sunday baptisms virtually disappeared by the mid-seventeenth century, the evidence from St. Olave's parish suggests continuation of this ancient custom, not its cessation. Frailty of newborns and social status of parents were also found to be positively linked to higher incidences of weekly baptisms, which relationships were previously documented for the London parish of St. Botolph's without Bishopgate during the late Elizabethan times.

Without question this study's findings only represent a very small part of 'a population data explosion' which one authority hoped would emerge during the 1970s.[24] And although two decades have elapsed since K. F. Helleiner argued that research in demographic history had reached a stage which required more 'processing' and less 'mining,' it is clear that minute study of English parish records still has much to recommend it on such matters. [25] In fact, until a substantially larger number of such records are analysed and the results published, it would appear that E. A. Wrigley's observation of more than a decade ago still holds true today: 'What remains to be done bulks much larger than what has been achieved so far in historical demography'.[26]

Notes

1. John Brownlee, 'The history of the birth and death rates in England and Wales taken as a whole, from 1570 to the present time,' **Public Health,** 29 (June-July, 1916), 211-222; E. A. Wrigley, 'Family limitation in pre-industrial England,' **The Economic History Review,** Second Series, X1X, No. 2 (August 1966), 82-109; 'Mortality in pre-industrial England: the example of Colyton, Devon, over three centuries,' **Daedalus,** 97, No. 2 (Spring 1968), 546-580; P. E. H. Hair, 'Bridal pregnancy in rural England in earlier centuries,' **Population Studies,** 20, No. 2 (November 1966), 233-243; 'Bridal pregnancy in earlier rural England further examined,' **Population Studies,** 24, No. 1 (March 1970), 59-70; Alan Macfarlane, **The family life of Ralph Josselin, a seventeenth-century clergyman. An essay in historical anthropology** (Cambridge, Eng., 1970), pp. 88-89; Mary F. Hollingsworth and T. H. Hollingsworth, 'Plague mortality rates by age and sex in the parish of St. Botolph's without Bishopgate, London, 1603,' **Population Studies,** 25, No. 1 (March 1971), 131-146; B. Midi Berry and R. S. Schofield, 'Age at baptism in pre-industrial England,' **Population Studies,** 25, No. 3 (November 1971), 453-463.

2. Berry and Schofield, **op. cit.,** in footnote 1, pp. 453-454.

3. Paper registers beginning in the year 1538 (when the system of parish registration was established by Thomas Cromwell's Injunctions) survive for the parish in Guildhall Library, MS. 4399. parchment copies used for this study which include engrossment of the paper registers are found in Guildhall Library MSS. 4400/1, 2. During much, if not all of the seventeenth century, St. Olave's was a moderately sized, well-to-do, intramural London parish. Named after its principal street, Old Jewry, which had been associated with the Jewish quarter in medieval London, it was situated near both the administrative and commercial seats of the City — the Guildhall to the northwest and the Royal Exchange to the east. Halls of the two great companies, the Grocers and the Mercers, stood just beyond its eastern and southern boundaries and close by was situated the cloth market at Blackwell Hall,

the flesh and fish market at the Stocks and the great market in West Cheap. The parish was also the site of the Old Wardrobe which replaced the Jews' houses formerly located there. At the outset of the English Revolution St. Olave's inhabitants were employed in more than thirty occupations, the largest numbers being engaged in such trades as those of merchant taylors, barber surgeons, grocers, clothworkers, and drapers respectively, with mercers, attorneys, upholsterers and apothecaries close behind. Henry A. Harben, **A dictionary of London** (London, 1918), pp. 83, 136-137, 270-271, 280-282, 404-405, 512-513, 454, 554-555; John Stow, **The survey of London,** eds. Anthony Munday, Henry Dyson, and others (London, 1633), p. 291; Thomas Cyril Dale, **Returns made by parishes, wards and livery companies of the City of London,** 6 parts (London, 1934-1938), pp. 18-22.

4. Hair argued that 'the Commonwealth Act of 1653, which attempted to introduce a system of civil registration, ordered births to be registered: though the Act was generally a failure, and lapsed in 1567, some parish registers record birth dates for all or some of the years between 1653 and 1659.' Hair, 'Bridal pregnancy in rural England in earlier centuries,' **op. cit.,** p. 234, n. 6. Hair was incorrect in claiming that the Act of 1653 lapsed in 1657. See Dorothy McLaren. 'The Marriage Act of 1653: its influence on the parish registers,' **Population Studies**, 28, No. 2 (July, 1974), 319-327. Berry and Schofield see the custom of birth and baptism registration chiefly as a phenomenon associated with the Commonwealth from 1653-1669 ...' Berry and Schofield, **op. cit.,** in footnote 1. p. 455.

5. C. H. Firth and R. S. Rait, **Acts and Ordinances of the Interregnum** (London 1911), 1, 583.

6. Knowledge of death dates was probably less important than birth dates for various reasons. Birth dates established one's age throughout life, determined parish of origin, and the interval between death and burial was generally shorter than that which might elapse between birth and baptism. Nor has any dispute regarding the wording of this part of the Ordinance been discovered either in the Journals of the House of Commons or House of Lords. On Thursday, 12 December 1644, Sir Robert Hardy reported to the House of Commons from committee on the amendments to the Ordinance for establishing the Directory including a clause 'for Registering the Time of the Baptising of Children, and their Parents Names; and for Registering of Burials,' which was passed. On Friday, 3 January 1644/5, the only change in phraseology in the section on registration of births, marriages, and burials was the insertion of the phrase 'or Chappelry' by the Lords prior to final passage of the Ordinance the following day. **Journals of the House of Commons,** III, 115, 722; IV, 9-10.

7. Guildhall Library, MS. 4415/1. f. 113^v.

8. **Ibid.,** fols. 117^v-118^v.

9. The four parishioners selected on 19 July 1646. were George Almery, John Frederick, John Mascall, and William Vaughan. **Ibid.,** f. 132^v. The election of elders took place under the Parliamentary Ordinance of 14 March 1645/6 which enabled congregations to choose elders and corrected some of the defects of an earlier Ordinance passed on 19 August 1645. Firth and Rait, **op. cit.,** in footnote 5, 1, 749-754, 833-838.

10. Berry and Schofield, **op. cit.,** in footnote 1, p. 454.

11. **Ibid.,** pp. 454-455.

12. The authors preferred percentile values to the mean and standard deviation which the long birth/baptism intervals would have affected disproportionately. They define the semi-interquartile range as 'approximately the period in days over which the middle quarter of the population were being baptised.' **Ibid.,** pp. 455-456.

13. During the period 1660-1667 the median birth/baptism intervals show that baptisms took place very soon after birth in 1660-1661 and 1664-1665, and somewhat later during the remaining years. Guildhall Library, Ms. 4400/2, pp. 29-33.

14. Reported intervals for the latest baptising English parishes in the latter part of the eighteenth century and early years of the nineteenth century ranged from about twenty-two to sixty-three weeks. Berry and Schofield, **op. cit.,** in footnote 1, pp. 457-461.

15. The six parishes included three in Lancashire (1646-1654), two in Sussex (1654-1657) and one in Leeds (1666) where the median intervals were three to five days, ten and fourteen days and nine days respectively. Hair, 'Bridal Pregnancy in earlier rural England further examined,' **op. cit.,** p. 66.

16. **Ibid.**

17. Berry and Schofield, **op. cit.,** in footnote 1, p. 460.

18. **Ibid.,** p. 462.

19. Hollingsworths, **op. cit.,** in footnote 1, pp. 137-138.

20. **Ibid.**

21. **Ibid.**

22. Baptisms occurred nearly 40 per cent (38.89 per cent) of the time on Sundays between 1660 and 1667 compared to 22.28 per cent during the early period, for a 74.55 per cent increase.

23. Four out of twenty-nine children who died under one year of age throughout the period 1645-1667 were baptised on Sunday, or 13.8 per cent. For the entire period Sunday baptisms occurred 25.9 per cent of the time.

24. R. Thompson, 'Seventeenth-century English and Colonial sex ratios: a Postscript,' **Population Studies,** 28, No. 1 (March 1974), 164.

25. K. F. Helleiner. 'New light on the history of urban populations,' **Journal of Economic History,** XVIII, No. 1 (March 1958), 57. The last quoted phrase is taken from the recent analysis of the role which infectious disease played in shaping human history, William H. McNeil's **Plagues and Peoples** (New York, 1976), p. 213.

26. Wrigley, 'Mortality in Pre-Industrial England,' **op. cit.,** in footnote 1, p. 577.

AGE AT BAPTISM: FURTHER EVIDENCE

Donald M. McCallum

The question of the variability of the birth/baptismal interval has again been discussed with the publication of the letter from Mr. Collins (LPS 19) but it was an observation in the article by Jackson and Laxton which, when referring to the East Somerset-West Wiltshire area, stated that, 'the actual date of birth is rarely stated in this part of the country,' that has prompted me to write with information concerning the parish of Bruton in East Somerset.

Bruton is an ancient town which was involved in the wool trade and then from the mid-eighteenth to the mid-nineteenth century was a centre of the silk industry. There was a population of approximately 1280 in 1670, nearly 1700 in 1791 and 2109 in 1851. Birth/baptism intervals can be calculated for two separate periods. The first was during the Commonwealth from 1654 to 1659, and the second from 1784 until 1812.

During the Commonwealth period there were two favoured ages for baptism. For 10 per cent of the children the ceremony was performed on the day of birth. A further 13 per cent of all baptisms were carried out on the twenty-eighth day, and most of the remaining baptisms were concentrated around that period (see Table 1).

In 1784 the registers reveal a different pattern with the most favoured age being before the infants were two days old. After 1795 the popularity of an early ceremony waned and baptisms were spread more evenly with the third and fourth weeks being slightly more favoured than any others.

Table 1 Interval in days (+ 0.5) by which the stated percentile of births was baptised: for the parish of Bruton in Somerset.

	25%	50%	75%	90%	N	IE[1]
1654-1659[2]	14	25	29	32	257	27
1784-1790	2	12	32	94	366	30
1791-1795	3	12	34	85	238	1
1796-1800	15	29	64	132	189	0
1801-1805	18	28	66	220	219	1
1806-1812	23	35	121	361	309	1

1. Incomplete entries.
2. Converted to 'new' years.

The rubric of the Prayer Book makes it clear that baptisms should preferably be performed on a Sunday or other Holy Day. It would be difficult to conform with that ruling while the preference was for very early baptism, but with a greater range of acceptable ages it could be expected that the ceremonies would be concentrated into Sundays. As can be seen from Table 2 the Bruton registers do not confirm such expectation.

Table 2 The percentage of baptisms performed on the different days of the week at various periods in the parish of Bruton in Somerset.

	Sun	Mon	Tues	Wed	Thurs	Fri	Sat	N
1654-1660	12	27	26	8	14	5	9	256
1784-1790	26	9	6	27	5	20	8	394
1791-1795	26	10	6	29	6	16	7	235
1796-1800	35	7	4	32	6	14	1	188
1801-1805	37	5	. 4	32	5	15	2	220
1806-1812	42	8	3	30	3	13	1	308
1827-1830	35	5	7	24	10	14	5	229
1831-1836[2]	7	2	3	60	3	23	2	333
1851-1854	7	12	5	38	5	27	6	195
1861-1864	3	5	8	47	3	32	3	192
1871-1879	8	4	5	41	2	35	4	353
1880-1887	38	3	2	26	3	24	5	303
1888-1892[1]	60	4	3	15	3	15	0	120
1891	0	4	13	0	17	4	61	23

1. 1891 was an abnormal year in that number of baptisms was low and their distribution throughout the week differed from all other years.

2. The distribution in the neighbouring parish Pitcombe for this period was as follows:

1831-1836	77	2	2	9	0	6	4	53

During the Commonwealth Mondays and Tuesdays between them accounted for half of the baptisms and the rest were distributed fairly evenly between the other days.

In 1784 Sundays and Wednesdays shared just over half of the baptisms between them, and their position became even more dominant as time passed, until 1830 when an abrupt change occurred. The popularity of Sunday baptisms fell, Wednesday remained popular and Friday gained in favour. In 1880 the pattern again changed with Sunday becoming the most common day.

There is no obvious reason why Sunday should not have assumed a more dominant position at an earlier period. A market was held on Saturdays but that was never a popular day. It could be argued that the distribution of baptisms shows that the Church in Bruton was in a healthy condition in that the parishioners did not relegate all of their religious duties to Sunday, but were prepared to visit and use the church on all days of the week. At the beginning of the nineteenth century 88 per cent of the parishioners lived in the town and had easy access to the church. Whether the customs which prevailed in Bruton were common in the area is not known, but in the neighbouring parish of Pitcombe, which had a smaller and more scattered population, Sunday was the most common day for baptisms during the period 1831 to 1836.

What is most remarkable about the findings of this small piece of local research is that what were apparently established practices could be discarded and new patterns of behaviour instituted. This occurred in 1796 with regard to the birth/baptismal interval although the distribution of ceremonies throughout the week was unaffected. Abrupt changes occurred to the distribution in 1831 and again in 1880. I do not have to hand any information about the eighteenth century incumbents but the change in 1831 coincided with the arrival of a new vicar. The later change however took place during the time of H. T. Ridley who, as vicar from 1868 to 1898, apparently officiated at the great majority of the baptisms during that period.

If other parishes have also experienced such sudden changes it will make the formulation of meaningful generalisations on this subject very difficult indeed.

Note

1. I have an article on the demographic history of Bruton and Pitcombe in the **Proceedings of the Somerset Archaeological and Natural History Society,** vol. 121, 1977.

AGE AT BAPTISM: FURTHER EVIDENCE

Ian G. Doolittle

Age at baptism has attracted considerable attention from historical demographers in recent years. They are naturally concerned with its implications for the adequacy of parochial registration, and they are anxious to make some form of statistical allowance for it.[1] Systematic analysis of the problem began in 1971 with an article by Berry and Schofield who presented a good deal of evidence from a wide range of printed registers.[2] In the intervening years this study has been supplemented by a number of contributions to this journal, notably the article by Jackson and Laxton which appeared in Spring 1977.[3]

These last two authors noted that Berry and Schofield were able to offer only a few sets of figures for the crucial period of the eighteenth century when the interval between birth and baptism appears to have grown appreciably wider. There is obviously a need to trace this development with as much precision as possible, and Jackson and Laxton have provided much useful data to this end. Further evidence, however, may well be of value, especially when it comes from a part of the country which has not appeared in the samples so far.

From 1721-1812 the registers of St. Mary Magdalen, Colchester (in Essex), provide an almost unbroken series of birth and baptism entries. The sample, naturally, is small but it does have the important virtue of continuity. In some decades, it is true, the number of incomplete entries exceeds the 10 per cent limit observed and recommended by Berry and Schofield,[4] but this does not vitiate the figures. The limit has been imposed on the reasonable assumption that clerks might have troubled to record birth-dates only in cases of unusually late baptisms. There are no fears of such a distortion in this instance. Most of the 'incomplete entries' do not lack the date of birth but are deficient in other respects. Apart from those which are simply ambiguous or unintelligible, some record 'split' events (with births or baptisms in other parishes) while others note births and not baptisms. Only in the decade 1741-50, when no more than thirteen of the twenty-seven entries give both birth and baptism, have the totals been disregarded.

The figures presented in the Table below have been calculated in accordance with the conventions first established by Berry and Schofield and later modified by Jackson and Laxton. The sole deviation from these precepts lies in the omission of the mean which could not be estimated with any confidence in view of the vagueness of some of the longest birth-baptism intervals. Some further preliminary remarks are necessary. It is comforting to note that private as well as public baptisms are recorded in the registers. A number of entries make mention of both birth and baptism and also a subsequent reception in the presence of the congregation. Then there is the question of the army's arrival in the parish. From 1795 are registered the baptisms of children belonging to soldiers stationed at the barracks nearby. These have been omitted from the tabulated figures.

In such an unavoidably small sample the results show some eccentricities, but there remain some trends which deserve to be noticed. The interval between birth and baptism conforms in rough fashion with the somewhat disparate findings of Berry and Schofield for this period, and there is likewise a general, though by no means a consistent, tendency for the interval to increase in the course of the century. There is as yet no agreement on the possible differences between baptismal habits in town and country, but certainly this evidence from a former industrial centre, and by this time a market town of some ten thousand inhabitants, corresponds with the intervals calculated by Jackson and Laxton for Liverpool rather than with the longer ones given by the same authors for East Somerset and West Wiltshire.

This short study also prompts some more general conclusions. It has been emphasised more than once that it is important to take account of local circumstances in assessing the pattern of baptismal practices.[5] This Colchester material only serves to reinforce these pleas for caution. Many of the pitfalls which await the unwary are encountered here. In the first place, there are some predictable features: some parents had all or some of their children baptised on the same day while others adhered to a consistent interval between birth and baptism. Then there are factors which, though important in other examples, appear to have had no impact in this case: the local fair, for instance, which took place on 21-22 July, prompted no rush of baptisms on those days.[6] (This phenomenon may perhaps be found to have been the preserve of rural rather than urban areas). Finally, there are factors which unfortunately cannot be traced: there are, for example, no returns for non-conformists,[7] though it is known that there were many dissenters, including Baptists, elsewhere in the town, and indeed in one parish an increase in baptisms in mid-century was explicitly ascribed to 'the decrease of the dissenters' or some other cause.[8]

These assorted considerations are familiar enough and require no elaboration. Only two points deserve special attention here. The first concerns the effect of heavy mortality. In time of widespread sickness — provided that the epidemic was not so severe that no-one dared venture outside[9] — anxious parents were eager to have their ailing or vulnerable children baptised as soon as possible. This was certainly true of the late 1730s when smallpox visited the town,[10] and this may account for the surprisingly short intervals recorded in that decade. The second factor relates to the influence of the incumbent. The church, or rather the chapel, of St. Mary Magdalen was heavily damaged during the Civil War, and it was not used again until 1721 after it had been refurbished at the expense of the rector, and master of the parish hospital, Palmer Smythies.[11] Before the restoration, parishioners went elsewhere to christen their children. This produced many delayed and multiple baptisms. On 28 March 1717, for example, the minister at neighbouring St. Leonard's conducted a mass christening of many Mary Magdalen children, including two teenagers. This pattern was repeated in later years. On 9 August 1720 there was a set of family baptisms involving youngsters well advanced in years, and the candidates on 19 September following were even older, with ages ranging from seventeen to fifty-two. Matters changed abruptly after 1 September 1721 and regular, early baptisms became customary under the eye of the long-serving Smythies, who remained rector until 1773.[12] In the early days of the new regime there were still some late baptisms, as a legacy, no doubt, of earlier negligence, and these cases may make the figures for 1721-30 unduly high. When allowance for this bias is made, a more regular increase in the birth-baptism interval during the century becomes apparent.

Such statistical adjustments, however, can easily become too sophisticated. It is essential always to bear in mind the reality which lies behind beguiling figures, and local circumstances of the kind described above can make nonsense of the most plausible of graphs and tables. National surveys must be regularly supplemented by sensitive local work, and to this truism of population studies the important question of the age at baptism is no exception.

Table   Age at baptism in St. Mary Magdalen, Colchester, 1721-1812.

Interval in days by which the stated percentile of births were baptised.

	25%	50%	75%	90%	Semi-inter quartile range	Number	Incomplete entries
1721-30	8	13	46	207	12	72	11[1]
1731-40	5	10	19	37	5	60	5
1741-50				Incomplete figures			
1751-60	16	24	44	83	9	25	3
1761-70	10	17	27	127	8	24	8
1771-80	14	22	73	173	35	24	4
1781-90	14	27	61	280	12	37	2
1791-1800	10	18	53	507	13	54	4
1801-12	12	25	65	195	21	96	6

Source: Essex Record Office, D/P 381/1/1-3.

Note 1.   This total includes the births of five children belonging to the incumbent, Palmer Smythies. The baptisms took place at St. Mary's at the Walls.

Notes

1. The study of most relevance here is E. A. Wrigley, 'Births and baptisms: the use of Anglican baptism registers as a source of information about the numbers of births in England before the beginning of civil registration,' **Population Studies,** XXXI (1977), 281-312.

2. B. M. Berry and R. S. Schofield, 'Age at baptism in pre-industrial England,' **ibid.,** XXV (1971), 453-63.

3. S. Jackson and P. Laxton, 'Of such as are of riper years? A note on age at baptism,' **L.P.S.,** 18 (1977), 30-6.

4. See also Dr. Schofield's reply to a contribution by H. Collins in **L.P.S.,** 19 (1977), 50-2.

5. See especially D. R. Mills, 'The christening custom at Melbourn, Cambs., **L.P.S.,** 11 (1973), 11-22. Evidence from the mid seventeenth century is supplied by D. Woodward, 'The impact of the Commonwealth Act on Yorkshire parish registers,'

L.P.S., 14 (1975), 18-24, and from the early nineteenth by R. W. Ambler, 'Baptism and christening: custom and practice in nineteenth-century Lincolnshire,' **L.P.S.,** 12 (1974), 25-7. Early pioneering work was done by L. Bradley, 'An enquiry into seasonality ...,' part 2 (Baptisms seasonality), **L.P.S.,** 5 (1970), 18-35.

6. The two baptisms on 21 July 1793 and a further one on the same day in 1805 are the only ones to occur on these dates in the entire period. For the fair, see P. Morant, **The history and antiquities of the most ancient town and borough of Colchester** ... (London, 1748), Book II, 77. It should perhaps also be noted here that two adults were baptised on Easter day 1723.

7. These are missing from the diocesan returns in the Guildhall Library, MS 9558.

8. This remark appears after the burial entries for 1793 in the register of All Saints in the Essex R.O., T/R 108/4.

9. See the evidence from Leeds in 1645 quoted by M. Drake, 'An elementary exercise in parish register demography,' **Economic History Review,** 2nd series, XIV (1961-2). 434 n.5.

10. Four baptisms in 1737, which all took place within three weeks of birth (and in one case on the same day), have the melancholy marginal addition 'dead' beside them.

11. This information is given in a note at the front of the first register, Essex R.O., D/P 381/1/1. There is a description of the derelict chapel in the visitation of 1705, Essex R.O., D/ACV 9a, f.64. Morant has some interesting comments in his **Colchester,** Book II, 21-2.

12. He was succeeded by his son John. Palmer was also rector of St. Michael's, Mile End, and he was the predecessor of Samuel Parr as master of the Royal Grammer School. See R. H. R. Smythies, **Records of the Smythies Family** (London 1912), 9, 14, 38-9.

BIRTH-BAPTISM INTERVALS IN SOME FLINTSHIRE PARISHES

Mary Cook

The monthly analysis of baptism registers is meaningful only in those parishes where birth is followed by baptism consistently within a short period of time. A crude method of making sure that the register under consideration is suitable for aggregative analysis is to conduct a one in ten systematic sample where a series of birth and baptism dates is given in the register. The result of such an analysis of two Flintshire registers in the late eighteenth century was 97 per cent of children baptised within a month of birth in Mold and 99 per cent of children in Northop.

These crude figures have been supplemented by the figures of Flintshire parishes in Table 1, which have been arrived at by following the techniques advocated by S. Jackson and P. Laxton in their article in **Local Population Studies,** 18, Spring 1977. I am also indebted to Dr. Laxton for his valuable advice.

Table 1   Interval in days (+ 0.5) by which the stated percentile of births was baptised two sample periods from Flintshire parish registers.

		25%	50%	75%	90%	N	IE[1]	Mean
Cilcain and Ysefiog	1686-90	2	4	7	9	148	0	4.6
Hope	1686-90	8	11	15	19	224	0	11.8
Mold	1686-90	4	7	9	13	210	0	7.5
Hope	1783-86	4	11	18	39	224	0	17.2
	1787-90	4	11	24	63	269	0	27.8
	1791-94	4	9	22	61	220	0	26.5
	1795-98	4	11	23	54	230	0	25.6
	1799-1802	4	12	25	55	243	0	26.4
Northop	1783-86	1	3	7	14	246	0	5.9
	1787-90	1	4	7	15	268	0	6.6
	1791-94	2	4	8	17	278	0	7.7
	1795-98	2	5	10	20	307	0	8.0
	1799-1802	2	6	9	17	299	0	7.3
Mold	1784-85	1	4	7	16	222	2	6.5
	1788-89	1	3	9	17	220	0	7.7
	1792-93	2	4	8	17	207	8	8.7
	1796-97	2	4	8	23	259	5	11.5
	1800-01	1	4	11	22	262	14	11.1

[1]Denotes the number of incomplete entries

The parishes of Cilcain and Ysefiog, Northop, Mold and Hope are situated on a line running roughly west to east in the north-east corner of Wales. Northop, Mold and Hope are about equal in area and are similar geographically and economically: all are mainly agricultural, mostly hill-farming with some richer land in the valleys; there has, however, also been coal and lead mining in the district since late medieval times. Assuming that the annual tables calculated every tenth year for baptisms and burials in the Parish Register Abstract are correct, it would seem that Flintshire experienced one of the highest rates of population growth during the eighteenth century and that there was considerable in-migration.

As there are no seventeenth century figures for Northop, Cilcain and Ysefiog have been included for comparison for these years, although they are small, more mountainous, parishes and therefore unlike the three large parishes.

All the parishes would seem to have had a tradition of early baptism, although there are some differences. In the early period baptisms in Hope were delayed in comparison with the other parishes but there is no marked skewing: the oldest baby baptised in all parishes in the early period was just twenty-nine days old. In the later period baptisms at Hope were again later than in the other parishes, but all parishes show a skewing of data, for there seem to be two conflicting trends at work. The 25 percentile is earlier in the late eighteenth century than in the late seventeenth century, but the mean age at baptism is markedly later and the age range at which baptism takes place is greatly extended. During the later period the oldest baby baptised at Northop was 124 days, at Mold 290 days and at Hope 989 days; (the last was the only case found where two children of the same family were baptised on the same day). The second oldest baptism at Hope was 399 days.

A possible explanation of the differences between the seventeenth and eighteenth centuries may be that in the latter these parishes comprised two sets of people, the old, establishd families who maintained the tradition of early baptism and the newcomers who were more loosely connected with the parish church and so felt less urgent need of early baptism. It is also possible that nonconformity made some parents reluctant to bring their children to be baptised in the parish church. This would need to be looked at more closely. The majority of newcomers to Flintshire at this time probably came from the more remote parts of Wales. It could be that such newcomers to the scattered mining villages of Flintshire would be more likely to be attracted to the fellowship of the village chapel than to the more distant and formal parish church, but would still want to have their children baptised in the church.

It is well known that parish registers become less reliable towards the end of the eighteenth century as a complete record of the local community. This study also shows that monthly totals become less meaningful during this period, even in parishes which have a low mean age at baptism. The implications for the aggregative analysis of parish registers are obvious but, as long as the disadvantages are borne in mind, such analyses should not be considered totally worthless. Indeed, it is hoped that this paper will make a small contribution to our understanding of the reasons for variation in the birth-baptism interval and to the possible classification of early and late baptism regions.

DISTANCE TO CHURCH AND REGISTRATION EXPERIENCE

Roger Finlay

The question of the accuracy of the parish registers is of great importance to the population historian studying the period after 1660 when it is generally agreed that some registers of baptisms, weddings and burials were becoming less reliable as guides to the numbers of births, marriages and deaths that actually occurred. One of the main conclusions about the standard of registration is that it varied considerably even between parishes which were situated close to each other.[1] Local social and economic conditions are often ignored when evaluating the reliability of parish registers as sources for population studies. An especially interesting area of England was the Furness district of north Lancashire (now Cumbria) where the parishes were very large. The subject of this paper will be registration at Hawkshead where a continuous record was kept from 1568. The Hawkshead registers will be compared with those for the neighbouring parishes of Cartmel and Ulverston.

A number of important features of the Hawkshead registers were remarked upon by H. S. Cowper and K. Leonard who edited the successive published parish register volumes.[2] These included details of place of residence, and at times occupations, as well as comments on unusual events such as violent deaths. The parish clerks also attempted to draw attention to established householders and to paupers. One of the features of the registers that is particularly suggestive of their effective compilation is that the burials of abortive children were frequently recorded even though there was no statutory requirement to do this. It is not exactly clear what the parish register means when it refers to the burial of abortives, but it seems reasonable to assume that such infants were dead at birth.[3] Abortives recorded in the Hawkshead register appear to have been stillborn and the two terms are used interchangably in this paper. The inclusion of children who were not born live is uncommon in English parish registers. The fact that the trouble was taken to record the burials of children who were stillborn would suggest that the baptisms of children who were liveborn were also conscientiously registered. Attention has been drawn to this unusual feature of Hawkshead registration experience by Roger Schofield and some of his data are given in Table 1. Over the half-century from 1661 to 1710, the foetal death rate calculated as the number of stillbirths as a proportion of live births was 75 per thousand whilst in one decade, 1691 to 1700, it reached almost 100 per thousand. These stillbirth rates are exceptionally high even for pre-industrial communities. For example, in London parishes of contrasting socio-economic characteristics before 1650, the stillbirth rate hardly exceeded 50 per thousand and this also appears to be the upper limit in nineteenth-century England. In Sweden in the period from 1756 to 1760, the rate was only 25 per thousand.[5]

Table 1: Deaths of unnamed and stillborn children in Hawkshead, Lancs., 1661-1710.

Dates	Baptisms (1)	Total burials (2)	Burials of unnamed (3)	Burials of abortives (4)	Total live births (1) + (3) (5)	Foetal death rate (4) / (5) × 1,000 (6)
1661-1670	320	444	5	25	325	77
1671-1680	229	364	6	15	235	64
1681-1690	263	360	5	18	268	67
1691-1700	273	370	9	27	282	96
1701-1710	256	265	1	18	257	70
1661-1710	1,341	1,803	26	103	1,367	75

Source: Schofield, 'Perinatal mortality' (note 4), p. 13.

Although the recording of stillbirths gives the impression that registration at Hawkshead was good, especially as there were no gaps in the parish registers, this conclusion is not confirmed by other statistical evidence. The register may have included all the baptisms which took place in the parish, but it was not necessarily a complete record of all the births that occurred. Where registers were generally well kept the major cause of deficiency will be the length of the customary interval between birth and baptism because some children may have died before they would have been christened. It is not known how long parents waited after birth before they took their infants for christening.[6] As there is little surviving information from which the interval between birth and baptism may be calculated, it is necessary to find an alternative way of measuring the extent to which there were more births occurring than baptisms actually recorded. It is known that infants are at greatest risk of dying immediately after birth and that this risk declines with increasing age. In many pre-industrial communities infant mortality rates were high and half the deaths would generally occur within the first month of life. If the interval between birth and baptism were a month, this could have the effect of reducing the infant mortality rate by half as a percentage of the births would not have been recorded as baptisms.

Infant mortality rates are frequently divided into two components. Endogenous infant deaths are those associated with the circumstances of the birth whilst exogenous deaths result from diseases and accidents picked up after birth. Since all endogenous deaths occur within the first month of life, very low endogenous infant mortality rates are indicative of birth under-registration.[7] Endogenous and exogenous components of infant mortality rates may be calculated by a graphical method utilising a bio-metric analysis of the data. If the cumulative infant mortality rate is plotted against the age at death represented on a scale $\log^3 (n+1)$ where **n** is age in days since birth, the graph after the first month results

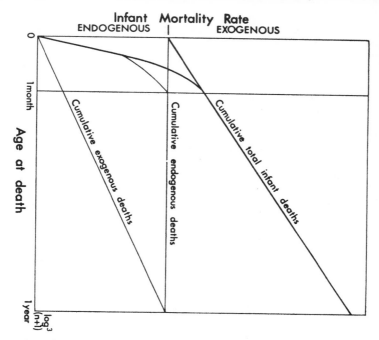

Figure 1: Biometric analysis of infant mortality.

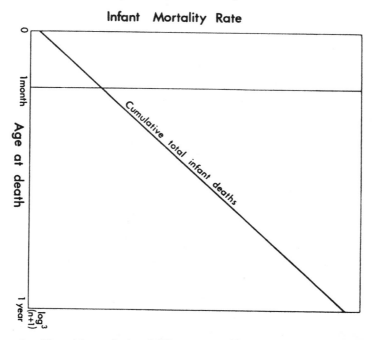

Figure 2: Biometric analysis of infant mortality if births are under-registered.

73

in a straight line as in Figure 1. If this plot is extended back to the intercept on the x - axis of the graph, a good estimate of the endogenous and exogenous components of the infant mortality rate is provided. Infants do not die from endogenous causes after the first month of life. This method has been shown to work using data not only from English and continental populations in the past but also from modern world populations. If the endogenous component of the infant mortality rate is very small, as in Figure 2, with the plot of the cumulative total infant deaths cutting the x - axis of the graph close to the origin, or even the y - axis, births must have been under-registered because an insufficient proportion of them resulted in endogenous infant deaths. Although it is not known how low the endogenous infant mortality rate could be whilst remaining consistent with effective registration of births, a rate of little

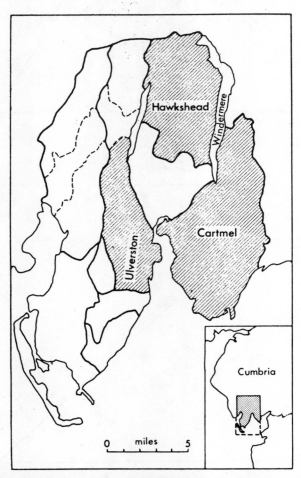

Figure 3: Furness registration areas, 1690-1709. The broken lines enclose chapelries within parishes which kept their own registers at this time.

74

more than zero as in Figure 2 clearly indicates poor registration of births. The observed distribution of infant deaths does not match up with the expected distribution.[8] Where the endogenous infant mortality rate is low, there is good reason to suppose that some births did not result in a corresponding entry in the baptism register. Any delay between birth and baptism, and especially an interval of up to a month would mean that the calculated endogenous infant mortality rate would be reduced because infants were at such risk of dying close to birth.

In the absence of family reconstitution methods, the infant mortality rate may be calculated as the number of deaths occurring within a year from birth per thousand live births. This will underestimate the true rate because it does not take into account the deaths of those infants who migrated from the parish with their parents during the first year of life although it is unlikely that this problem will affect the results to any marked extent. It was assumed that infants recorded in the burial register without having been named had been born in the parish but had probably died before they could have been taken to church for christening. The existence of these infants dying unnamed therefore indicates that there were more births than baptisms. To set the material for Hawkshead into perspective, the data will be compared with those for two neighbouring parishes, Cartmel and Ulverston, where abortives were not recorded. Cartmel and Ulverston were bounded by the coast of Morecambe Bay on at least one side, and the locations of all these parishes are shown in Figure 3.[9] The data will refer to the two decades 1690 to 1709.

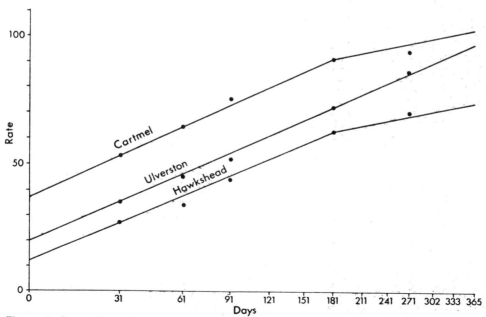

Figure 4: Cumulative infant mortality rates per thousand live births 1690-1709.

Table 2: Infant mortality rates per thousand live births, 1690-1709.

	Hawkshead	Cartmel	Ulverston
Total	74	103	96
Exogenous	62	66	76
Endogenous	12	37	20
	(528)	(1,084)	(637)

The number of live births from which each set of rates was derived is shown in brackets underneath them.

Table 3: Distribution of infant deaths within the first year of life.

Parish and dates		Days 0*	0	1	2	3	4	5	6	Weeks 1	2	3
Hawkshead 1690-1709	Number	3	2	2	0	0	0	0	0	4	2	1
	Cumulative %		13	18	18	18	18	18	18	28	33	36
Cartmel 1690-1709	Number	5	1	11	6	3	4	4	1	10	9	3
	Cumulative %		5	15	21	23	27	30	31	40	48	51
Ulverston 1690-1709	Number	0	1	3	0	1	2	0	3	5	1	6
	Cumulative %		2	7	7	8	11	11	16	25	26	36
16 parish sample 1680s	Number	18	2	8	14	9	3	7	8	26	22	14
	Cumulative %		8	11	16	20	21	23	27	37	45	50

*These are infant burials for which there was no corresponding baptism entry.
Sources: see text.

Months 1	2	3	4	5	6	7	8	9	10	11	Total Infant deaths	Total of related births
4	5	8	2	0	3	0	1	0	2	0	39	528
46	59	79	85	85	92	92	95	95	100	100		
12	13	8	5	3	0	1	3	5	2	3	112	1,084
62	73	80	85	88	88	88	91	96	97	100		
6	5	5	4	3	4	4	1	0	4	3	61	637
46	54	62	69	74	80	87	89	89	95	100		
26	17	24	9	10	7	9	6	9	8	4	260	1,747
60	67	76	80	83	86	90	92	95	98	100		

Endogenous and exogenous components of infant mortality rates calculated by the graphical method are shown in Table 2 and Figure 4 for the three parishes. In this diagram, the total infant mortality rate at Hawkshead after the first year was 74 per thousand live births, and 27 after the first month, whilst the endogenous rate was only 12. This is represented by the point where the line joining the various observations intercepts the vertical axis on the graph. Infant mortality rates were clearly low in this area. At Hawkshead, the total rate is suspiciously low and the endogenous rates at both Hawkshead and Ulverston strongly suggest that births were not being adequately registered. A far smaller proportion of deaths were occurring in the first month of life than might be expected. This point is underlined in Table 3 which presents the data more fully. It is clear that in Hawskhead and Ulverston very few infants died within the first week after baptism compared with Cartmel where registration experience was quite adequate and very similar to a sixteen-parish national sample in the 1680s.[10] Comparison of the data for Cartmel with the national sample suggests that the quality of the baptism register for Cartmel was better than in the other two parishes, according to the assumptions made in this essay. However, there was some slight under-registration at Cartmel because there were insufficient burials of unnamed infants for which there was no corresponding baptism entry to account for those deaths which occurred in the period between birth and baptism.

Table 4: Size of parishes and population in 1801.

Parish	Acres	Population
Hawkshead	19,252	1,585
Cartmel	22,960	4,007
Ulverston	13,706	4,422

Source: British Parliamentary Papers, 1852-53, LXXXVI, Census of Great Britain 1851, Population Tables I, vol. II.

Another factor which has an important bearing on the question of the incompatibility between the apparently good Hawkshead registers and the low level of endogenous infant mortality is the size of the parishes in this region. As Figure 3 and Table 4 clearly illustrate, these Furness parishes were very large in area.[11] In relation to possible total population size this was especially marked at Hawkshead where the inhabitants were dispersed in individual farms or small hamlets scattered in the valleys throughout the parish. Relatively few people lived close to the church and many had to travel some miles across difficult countryside to register baptisms and burials. To some extent this was also true of Cartmel and Ulverston but these parishes contained far less fell country than Hawkshead. It would clearly have been hazardous to have taken newly born children from outlying farms several miles to the parish church at Hawkshead to be christened.

Many years ago, J. D. Chambers realised that the size and shape of parishes could affect registration in that people living a very long way from church might find it difficult to register vital events. He commented:

> In the Marsh parishes in Lincolnshire, for instance, where the church may be five miles from the outlying farms, the failure to baptise the newly born was a much more common occurrence than to bury the dead, and this is reflected in the greater frequency with which burials outstripped baptisms.[12]

Much the same point was made by M. L. Armitt in her history of the upland parish of Grasmere, directly to the north of Hawkshead:

> The Ambleside folk, when in 1674 they petitioned their bishop for the right of burial in their chapel, stated that 'by reason of the heat in summer and the great snowes and sudden inundations of water in winter it is very difficult and dangerous to carry their dead thither (to Grasmere) for burial'; yet their distance from the church was nothing like that of the Langdale folk.[13]

Doubtless they also found the journey to Grasmere to baptise their children a problem.

It is not clear how the registers were compiled in these large parishes. Chapelries were established in most large Lancashire parishes to enable local people to worship regularly without making a long journey to the parish church. For example, in Ulverston parish, the chapelries of Church Coniston and Torver in the north kept registers from 1599, and these were excluded from the analysis of the Ulverston registers. There were no other chapelries which kept their own registers in the parishes and the period analysed in this essay. However, the original registers kept in the parish chests at Hawkshead and Cartmel are parchment copies of either original paper registers or rough notebooks in which the records of baptisms, weddings and burials were entered as they occurred. In Cartmel, there were four chapelries at Lindale, Flookburgh, Staveley and Cartmel Fell which did not keep registers but could have baptised, married and buried people and then sent a record of these events to the Priory Church each year to be entered in the parish registers. The Bishops' Transcripts of the registers for the later eighteenth century suggest very strongly that this is what happened,[11] but it is not very clear how early this practice had begun. The chapelries were also licensed for marriages. The marriage licences were sometimes valid only for particular chapels after 1718, when the licences first name the churches for which they were valid. Many of the marriages which took place in the chapelries were recorded in the parish registers in the same way as if the wedding had been celebrated in the Priory Church.[15] Nevertheless there is some evidence to suggest that local people in Cartmel registered vital events in the chapel in which they worshipped and these records were then transferred to the central parish registers.[16] In contrast, there were no chapelries before 1733 in Hawkshead, which made all inhabitants use the parish church.[17]

The problem of distance to church in Hawkshead may be pursued further in Figure 5 which shows the residence of all infants and abortives buried.[18] This map is especially interesting because it confirms that relatively few people lived in Hawkshead Town during this period but that the population was scattered throughout the parish in the lowland valleys. The fact that people living a long way from the parish church, for example at Satterthwaite or Skelwith, bothered to register events there is significant for it demonstrates quite clearly that registration was effective wherever possible since many people preferred the parish church to neighbouring churches at Colton, Ambleside and Church Coniston to which access may have been more convenient. Nevertheless, because of the distances to church it might be expected that a fair proportion of infants would have died unbaptised unless they were christened privately at home and this did not appear in the parish registers. Secondly, the map is important as it suggests that people living in the main settlements at Hawkshead Town, Monk Coniston and Sawrey were more likely to have had their infants christened than those in Skelwith, Grizedale, Satterthwaite and Dale Park where nearly all the recorded infant deaths were of abortives.

It could be argued that women from lower social status families would be more likely to have conceptions resulting in stillbirths or abortives than their wealthier neighbours. If the distribution of social groups within

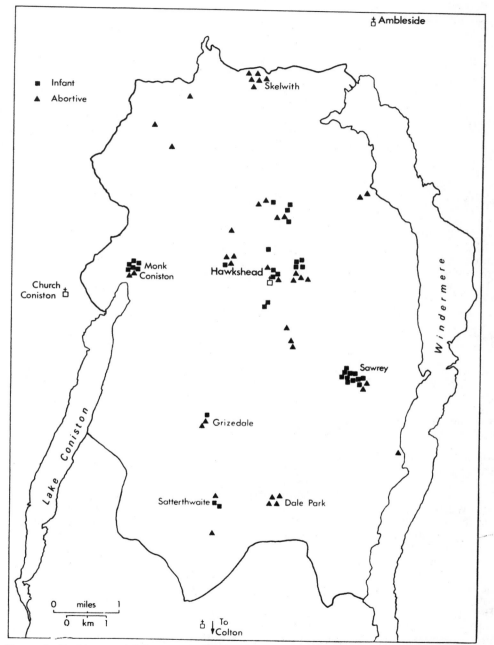

Figure 5: Residence of infants and abortives buried at Hawkshead, 1690-1709.

Hawkshead were such that people of higher social status lived closer to the church and that the poorer people mainly inhabited the peripheral parts of the parish which were least accessible to the centre, Figure 5 would really represent only a map of social areas within Hawkshead. It is difficult to substantiate this point but it seems that wealthier and poorer people did not live in different parts of the parish. For 24 of the 87 burials of infants and abortives, or 28 per cent, it was possible to link probate inventories of fathers of these children to the names recorded in the parish registers.[19] For 10 abortives, the mean wealth at death was £139.71 and for 14 infant burials, it was £197.64. Since one of the latter fathers was worth £1,656.37 at death, this person was eliminated and the mean wealth of the remainder was £85.43. The inference to be drawn from this is that the parents of both abortives and infants buried were of similar social status. Wealthier and poorer people in Hawkshead do not appear to have inhabited distinctive areas of the parish at this time.

This method of reasoning is obviously inconclusive in that it is based on a small sample of abortives and infant burials whose fathers could be linked to an inventory and also because of the question of the representativeness of the inventory sample as a guide to social status. Although they exclude many of the poorer sections of the community, inventories do survive for large numbers of people in the Cumbrian area at least till 1750. Nevertheless, the recording of abortives and infant burials was not obviously socially biased.

Table 5: Low and high estimates of Hawkshead infant mortality rates, 1690-1709.

	Low	High	Mid-Point
Total	74	151	113
Endogenous	12	93	53
Exogenous	62	58	60
	(0)	(48)	(24)

The number of abortives included in each set of calculations is shown in brackets underneath. See text for method of calculation.

Indeed, the argument about the accessibility of the parish church from some parts of Hawkshead may be pushed a stage further by suggesting that the abortives recorded in the burial register at Hawkshead were in fact the record of children which had been born live but died shortly afterwards and had been too weak to have been taken for christening in church. This would explain why so many endogenous infant deaths were missing from the registers. But since there were 48 abortives recorded in the burial register between 1690 and 1709, if all the abortives were liveborn, the endogenous infant mortality rate would have been very high indeed. A more plausible explanation is that some of the abortives were stillborn and some were liveborn. There is insufficient information given in the registers to distinguish which had been born live. Because of this, low and high estimates of the Hawkshead infant mortality rate are given in Table 5. In the low estimates it was assumed that all the abortives were stillborn, whilst in the high estimates all were liveborn. The mid-point represents the situation where half the abortives were stillborn and half were liveborn. The resulting rates were similar to those for Cartmel where registration was apparently better, but with a higher endogenous component which takes account of the interval between birth and baptism. If the underbaptism rate were calculated as the number of dummy births (3) and liveborn abortives (24) per thousand live births (552 + 3 + 24), there would be 27 underbaptisms and 552 live births giving a rate of 49 per thousand. The multiplier from baptisms to births at Hawkshead would therefore be 1.05 (552/525). This applies only to the period from 1690 to 1709. Local topography and distance were important in determining whether a child dying soon after birth would have been baptised.

The suggestion that some, but not all, of the abortives contained in the Hawkshead burial register were born live but died very shortly afterwards is consistent with most of the known features of registration. If half the 48 abortives were stillborn, the stillbirth rate would be reduced from 91 per thousand to 43 per thousand live births which is similar to other pre-industrial populations and is still consistent with good registration. The infant mortality rate is much less suggestive of defective registration if half the abortives were born live but died very soon after birth. The reason that so many infants died unnamed at Hawkshead where registration was apparently generally good, but less satisfactory in reality, may therefore have been related to the size of the parish and the nature of the countryside. This does not, however, enable those abortives which may have been born live to be identified. At Ulverston, registration was less good than at Hawkshead because the endogenous infant mortality rate was low and stillbirths were not included. Figure 4 clearly illustrates that the most useful register was for Cartmel.

Parish sizes may therefore have had an important effect on registration and their large areas may be one of the reasons for defective registration at Hawkshead and Ulverston.[20] As the case of Hawkshead demonstrates, the geographical extent of the parish, the scattered population and the difficult countryside meant that there were problems in compiling the register effectively, even though the inclusion of stillbirths strongly suggests that the parish clerk tried very hard to ensure that there was some record of all infants born in the parish. Doubtless there are other explanations of the abortives which would merit consideration. Local customs were of some importance in determining how problems encountered in individual areas were to be overcome.[21] And it is important to realise that there were other factors affecting registration experience in Hawkshead at this time. Whether the Hawkshead abortives were live or dead born is of great importance for the calculation of rates of fertility and mortaliy in the parish but whatever viewpoint is preferred, as Roger Schofield argued, these deaths were clearly perinatal, that is occurring close to birth.[22]

One of the intriguing features of English historical demography is that the main data sources vary in their consistency both across space and through time. Much of the work that has been accomplished relates to the Midlands and the South. The different countryside encountered in parts of the North presented some special problems for the compilation of the parish registers, amongst which are included the very large size of the parishes. Thus population historians should be aware not only of the deterioration in the quality of the parish registers during the period of the industrial revolution in some areas, but also in the equally wide variations which could be apparent between individual parishes and areas. In Hawkshead and its neighbourhood, the large geographical extent of the parishes, and the scattered settlement pattern presented a special challenge for the parochial registration system. The recording of abortives in Hawkshead allows some insight to be gained into the problem of how perinatal deaths could be incorporated into the parish registers.[23]

NOTES

1. This point emerges from a study of West Riding parish registers. M. Drake, **Historical demography: problems and projects,** Milton Keynes, 1974, pp. 47-63. There are useful comments on local demographic variations in P. G. Spagnoli, 'Population history from parish monographs: the problem of local demographic variations', **Journal of Interdisciplinary History,** 7, 1977, pp. 427-52.

2. H. S. Cowper, **The oldest register book of the parish of Hawkshead in Lancashire 1568-1704,** London, 1897; K. Leonard and G. O. C. Leonard, **The second register book of the parish of Hawskhead 1705-1787,** mimeo., 1966-68; K. Leonard, **A register of marriages in the parish of Hawkshead, Lancashire 1754-1837,** London, 1969; and K. Leonard, **A register of births and baptisms, deaths and burials 1788-1812 and of baptisms and burials 1813-1837 in the parish of Hawkshead Lancashire,** London, 1971. The other registers used in this study were R. Dickinson, **The registers of the parish church of Cartmel 1660-1723,** Lancashire Parish Register Society, 96, 1957; and C. W. Bardsley and L. R. Ayre, **The registers of Ulverston parish church,** Ulverston, 1886.

3. Typical burial entries from the Hawkshead register for 1692 are:
'November   8: An Abortive son of George Riggs of Satterthwait.
            14: An abortive daughter of George Taylors of Grysdall.'

4. R. S. Schofield, 'Perinatal mortality in Hawkshead, Lancashire, 1581-1710', **Local Population Studies,** 4, 1970, pp. 11-16.

5. R. A. P. Finlay, 'The accuracy of the London parish registers, 1580-1653', **Population Studies,** 32, 1978, Table 8, p. 106; and D. V. Glass, **Numbering the people,** Farnborough, Hants, 1973, pp. 182-3, 195-6.

6. The Hawkshead parish register does not contain sufficient information to calculate the birth-baptism interval at this time. In the period from 1778 to 1786 it was very similar to the average for a sample of parishes for which this measure could be calculated. B. M. Berry and R. S. Schofield, 'Age at baptism in pre-industrial England', **Population Studies,** 25, 1971, pp. 453-63.

7. For detailed discussions, see E. A. Wrigley, 'Births and baptisms: the use of Anglican baptism registers as a source of information about the numbers of births in England before the beginning of civil registration', **Population Studies,** 31, 1977, pp. 281-312; J. Knodel and H. Kintner, 'The impact of breast feeding patterns on the biometric analysis of infant mortality', **Demography,** 14, 1977, pp. 391-409; M. Poulain and D. Tabutin, 'Mortalité aux jeunes âges en Belgique de 1840 à 1970', **Population et Famille,** 42, 1977, pp. 49-86; and Finlay, 'The accuracy of the London parish registers' (note 5).

8. For example, in Belgium in 1841-5, the endogenous infant mortality rate was 38 per thousand and the total infant mortality rate was 157 per thousand so 24 per cent of all infant deaths were endogenous. Examination of calculations made from accurate civil statistics show that the endogenous rate in Figure 2 is too low to be plausible when considered in relation to the exogenous rate. See Poulain and Tabutin 'Mortalité aux jeunes âges en Belgique' (note 7), Table 3, p. 59 and Graph 4, p. 60; and Wrigley, 'Births and baptisms' (note 7), Table 13, p. 299 and Table 14, p. 302.

9. In this discussion, Ulverston excludes the chapelries of Church Coniston and Torver in the northern part of the parish which registered events separately.

10. The data for the 16 parish sample are drawn from Wrigley, 'Births and baptisms' (note 7), Table 7, p. 291. Professor Wrigley argued that the number of baptisms ought to be inflated by about 5 per cent in the period 1650-99 and 7½ per cent in 1700-49 to account for under-registration of births in a national sample (**op. cit.,** p. 310). For Hawkshead, the data differ from Dr. Schofield's in that the baptisms and burials of illegitimate children are not included.

11. The large size of parishes in Lancashire compared with the remainder of the country is brought out very clearly in a map showing the average size of parishes by registration districts in 1851 in J. B. Harley, 'England **circa** 1850', in H. C. Darby, ed., **A new historical geography of England,** Cambridge, 1973, Figure 109, p. 532.

12. J. D. Chambers, **The Vale of Trent 1670-1800, Economic History Review** Supplement, 3, 1957, p. 19.

13. M. L. Armitt, **The church of Grasmere: a history,** Kendal, 1912, p. 30. Also see A. P. Brydson, **Some records of two Lakeland townships (Blawith and Nibthwaite),** Ulverston, n.d., pp. 109-10; and M. L. Armitt, **Ambleside town and chapel,** Kendal, 1906, pp. 41-3.

14. Lancashire Record Office, DRC2/7-9.

15. R. Stewart-Brown, W. F. Irvine and R. Dickinson, eds., **Lancashire marriage bonds,** Lancashire and Cheshire Record Society, 75, 1920; 80, 1925-6; 81, 1926-7; 83, 1933; and 100, 1949.

16. In Cartmel, the exception to this statement was in Cartmel Fell, on the eastern shore of Lake Windermere and somwhat peripheral to the main part of the parish. Here, the Friends' Meeting House, which had been established at Height in 1677, was especially strong, and early impressions from a family reconstitution study of the whole parish suggest that family reconstitution forms are incomplete for many inhabitants of Cartmel Fell, especially when compared with wills.

17. The information about the chapelries was taken from the **Victoria County History, Lancashire,** 8, 1914, pp. 254-85, 342-63, 370-82.

18. This may exclude 3 liveborn infants and 2 abortives buried at Hawkshead but resident outside the parish and 2 liveborn infants and 3 abortives whose residence was not given in the registers.

19. The probate inventories are at Lancashire Record Office, filed with Richmond wills, Furness deanery, WRW. There is a discussion of Hawkshead probate inventories in J. D. Marshall, 'Agrarian wealth and social structure in pre-industrial Cumbria', **Economic History Review,** forthcoming.

20. Other factors could of course have affected registration. One was the rise of non-conformity and the most important group in Hawkshead were the Quakers who had a burial ground in the parish at Colthouse. Although this essay is concerned with Anglican registration, the experience of nonconformists may have had a bearing on Anglican registration in that some people may have used more than one system. During the period, there were 29 burials of Friends and 609 of Anglicans so the Quakers accounted for only 4.5 per cent of all burials. There is no evidence that **there were any infant burials at Colthouse at this time of children baptised in the** parish church. E. J. Satterthwaite, **Records of the Friends' burial ground at Colthouse, near Hawkshead, Lancashire,** Ambleside, 1914.

21. Compare D. R. Mills, 'The christening custom at Melbourn Cambs.', **Local Population Studies,** 11, 1973, pp. 11-22; and D. M. Woodward, 'The impact of the Commonwealth Act on Yorkshire parish registers', **Local Population Studies,** 14, 1975, pp. 15-31.

22. Schofield, 'Perinatal mortality' (note 4).

23. This research is part of a project which has been funded by the Social Science Research Council, Grant No. HR 5141/1. I am grateful to Christopher Charlton, John Marshall and Richard Wall for their help with this paper.

AN ENQUIRY INTO SEASONALITY IN BAPTISMS, MARRIAGES AND BURIALS

L. Bradley

Part 3. Burial Seasonality

The 'political arithmeticians' from Graunt (1) onwards, attempting to investigate the structure, the size and the changes of the population in the immediate past and to forecast future changes had, of course, to concern themselves with the available statistics of births and marriages as well as of deaths.   Nevertheless, it would appear that, in the 17th and 18th centuries, mortality statistics received the greater share of attention.   They were used for two main purposes.   In the first place, in addition to a natural curiosity about the normal span of human life, there was a strong practical interest arising out of the growing practice of life assurance and the rapid development of annuities, from the sale of which some governments derived a considerable income.   Both of these demanded the construction of reliable Life Tables, that is, of Tables showing how many out of a group of, say, 10,000 persons born at the same time could be expected, on the average, to have survived at the end of each completed year of life (2). For this, annual mortality statistics were required, but no consideration of seasonality was involved.   In the second place, doctors and others concerned with the public health were increasingly using detailed observation and elementary statistical methods to investigate the incidence, both in terms of geography and of the seasons, of the fatal diseases.   A good example is Thomas Short, a Sheffield physician, who, in his New Observations on the Bills of Mortality (1750), used burial statistics taken from a considerable number of parish registers and from the London Bills of Mortality (3) to discuss the relation between the incidence of disease and the geographical and climatic

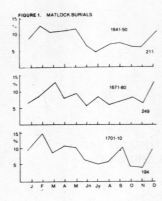

FIGURE 1. MATLOCK BURIALS

1641-50   211

1671-80   249

1701-10   194

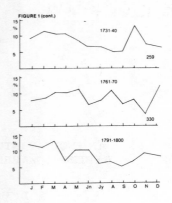

FIGURE 1 (cont.)

1731-40   259

1761-70   330

1791-1800

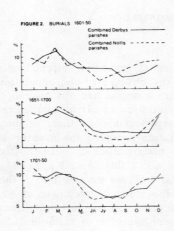

FIGURE 2. BURIALS 1601-50

Combined Derbys parishes
Combined Notts parishes

1651-1700

1701-50

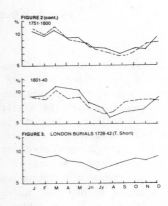

FIGURE 2 (cont.)

1751-1800

1801-40

FIGURE 3. LONDON BURIALS 1728-42 (T. Short)

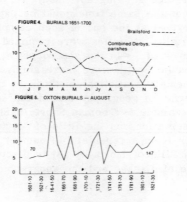

FIGURE 4. BURIALS 1651-1700

Brailsford
Combined Derbys. parishes

FIGURE 5. OXTON BURIALS — AUGUST

70   147

characteristics of the parishes, the varying pattern of mortality with
age and the seasonal incidence of disease - as well as the moral
failures to which he ascribed much of the high rate of disease and
death.   Some of the issues are still matters of controversy.   The
recent article by Professor J.D. Chambers in L.P.S. No. 3
('Some Aspects of E.A. Wrigley's Population and History) revives the
argument over the relative importance of 'crises of subsistence' and
epidemic disease in limiting population growth.   Can a discussion of
the seasonality of mortality throw any light on this controversy?

In his consideration of the seasonal incidence of disease, Short had to
rely entirely on the London Bills of Mortality for his statistics, since
his information from parish registers gave him only annual totals of
burials.   Unfortunately, the London Bills are hardly likely to be
typical for the country; the age of distribution of the population, the
living conditions and a number of other factors were exceptional.
What might he have found if he had been able to study monthly burial
totals from the parish registers?

An observed pattern of burials

Looking at the twelve parishes which I have studied, the decadal graphs
for the parishes taken separately suggest a marked seasonal pattern
throughout the period (1600-1840), with a peak of burials in the early
spring and a trough in summer and early autumn (Fig. 1) though, as
would be expected, the precise shape of the graph varies from parish
to parish and from decade to decade.   If we combine the figures for
the six Derbyshire parishes and also for the six Nottinghamshire
parishes over 50-year periods (to reduce short-term and local effects),
the seasonal pattern is very clear, as is shown in Fig. 2.   The
pattern remains fairly constant throughout the period, except that the
spring peak tends to persist into April, and even into May, towards
the end of the period.   Although there is some tendency for the
graphs to flatten towards the end of the period, this is far less marked
than it was in the case of marriages and baptisms.   In the combined
Nottinghamshire parishes, the range (the difference between the highest
and the lowest monthly percentages for a given period) certainly decreases
though not to the same extent as was found (L.P.S. No. 5) in the
combined baptism graphs.   In the combined Derbyshire parishes,
the range for 1801-40 is actually greater than for any earlier period
(Table 1).   Burials were still subject to marked seasonal influences
right up to the end of the period.

Table 1

	1601-1650	1651-1700	1701-1750	1751-1800	1801-1840
Nottinghamshire parishes	4.3%	5.0%	4.4%	3.9%	3.6%
Derbyshire parishes	3.7%	3.4%	4.1%	3.7%	4.8%

It is interesting to find that Thomas Short (op.cit.), using the London Bills of Mortality for 1728-42, with a total of 405,951 burials, found a similar seasonal pattern, but with January as the peak month and with a smaller range of 2.4% (Fig. 3).

As would be expected, this general long-term pattern is very considerably modified in every parish. There is, in fact, no single month of the year which is not, in some decade, for some parish, the peak month for burials, and no month which is not, at some time, the trough. In BRADBOURNE, BURTON JOYCE and CROPWELL BISHOP the decadal totals of burials in the early decades are small and the element of chance will account for some of the deviations. In BRAILSFORD and OXTON (with decadal totals ranging, in both cases, between 60 and 160), the deviations are frequent and often marked (Fig. 4). In the remaining seven parishes the deviations, though they can be striking, are much less frequent.

The deviations from the general long-term pattern are of two kinds.

(a) Many of them consist merely of a shift of the peak or trough by a month or two either way, retaining the general shape of the graph, but displacing it slightly. In any parish, the peak month or the trough month will vary from decade to decade (Fig. 1), but it is noticeable that OXTON tends to an earlier peak and GEDLING to an earlier trough than other parishes.

(b) Other deviations are of a quite different kind, the graph showing a large percentage of burials in a month which normally has few (Fig. 1, Sept. 1701-10). A striking example is found in OXTON 1641-50, when August contributed 22.0% of the decadal burials, though this month normally contributed less than the average of 8.3% (Fig. 5).

Interpretation

In considering how these facts may be interpreted, we are spared one of the difficulties which attended the discussion of baptism seasonality. Burial normally follows very soon after death, so that the burial distribution is virtually a death distribution. This is unaffected by some of the factors, such as custom and church law, which we have previously had to consider, so that when we ask such questions as why the normal long-term pattern shows a spring peak, or why there was that exceptional August peak in OXTON 1641-50, we are, in effect, asking questions about the causes of death. Remembering that the parish registers rarely give the cause of death, we ask whether our enquiries can help us to identify the operative causes, not, of course, for individuals, but in the gross.

The major causes of death will affect the burial distribution in two ways. There will be the normal seasonal diseases, such as the respiratory diseases in winter, operating with fair regularity year after year, though exceptional circumstances, such as an unusually severe winter or an exceptionally cold autumn, will affect their precise timing. These will be responsible for the long-term general pattern. In addition, there may be exceptional mortalities caused by epidemic outbreaks (4) such as epidemics of plague or smallpox. These epidemics are far less predictable, if indeed they can be predicted at all, and they will cause the short-term peaks which radically modify the general pattern.

Certain diseases are well known to have a seasonal incidence. Taylor and Knowelden (Principles of Epidemiology, London, 1964) list scarlet fever, diptheria and dysentery as having their highest incidence in the cold months. They add, "Most infectious diseases have their own characteristic seasonal variations in incidence but, apart from the well known winter incidence of bronchitis, few non-infectious diseases show clear-cut seasonal changes. .... Most of the deaths from measles, whooping cough and influenza result not from the primary infection, but from secondary pneumonia. As the incidence of pneumonia is greater in the winter months, the mortality of these diseases will also be high at this season." Shrewsbury (A History of Bubonic Plague in the British Isles, C.U.P., 1970) suggests a winter peak for smallpox, but he may be referring to endemic smallpox, which is unlikely to be present in parishes as small as those which we are now considering. Deaths listed in the Bills of Mortality as due to age are likely to have been heavier in winter than in summer. On the other hand, some fevers and also gastro-intestinal diseases (a major cause of mortality amongst infants in unhygienic conditions) have their greatest incidence in the hotter months.

Professor Knowelden suggests that 'crises of subsistence' might be expected to have their greatest effect at the end of winter and in the spring and early summer and says (5): "This is certainly the period in which vitamin C deficiency has been greatest and scurvy has appeared. It could be that the infection was secondary to semi-starvation and that the seasonal pattern was not one of the infectious disease itself."

The fact that so many of the seasonal causes of death have a winter peak is a reasonable explanation of the general long-term pattern which we have found - an explanation which has long been accepted. Unfortunately, more detailed analysis, the identification of specific causes in any particular parish, hardly seems possible without much more information than the parish registers afford. The number of possible causes with similar seasonal characteristics, the way in which they are inter-related (so that, for example, pneumonia may be a secondary infection following any of several primary infections) and the effects of abnormalities in the weather make the problem of identification too complex.

The one analysis which might have been possible - the distinction between the diseases of childhood and those of later life - is frustrated because parish registers do not give the age at death. Our graphs give the seasonal distribution of all deaths, irrespective of age; but the major causes of death are not the same for all age-groups. The London Bills of Mortality did, from 1728, give the ages at death, and Thomas Short quotes statistics from them in age-groups. In Table 2, adapted from Short, the figure 1 indicates, for each age-group, the month of greatest mortality, and 12 the month of least mortality. It will be seen that it is not until after the age of five that the winter peak becomes established. This London pattern cannot, of course, be taken as representative of the whole country. Smallpox, for example, would be endemic, probably seasonal and largely a disease of children in London, whilst in our smaller communities it would be epidemic, less likely to be seasonal and affecting a greater proportion of adults. But whatever the size of the parish, age differences in mortality could be considerable and ignorance of them seems to me to make further analysis impossible.

TABLE 2

Mortality rank-order of months for different age-groups - London 1728-42.
(from Thomas Short's discussion of the London Bills of Mortality, 1750).

Note: The column headed 'A' shows the percentage of the total burials contributed by each age-group.

	A	Jan	Feb	Mar	Apl	May	Jun	Jly	Aug	Sep	Oct	Nov	Dec
Under 1 year	36.7	6	7	5	3	9	11	12 (Least)	4	2	1	10	8
2 – 5 years	8.9	12 (Least)	8	1	3	2	5	10	9	4	6	11	7
6 – 10 years	3.6	1	3	5	=11	4	6	7	9	=11	8	10	2
11–20 years	3.1	1	2	8	9	10	7	11	12	5	6	4	3
21–30 years	7.6	1	3	2	4	7	9	11	12	8	10	5	6
31–40 years	9.2	1	7	2	5	8	11	10	12	9	6	4	3
41–50 years	9.3	1	4	3	7	8	10	12	11	9	6	5	2
51–60 years	8.2	2	4	1	8	6	12	11	9	7	10	5	3
61–70 years	6.2	1	2	5	7	6	10	11	12	9	8	4	3
71–80 years	4.5	2	1	4	6	8	10	12	11	9	7	5	3
81–90 years	2.3	1	2	3	7	8	10	11	12	9	6	4	5
91–100 years	0.4	1	2	6	4	5	10	8	12	11	9	7	3

I have suggested that the exceptional short-term peaks which are contrary to the long-term pattern may be due to epidemic outbreaks of disease. The decadal burial totals, however, are not adequate for their investigation, since epidemics are isolated events, and we have to return to the year-by-year monthly distributions on the Cambridge Group aggregation forms (L.P.S. No. 4, pages 23). Here we can pick out the months of exceptionally high mortality, and since epidemics are normally severe outbreaks of a single disease, we might expect to have some hope of identifying the specific cause. GEDLING, for example, had 192 burials in the decade 1611-20. Of these, 42 occurred in 1616; and of these 42, 8 (19%) occurred in August, 5 (11.9%) in September and 7 (16.7%) in October. This suggests an epidemic - but of what? Shrewsbury (op.cit) says; "When a parish register shows an excessive number of burials in a year and a monthly analysis shows that more than 50% of these is contributed by any three successive months of the plague season, June to October inclusive, the record is suggestive of an outbreak of plague. When more than 66% of the total annual burials occur in the three months July to September inclusive, this almost certainly indicates plague." (6). The GEDLING 1616 figures are, then "suggestive of plague". But there are other possibilities. In a village where there had been no serious epidemic for several years previous, the number of persons who had acquired immunity from smallpox (by an attack from which they had recovered) could be quite low, and these figures do not appear to be inconsistent with an outbreak of smallpox. Consideration of the annual figures of baptisms and burials suggests that the population of GEDLING at this period would be between 500 and 600. Of these, as many as 70 could be under the age of five, and the figures are not inconsistent with an outbreak of a gastro-intestinal infection amongst young children. Plague, on the other hand, according to Hirst (7), mainly occurs in persons aged between 10 and 35 years, and the very young and the very old are little affected. Again, it hardly seems possible to ascribe the incidence of this unusually high mortality to any specific disease with any degree of certainty. The very high August peak in OXTON 1641-50, already mentioned, was entirely due to the year 1646 when, out of an annual total of 35 burials, 1 took place in July, 19 (54%) in August, 9 (26%) in September and 3 (8.6%) in October. This is, perhaps, more characteristic of plague, but the ascription still cannot be certain.

Dr. Schofield approaches the examination of years of exceptional mortality in a similar way in his interesting article in the last issue of Local Population Studies (No. 5, page 10). He defines years of

See p 31 wms 3-5

the burial distribution for a considerable number of parishes in which such crises are reputed to have happened.

Conclusion

My attempts to use burial seasonality to identify possible causes of death have been unsuccessful and have produced only confirmation of general statements about groups of diseases – statements which were already well known! But the attempt to arrive at more positive conclusions revealed a number of pitfalls into which one can incautiously fall, and I have thought that it might be useful to share the experience. Other researchers, who have access to registers which give more than the usual amount of information about burials, may well find a study of burial seasonality rewarding. In the larger towns, the seasonal pattern of burials in years of high mortality (6) may well give more positive identifications of the cause than is possible in the parishes with which I have been dealing. And even if the cause of an epidemic cannot be determined, the dating of epidemics by examination of the monthly burial figures may be of importance in relation to the history of the parish.

I would stress again that these articles have been an attempt firstly to demonstrate the possibility that a study of seasonality might be used to throw light on the demography and the history of a parish or group of parishes and secondly to expose the difficulties and the necessary precautions relevant to any study of this nature. Limitations of space make it quite impossible to apply the method in detail to even a single one of the parishes for which I have statistics, even had the detailed investigations been completed.

I am deeply grateful to the individuals and the Population Studies Groups who have allowed me to use the results of their studies, and to a number of experts in various fields (and in particular to Mr. Christopher Charlton) for helpful criticism and suggestions.

NOTES

1. John Graunt, <u>Natural and Political Observations on the Bills of Mortality</u> - published 1662.

   Gregory King, <u>Natural and Political Observations upon the State and Condition of England</u> - completed in 1696 and circulated in manuscript, but not published in full until 1802, in an appendix to G. Chalmers, <u>An Estimate of the Comparative Strength of of Great Britain</u>.

2. A number of Life Tables had been constructed in the 17th century, but the mathematician and astronomer, Edmund Halley, is credited with the first enunciation of satisfactory principles for their construction (Phil. Trans. Roy. Soc., Vol. 17, 1692-3). His own Life Tables, though they were faulty, completely adequate statistics not being then available, remained the best available for at least fifty years.

3. Bills of Mortality were kept regularly in London from 1605. They were weekly summaries of the numbers of baptisms and burials, with the causes of death. From 1728 the age at death was also recorded. Other large towns followed suit at various times, though the amount of detail given was not always the same. There is considerable variation in the accuracy of the figures and they take no account of migration.

4. A disease is epidemic when it occurs in isolated severe outbreaks, separated by periods in which it is absent or almost so. It is endemic when it is continually present to a substantial extent, though its severity will vary. The same disease may be endemic in certain circumstances and epidemic in others. Smallpox, for example, tended to be endemic in the larger towns but epidemic in small towns and villages. A person who recovered from an attack of smallpox acquired virtual immunity from further attacks. In a large town there would be a continuous supply of new susceptible persons by birth and migration into the town, whilst in a small community the disease could run its course until all the inhabitants were either dead or immune, and could not recur until there were both new susceptible persons and a new source of infection from outside.

5. In a private communication.

6. See, for example, the histogram on page 463 and the Table on page 476 of A History of Bubonic Plague in the British Isles (Shrewsbury, Cambridge 1970) showing weekly numbers of plague deaths in London, 1665.
    OR   Appendix 2 of Historical Demography - Hollingsworth, London 1969.

7. L. F. Hirst, 'Plague' in Brit. Encycl. Med. Pract. IX - 1936.

8. N.T.J. Bailey, The Mathematical Theory of Epidemics - London, 1957
    M.S. Bartlett, 'Measles periodicity and Community Size' in
    J. Roy. Stat. Soc., A120 (1957).
    and many subsequent books and articles.

"CRISIS" MORTALITY

Roger Schofield

One of the most striking features of some parish registers is the recording of unusually large numbers of burials over short periods of time. We can easily imagine the dramatic impact of such "crisis" mortality on both families and communities, but "crisis" mortality has also featured in the more abstract debate over the reasons for the course of population change in the past. Some writers, for example J.D. Chambers in L.P.S. No. 3, have stressed the importance of this kind of mortality for the relative stability of the population in the seventeenth century, and pointed to its disappearance in the eighteenth century as a powerful agent of population growth.[1] Although "crisis" mortality deserves to be studied in detail, there is something to be said for taking a relatively simple definition of a "crisis" and using this to get some idea of the prevalence of epidemics in a parish, or in a group of parishes, at different periods in the past.

If we decide to work in this rather summary way, the first thing we need to do is to discover the years in which unusually large numbers of burials were recorded. By proceeding on a yearly, rather than on a monthly, basis, we shall lose some detail and in particular we may be in danger of missing "crisis" periods which run through December and January and thus get split between two calendar years. We should probably lose fewer "crisis" periods in this way if we were to start the year at a date when burials were usually relatively low, say on May 1st; but the calendar year is adequate for most purposes. In order to be able to tell whether any particular year witnessed an unusually large number of burials or not, we need to have some idea of what the usual annual number of burials would have been for that date. One reasonable way of discovering this would be to take a fairly long moving average, say of eleven years, centred on the year in question. This is probably better than taking a period of eleven years proceeding that year because if there were a rising or falling trend in the annual number of burials, possibly because the population were growing or declining, a figure based on the preceeding eleven years would lead us to expect too few burials in the current year in the case of a rising trend, and too many burials in the case of a falling trend. The moving average, on the other hand, includes years both before and after the year in question and therefore takes changes in trend into account. We might complicate the issue by excluding the year we are testing when we calculate the moving average in case it should turn out to be a "crisis" year and give us an inflated notion of the average annual number of burials. But by the same token, we also ought to exclude from our calculation of the moving average any of the surrounding years which can be shown to be a "crisis" year. Unfortunately, this would both involve us in a somewhat circular argument, and also make it more difficult to adopt a short-cut 'running' method of calculating the moving average.

In any case, we can get round this difficulty in the next stage of the argument, for we now have to decide whether the number of burials recorded in any one year is so much higher than the average annual figure as to warrant our calling it a year of "crisis" mortality. Since we are approaching the subject in an impressionistic and subjective manner, we shall have to take some arbitrary decision as to how large this discrepancy should be. Indeed, both the number and the nature of the "crises" that we find, will depend far more on our choice of the factor by which the annual number of burials must exceed the average annual number, than on the way in which we calculate the average annual number. So there is little point in spending much time on arithmetical refinements. Thus if we decide to take a short cut and include all years in calculating the moving average, rather than omit "crisis" years, we can offset the tendency to discover too few crisis years that this entails by accepting a less extreme deviation from the average as our definition of a "crisis".

Since the factor, by which the annual number of burials should differ from the average annual number, is so critical to the discovery of a "crisis". how should we set about choosing it? It would scarcely be sensible to make the factor one, for then we should classify as "crisis" years all those years in which the number of burials at least reached the average, and we should end up with about a half the period we are studying as years of "crisis" mortality. If, on the other hand, we take some large factor, such as four or five times the average annual number of burials, we shall find few crisis years, often none at all. There is obviously no one right answer to this question; it all depends on how strictly we want to define a "crisis". Since, within limits, we can please ourselves, we might as well choose a convenient figure, such as twice the average annual number of burials. In practice, a factor of two picks out a reasonable group of "crisis" years in most parishes, very much the sort of years one might notice oneself by looking over a set of aggregative returns. To be sure, if we were to take a factor of 1.5, we should get more "crisis" years, and with a factor of three we should get markedly fewer "crisis" years: but providing everyone is aware that there is nothing sacred about the figure 2. it affords a simple and reasonable, though arbitrary, definition of "crisis" mortality. In any parish there will be the odd year in which the number of burials, although higher than usual. is just under twice the expected figure, and it may seem unfair not to call it a "crisis" year when another year. with only a few more burials, is just more than twice the expected average figure and therefore qualifies for the title. But arbitrariness of this kind is the penalty one has to pay for being able to get a quick and relatively effortless overall view of the situation.

I thought it might be constructive to apply a superficial approach of this kind to discover the patterns of "crisis" mortality recorded on the aggregative analysis forms for the 550 odd parishes now in the Group's collection. Others may be interested to compare their own findings with the results presented below. Although the method of calculation is a summary one, the amount of work involved in applying it to 550 parishes is rather large. I therefore decided to take a sample. In order to get a reasonable geographical spread I took advantage of the fact that we keep the aggregative returns arranged alphabetically under county, and I systematically picked out every tenth parish. In fact this simple procedure did not always work, because some parishes had burial registers which either started too late to be useful, or were obviously defective for a number of years, especially in the 1640s and 50s. These parishes were rejected and I took the next suitable parish. The parishes in the sample were therefore those with consistent burial registration which began relatively early, for example 40 out of the 54 burial registers in the sample had begun by 1570 and all had begun by 1613. It should also be stressed that the original group of 550 odd aggregative returns do not in any way constitute a scientifically drawn sample of all the parishes in the country. For example there are too few London parishes and too many from Bedfordshire, too few very small parishes and too many market towns, and this imbalance is reflected in the sample of 54 burial registers. Nonetheless the collection covers a fair variety of different kinds of parish in all parts of the country, as is clear from Table 1.

The definition of "crisis" mortality which I used was an annual total number of burials more than twice the average annual number of burials for that year. For reasons of speed and convenience I decided to use the information contained on the standard aggregative analysis forms, so the annual totals were taken directly from the forms and refer to calendar years. The average annual numbers of burials were determined by an even more summary method than the one of moving averages discussed above. If there were no obviously defective years on a 20-year aggregative analysis form, then the average number of burials for each year on the form was taken to be one twentieth of the total number of burials recorded on the form. If certain years were deficient or omitted, as at the beginning of registration, then the average figure was adjusted accordingly. This procedure fails to meet many of the objections which we considered earlier on, and a full scale study would have to do better than this. Yet in view of the arbitrary definition of "crisis" mortality which I am using, this particular collection of corner-cutting devices may perhaps be acceptable for a preliminary survey of the field.

TABLE 1.

COUNTY	PARISHES
Beds.	Blunham with Mogerhanger, Kempston, Cranfield
Berks.	Winkfield
Cambs.	Cottenham
Cheshire	Wilmslow
Cornwall	St. Columb Major
Derbyshire	Dronfield
Devon	Colyton, Widecombe on the Moor
Durham	Whitburn
Essex	Great Baddow, Bradwell Juxta Mare
Glos.	North Nibley
Hants.	Aldershot, Odiham
Herefords.	Lugwardine
Herts.	Watford
Kent	Chislehurst, Tenterden, Cranbrook
Lancs.	Hawkshead, Rochdale, Warton
Leics.	Desford, Loughborough
Lincs.	Gainsborough, Horncastle
Middx.	New Brentford
Norfolk	Shipdham
Northumbs.	Berwick-on-Tweed
Notts.	Gedling
Oxon.	Banbury
Shropshire	Shrewsbury (St. Alkmund), Pontesbury
Somerset	Congresbury
Suffolk	Mendlesham, Horringer
Staffs.	Sedgley, Barton under Needwood
Surrey	Abinger, Cranley
Sussex	Eastbourne, Frant
Warwicks.	Alcester, Solihull
Wilts.	Bishops Cannings
Worcs.	Kings Norton
Yorkshire NR	York (St. Michael le Belfry)
ER	Hull (St. Mary's)
WR	Conisbrough, Rilston, Thornton in Lonsdale, Hartshead

Table II summarises the number of "crisis" years found for each of the 54 parishes over a period running from the start of burial registration in each parish up to 1809.

TABLE II

NUMBER OF YEARS OF "CRISIS" MORTALITY
FROM START OF BURIAL REGISTRATION (1538-1613) TO 1809

No. of "crisis" years	No. of parishes	Parishes
0	4	Dronfield, Rochdale, Pontesbury, Bishops Cannings
1	5	Winkfield, Cranbrook, Desford, Horncastle, Hull (St. Mary's)
2	10	Cottenham, St. Columb Major, Great Baddow, Watford, Tenterden, Gainsborough, Berwick-on Tweed, Sedgley, Cranley, Hartshead
3	7	Widecombe on the Moor, North Nibley, Chislehurst, Hawkshead, Barton under Needwood, King's Norton, York (St. Michael le Belfry)
4	8	Cranfield, Wilmslow, Warton, Loughborough, New Brentford, Shrewsbury (St. Alkmund), Mendlesham, Rilston
5	3	Banbury, Eastbourne, Alcester
6	4	Colyton, Whitburn, Odiham, Thornton in Lonsdale
7	4	Bradwell Juxta Mare, Gedling, Solihull, Conisbrough
8	2	Kempston, Shipdham
9	0	-
10	1	Congresbury
11	2	Abinger, Frant
12	2	Blunham with Mogerhanger, Lugwardine
13	0	-
14	2	Aldershot, Horringer

We should not pay too much attention to the absolute number of "crisis" years recorded, because this clearly depends on how we have defined a "crisis"; but the Table is interesting in the wide variety of experience it reveals amongst the 54 parishes. With this definition of a "crisis", and over a period of about $2\frac{1}{2}$ centuries there are at one extreme four parishes (Bishops Cannings, Wilts; Dronfield, Derbys; Pontesbury, Salop; and Rochdale, Lancs.) with no years of "crisis" mortality, while at the other extreme Aldershot, Hants and Horringer, Suffolk have 14 years of "crisis" mortality. This comparison between parishes is not altogether fair, because those which have burial registers beginning early in the 16th century will have a greater opportunity to score a greater number of "crisis" years. But this does not seem to have lead to any great distortion, for if we take, for example, the 7 parishes for which burial registration is available before 1540, four of them (St. Columb Major, Pontesbury, Gt. Baddow, Watford) had less than three crisis years, while the other three were distributed over the rest of the range (Colyton and Odiham (6), and Lugwardine (12). Another way in which the comparison between parishes may be less than fair lies in the fact that one extra burial in each year will have a greater proportional impact on a very small parish, with a very small average annual number of burials a year, than on a large parish, with a large average annual number of burials. Since we are defining "crisis" as being twice the annual average, then purely random fluctuations in the number of burials each year will be more likely to create spurious "crises" in small parishes than in large parishes. A more careful study of "crisis" mortality would make some correction for this fact. We are, however, presently in some difficulty, for the eleven "small" parishes in the sample, with a population of under a thousand in 1811, have twice as high a proportion (64%) with six or more "crisis" years than is the case (31%) in the whole set of 54 parishes. Because no precautions have been taken to eliminate the greater effect of random fluctuations on small parishes, we cannot tell whether this was responsible for the difference we have observed, or whether small parishes were genuinely more subject to "crisis" mortality.

Amongst the whole group of parishes, about half had less than four years of "crisis" mortality over a period of about $2\frac{1}{2}$ centuries. Although this result reflects my arbitrary definition of a "crisis" as twice the expected average annual number of burials, this level is not a particularly high one. Normal rural death rates at this time probably rarely exceeded 30 per thousand, implying that at most about 3% of the population died in a normal year. Thus what I have called a "crisis" year was reached when more than about 6% of the population died in a year. In some of the "crises" experienced by some of these parishes the burial figures suggest that the proportion of the population dying was very much higher than this, for example in Colyton in 1645-6 probably about 20% of the population died; but

TABLE III

ANNUAL FREQUENCE OF "CRISIS" MORTALITY IN 54 PARISHES

Note: Figures in brackets refer to original data when missing registration requires numbers to be raised (see text)

Decade	Years 0	1	2	3	4	5	6	7	8	9	Decadal Total
1540s	–	–	6(1)	–	5(1)	5(1)	–	–	–	–	16 (3)
1550s	–	–	–	–	–	–	–	13(3)	25(6)	11(4)	49 (13)
1560s	–	–	–	–	3(2)	–	3(2)	1	1	1	9 (7)
1570s	–	3(2)	–	1	4(3)	–	2	1	1	1	13 (11)
1580s	–	–	4	–	1	–	1	3	4	1	14
1590s	3	2	1	2	1	1	–	11(10)	3	1	25 (24)
1600s	1	–	1	4	2	–	5	–	–	1	9
1610s	2	1	1	2	2	1	–	2	–	–	17
1620s	1	–	1	5	–	1	1	–	3	1	7
1630s	–	2	1	–	1	–	–	1	–	–	10
1640s	2	–	2	8	3	3	1	1	7	2	18
1650s	–	–	1	1	1	1	–	3	–	–	17
1660s	1	1	1	–	1	1	–	3	1	5	8
1670s	1	2	1	–	2	–	–	–	1	1	9
1680s	1	1	–	–	2	–	1	–	–	–	9
1690s	1	1	–	–	–	1	–	–	2	–	3
1700s	–	1	–	2	1	–	1	2	–	–	9
1710s	1	1	–	–	–	–	1	–	4	6	3
1720s	2	–	–	–	–	–	–	3	–	–	15
1730s	2	2	–	–	–	–	–	3	1	–	7
1740s	2	2	5	1	–	1	1	1	1	1	13
1750s	–	–	–	–	–	–	–	–	1	–	2
1760s	2	1	–	2	–	–	–	1	–	1	7
1770s	–	1	–	–	–	1	–	1	–	–	2
1780s	–	–	–	2	2	1	–	–	–	–	5
1790s	–	–	–	1	–	1	–	–	–	–	2
1800s	–	1	1	–	–	–	–	–	–	–	1

104

in many other cases the proportion dying in a "crisis" was not much above the 6% mark.

Perhaps more interesting, however, is the distribution of "crisis" mortality over time. Table III shows how many parishes experienced "crisis" mortality in each year from 1540-1809. The figures are on a uniform basis from 1613, for by then burial registration is available for all 54 parishes. The original figures (given in brackets in the table) for the years before 1613 are based on an increasing number of parishes as more and more parishes begin to have burial registration available. These original figures have been made comparable to the figures for later years by multiplying them by the ratio between the number of parishes in observation in each year and the full complement of 54 parishes. (Corrected number of "crisis" parishes

$$= \frac{\text{Original no. of "crisis" parishes}}{\text{No. parishes with burial registration}} \text{ X 54}).$$

This correction is better than nothing, but we should remember that when we make comparisons involving any of these early years for which the number of parishes is rather small, we are assuming that the missing parishes would have had the same experience as those for which burial registration happens to have survived. This point is of some importance, for the corrected calculations show that some of the most popular years for "crisis" mortality lie in this early period, when only a small fraction of the registers are in full observation.

The final column of the table gives the number of "crisis" years experienced by a full set of parishes in each decade. These figures provide a convenient summary view of changes in the incidence of "crisis" mortality from the sixteenth to the nineteenth century. The decades in which relatively few parishes experienced "crises" should give an indication of the "background" level of "crisis" mortality. The table suggests a marked change in this "background" level around 1700. Before 1700, the decadal numbers of "crises" were rarely below 8 while from 1710, with two exceptions, they never reached a total of 8. Decades with numbers of "crises" in excess of this "background" level were much more frequent up to the 1650s. The later sixteenth century scored particularly highly, while in the early seventeenth century, three decades (1610s, 1640s and 1650s) witnessed unusually large numbers of "crises". After 1660 the picture was very different, for only the 1720s and the 1740s disturbed the generally declining trend in the decadal number of "crises".

Table 3 also enables us to see which were the years, or groups of

TABLE IV

"CRISIS" MORTALITY PERIODS

SINGLE YEARS

Years	No. of parishes Corrected	(original)	Years	No. of parishes Corrected	(original)
1558	25	(6)	1544 ⎤		(1)
1557	13	(3)	1545		(1)
1559	11	(4)	1616	5	
1597	11	(10)	1623		
1643	8		1679		
1658	7		1742 ⎦		
1729)			1574 ⎤		(3)
1542)	6	(1)	1588	4	
			1592		
			1603 ⎦		

GROUPS OF 3 YEARS

Years	No. of parishes Corrected	(original)	Diseases
1557-9	49	(13)	Influenza
1597-9	15	(14)	Famine; dysentery, fevers, plague (North)
1643-5	14		Typhus, plague
1727-9	13		Fevers, influenza
1657-9	12		Influenza, fevers
1544-5	10	(2)	? Plague
1740-2	9		Spotted fever
1586-8 ⎤			Plague, and ? fevers
1592-3			Plague
1614-16	8		? Fevers
1679-81 ⎦			Agues

years, in which "crisis" mortality was most widespread. This information is summarised in Table IV since epidemics did not always strike parishes in the same years, the table presents the information for groups of 3 years as well as for single years. 1558 is by far the most common year for "crisis" mortality and 1557 and 1559 are second and third respectively; but once more we should remember that these are corrected figures based on relatively few parishes. These disputable years apart, 1597 emerges as the individual year in which crisis mortality was most widespread, some 11 parishes, or one in five of the sample, being affected. The rest of the field lags some way behind, led by 1643, 1658 and 1729. Not surprisingly the group of 3 years which emerges as the clear winner is that of 1557-9. If the 13 to 19 parishes on which the results for this period are based are representative of the whole group of 54 parishes, then this mortality was over 3 times more widespread than "crisis" mortality at any other time in the $2\frac{1}{2}$ centuries studied. The rest of the field follows in a bunch, led by 1597-8 with 15 parish-years of "crisis" mortality, followed by 1643-5, 1727-9, 1657-9, 1544-5 and 1740-2. It is interesting to find the two early eighteenth century "crisis" periods so high up the list.

In 1750 Thomas Short conducted a somewhat similar survey of about 200 parish registers, and amongst other things identified what he described as "sickly" years. [2]   Short's work suffers from the disadvantage that, although he included parishes from all over the country, a substantial proportion came from the adjacent counties of Yorkshire and Derbyshire. Short also seems to have defined as "sickly" a year in which a significant, although unstated, proportion of the parishes registered more burials than baptisms. Short's definition of a "sickly" year is therefore rather wider than my definition of a "crisis", for parishes can record more burials than baptisms over a number of years because of a generally higher level of mortality, without there being any sudden surge in the number of burials. It is therefore perhaps not surprising that he should find some years in which there is no sign of "crisis" mortality as I have defined it (1669-74, 1698-9, 1722-3) and that he should ignore some of the years which score quite highly on my criteria (1586-8, 1592-3, 1602-4, 1614-16). Otherwise he confirms the "crisis" periods I have found.

The final column of the second part of table IV gives the diseases which are thought to have been associated with each of the major years of "crisis" mortality. These have been taken from Creighton's History of Epidemics, [3] and are in many cases only guesses. Often the identification has been made on the basis of evidence from only one or two places, and it is of course possible that other parishes may have experienced "crisis" mortality in the same year, or group of years, for quite different reasons. What is striking, however, is that so few of the well-known London plagues (1563, 1592-3, 1603, 1625, 1636 and 1665-6) appear to have been widespread throughout the country. Plague epidemics usually involved large numbers of burials, and certainly left their mark on the burial registers of London and other large towns, such as Bristol and Norwich. For most of the rest of the country, however, heavy mortality seems rather to have been associated with what were probably fevers and influenzas of various kinds.

In conclusion it might be worthwhile stressing once again that for reasons of convenience I elected to study unusually high mortality by the simple expedient of defining an arbitrary level and calling everything above that level "crisis" mortality. There may therefore be occasions on which a parish register appears to record a significantly higher number of burials than normal, but insufficient for the occasion to qualify as a "crisis" year. A fuller study of aggregative mortality should therefore examine the whole range of variations in the numbers of recorded burials. In this way it would be possible to distinguish between parishes which frequently experienced relatively modest increases in the number of burials, and those which were subjected, perhaps more rarely, to the most substantial increases in mortality, which we have been considering here. It would also be possible to calculate and compare the mortality 'profiles' of individual years by observing how many parishes were affected at different levels of severity. In contrast, the present scheme was designed to give a quick bird's-eye view of the situation. But it would, I think, be surprising if a fuller study failed to confirm some of these preliminary results, particularly the identification of the main periods of widespread heavy mortality, and the wide range of experience of heavy mortality amongst individual parishes.

NOTES

1. J. D. Chambers. 'Some aspects of E. A. Wrigley's Population and History', L.P.S. No. 3, 21-2.

2. Thomas Short. New Observations on the Bills of Mortality (1750), 22-30, 44-9, 85-9, 90-109, 187-191.

3. Charles Creighton. A History of Epidemics in Britain, 2 vols. (1894), reprinted with an introduction by D. E. C. Eversley (1965).

"Crisis" Mortality in Nine Sussex Parishes

Derek Turner

In *LPS* 9 Dr. Schofield suggested a quick method of discovering something about "crisis" mortality from parish registers. This note describes the result of applying his method to nine Sussex parishes and makes some suggestions for extending it to provide a slightly different viewpoint of crisis mortality. The nine parishes were chosen for no better reasons than that the registers were available in print and that aggregative analysis had already been undertaken. The distribution of the parishes within Sussex is shown in the accompanying map.

In the first analysis Dr. Schofield's definition of a crisis mortality year was used, that is a year in which the number of burials was double or more than double the average number of burials per year averaged over twenty years. Table 1 shows the number of crisis years so defined and also the size of the parish. Because of the wide variation in the period of years covered in the registers, the number of crisis years is not strictly comparable, but the figures do tend to support Dr. Schofield's view that the smaller parishes experienced more crises than the larger ones. Dr. Schofield has however suggested that some of the apparent crises might in the smaller parishes be due to random fluctuations in yearly burials. My subjective impression in studying the figures suggested however a different hypothesis to explain the difference between larger and smaller parishes, namely that the crises indicated in the smaller parishes were genuine but that genuine crises of roughly the same order of magnitude in the larger parishes were not being picked out because in years of unusually high mortality the number of burials often just fell short of twice the normal average. I therefore undertook a second analysis, using as my definition of crisis a figure of one and a half times the normal average. Also, to make the figures for each parish roughly comparable, I produced sets of figures for two different periods and excluded Angmering altogether. For the sake of convenience I called years with double the normal average 'major crises' and those with one and a half times the average 'minor crises'. These terms should not be taken too literally. The difference in the proportion of the population dying in 'major' and 'minor' crises might not be more than 2%. The results of my second analysis are set out in table 2.

This produced some interesting results. For the later sixteenth century the smaller parishes had about five major crises but virtually no minor crises; in the larger parishes the situation was more or less reversed. The total number of crises was much the same for both larger and smaller parishes. For the seventeenth and eighteenth century the situation was rather different. The smaller parishes still had noticeably more major crises and they also had slightly more minor crises, so that overall Dr. Schofield's findings were confirmed though the difference between larger and smaller parishes was not as marked as it would have been if only major crises had been recorded.

Dr. Schofield's national sample also showed that the number of (major) crises decreased as time went on. Using his crisis definition, the Sussex parishes showed a similar pattern. Analysis of the minor crises however produced a strikingly different pattern, as table 3 shows. Certainly overall the number of crisis years tended to fall but this reduction was entirely brought about by the decrease in major crises. In fact there were actually more minor crises in the eighteenth century than in earlier centuries.

It must be emphasised that these Sussex parishes do not constitute a proper random sample nor are there enough of them for the statistics to be more than suggestive. Nevertheless this brief analysis does seem to support Dr. Schofield's findings part of the way. However, in case any reader of his article should have rashly inferred that the decline in crisis mortality years provided a convincing explanation for the rapid population growth of the late eighteenth century, the evidence of the minor crises in Sussex shows that the answer is not quite so simple.

One final point is worth making. On only nine occasions did any parish record the deaths of three times the normal average and six of these occasions occurred in 1558/9. Even in these years the proportion of the population wiped out probably did not greatly exceed ten percent. Crises there may have been but in a quarter of a millenium in Sussex, none of the parishes analysed suffered a demographic catastrophe. If these parishes are typical of the region it does seem that it was a downward drift of the general level of mortality rather than any dramatic disappearance of the killer epidemics that had a significant effect on population trends, yet this may well not be true of other areas of the country. It would be interesting to know how the pattern in other regions compares with Sussex and Dr. Schofield's national sample.

Derek Turner

TABLE 1

Number of Crisis Years and Size of Parishes

Parish	Acreage**	Baptisms 1601-20*	No. of Crisis Years	Register Coverage
Angmering	4,200	301	5	1593-1687
Ardingly	3,817	170	12	1558-1810 (less 1650-1663)
Balcombe	4,786	193	18	1558-1810 (less 1646-1707)
Bolney	3,546	156	14	1541-1810
Cowfold	4,458	219	8	1558-1810 (less 1643-1649)
Cuckfield	11,167	816	1	1597-1810 (less 1674-1677)
East Grinstead	15,071	1051	1	1575-1810 (less 1639-1653)
Horsham	10,770	1257	2	1541-1635
Worth	13,400	497	6	1558-1810

*Though birth rates would have differed from parish to parish, these figures give a rough idea of comparative population size.   **Source: Lower, *History of Sussex,* 1870.

TABLE 2

Number of 'Major' and 'Minor' Crises per Parish

Parish (in order of size)	No. of Crises, 1559-1597			No. of Crises 1598-1810		
	Major	Minor	Total	Major	Minor	Total
Horsham	2	4	6			
East Grinstead	0	2	2	1	6	7
Cuckfield				1	11	12
Worth	1	4	5	6	8	14
Cowfold	2	1	3	5	18	23
Balcombe	5	1	6	13	12	25
Ardingly	6	0	6	6	12	18
Bolney	5	1	6	9	15	24

TABLE 3

Number of 'Major' and 'Minor' Crises per half century

Period	E. Grinstead	Cuckfield	Worth	Cowfold	Ardingly	Balcombe	Bolney	Total Crises		Combined
								Minor	Major	
1550-99	2	?[1]	7	11	7	5	7	12+	27+	39+
1600-49	2	4	6	3	4	8	6	15	18	33
1650-99	3	3	0	5	5	?[2]	6	10+	12+	22+
1700-49	1	3	2	7	5	6	6	21	9	30
1750-99	1	2	1	6	3	8	2	15	8	23

Notes (1) If Cuckfield behaved consistently it probably had about 1 major and 4 minor crises 1550-99 bringing the period total up to 44.

(2) If Balcombe behaved consistently it probably had about 4 major and 4 minor crises 1650-99 bringing the period total up to 30.

MAP OF MID-SUSSEX SHOWING POSITION OF PARISHES ANALYSED

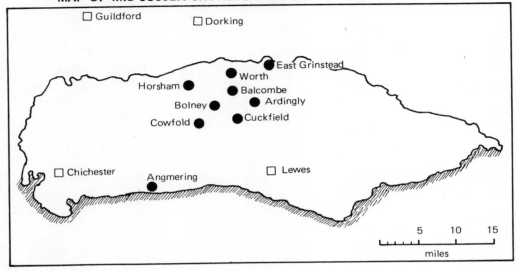

Common Law Marriage : a possible cause of under-registration

In the course of work on the parish registers of Eyam, Derbyshire, I have come across a number of cases which may have some relevance to Dr. Wrigley's very interesting article in *LPS* No. 10 on clandestine marriage.

In the aggregative survey, I noticed very high baptism/marriage ratios in the decades 1641-50, and 1651-60, but thought at first that they were probably due to errors in registration. Later, in the reconstitution, I found that there were fewer baptisms recorded of illegitimate children than one would expect. Moreover, I found a number of cases in which a succession of children were baptised to, say, Christopher and Sarah Smith, followed after a brief interval by a succession of baptisms to Christopher and Mary Smith. In other words, all the appearance of a remarriage except that there was no record of the marriages or of the burial of Sarah. There were, in my opinion, too many such cases to be due to under-registration. One possibility, of course, was that the marriages and the burial of Sarah took place in neighbouring parishes. I carefully examined the printed register of a large neighbouring parish with which Eyam had close connections, but was unable to trace any of the missing marriages or burials, though other marriages, burials and baptisms of Eyam residents were recorded. At this stage I began to wonder whether there might have been, in Eyam at this period, a considerable degree of common-law marriage, with an incumbent prepared to baptise the offspring.

I understand that Mr. E.P. Thompson has been investigating cases of "wife-selling" and has concluded that in many, if not most, cases the selling was not a commercial proposition but a sort of formal act of divorce. Could it, I wonder, have been related to common-law marriage?

Leslie Bradley

EASINGWOLD MARRIAGE HORIZONS

Bessie Maltby

The problem of how mobile people were in the past is of interest in many contexts, yet it remains a difficult one to solve, largely because there is so little direct evidence. One indirect approach is to study the distance over which people found their marriage partners, or as it is rather quaintly known in technical language: the marriage horizon. The marriage registers are used to discover the residence of the marriage partners, though of course it is chiefly the husbands from other parishes who can be traced from one register, as it appears to have been the custom for the wedding to take place in the bride's parish. This kind of analysis can emerge as a useful by-product of family reconstitution, as with the present study of the Easingwold register.

Easingwold, a small town in the North Riding of Yorkshire, situated in the ancient Forest of Galtres, near the Howardian Hills, is a parish for which family reconstitution has recently been completed. It is a parish with only one main centre of population - Easingwold itself. Raskelf, an extra-parochial chapel lies to the southwest, and has always been a comparatively small community. None of the adjoining parishes possesses a town of the size of Easingwold. The nearest large settlement is York, thirteen miles away, and there are traces of a considerable number of Easingwold girls marrying in parishes in that city.

The first note of parish of residence in the Easingwold register is in 1644, and thereafter where one partner or both came from outside the parish this appears to be stated. However, from 1669 to 1685, when with a different clerk the information is in Latin, there are only two references to other parishes. Thereafter the register reverts to its original form. The words "of this parish" are not consistently used until 1713 but the family reconstitution already done bears out the belief that where no place of origin is given the parties are from Easingwold.

In the following table the distances have been calculated from Easingwold itself.   Apart from a long, narrow tail to the South, Easingwold stands very approximately in the middle of the parish.   In calculating the percentages, 63 marriages from the period 1669-1685, when residence is not recorded in the register, have been excluded.

Marriage Horizon: Easingwold (1644 - 1812)

	No. of marriages	Proportion of all marriages (± 0.5%)
Partner from up to 10 miles away	241	23%
Partner from over 10 and up to 20 miles away	68	7%
Partner from over 20 miles away.	32	3%
TOTAL: Partner from another parish (65 of these were women)	341	33%

The analysis confirms the generally accepted view that, while many partners were found from outside the parish, they mostly came from within a radius of ten miles.   In Easingwold, approximately 10% took their partners from more than ten miles away, and this suggests a slightly wider movement than Dr. Eversley states to be the general conclusion from studies so far made (1).   However Dr. Eversley's calculations were based on a fifteen mile radius, and this extra five miles might well account for about two-thirds of the 68 marriages in the 11-20 miles distance group, making the number of marriages over fifteen miles about 5% of all marriages at Easingwold.   There is no indication of more marriages involving distant partners between 1683 and 1746 than later - if by distant is meant from more than 10 miles away.   At Bickenhill, a village a few miles to the south-east of Birmingham, there were many more marriages involving partners from a distance during the period 1683-1746 than was the case later in the eighteenth century, when such marriages became very rare (2).

There is no indication of such a pattern at Easingwold, for even when the 'irregular' marriages are taken into account (i.e. marriages where both partners came from outside the parish) the proportion of marriages involving a distant partner (taken here to mean from more than 10 miles away) remains roughly constant from 1683 to 1810.

Period	Marriages with 'distant' partner	
	No.	% of all marriages
1683-1796	38	10
1747-1810	67	12

There were of course more 'outsiders' married in Easingwold before the 1754 Hardwick Act than later, but most of them were from adjoining parishes, with smaller settlements.

The first marriage partner from outside the County is noted in 1729, a man from Horncastle (Lincolnshire); the next from Hamsterley (Co. Durham) in 1761, and Calverton (Nottinghamshire) in 1771. There were bridegrooms from London in 1773, 1782 and 1812. Darlington (1784), Sunderland (1806) and Scawby (Lincolnshire) complete the spouses recorded from other counties, but some of the Yorkshire partners from the West and East Ridings came from as long distances, for example, Bridlington (1710), Scarborough (1783), Hull (1786), Huddersfield (1792) and Sheffield (1803).

That Easingwold has since Roman times been on the route from London to Newcastle and had coach transport from 1734 to London and from 1706 between York and Easingwold does not seem to be reflected in the marriage partners chosen by the women of Easingwold. It would be interesting to know whether the men of Easingwold went any further afield for their wives. The probable origins of a few (the parish of their fathers) can be traced from details in the baptismal and burial registers - Keswick, Glasgow, Ridgley (Staffs), Newcastle, Derby, Bristol, Warwick, London, Cleethorpes (Lincs.), Carlisle and Whitby. A number of these were, however, married to men whose fathers also came from distant places. How long the husbands had been in Easingwold it is often not possible to discover. Indeed, there is some indication from occupations of some of them that their stay in Easingwold was likely to be temporary, e.g. itinerant preacher, waterman and postboy.

Although choice of marriage partner is only one aspect of mobility, and in a centre with such good communications as Easingwold possibly a minor one, it does give us an indirect insight into mobility in the past.   At Easingwold most marriages took place between people who were resident in the parish, and marriage partners from outside the parish came from a relatively short distance away.   It would be interesting to know whether other parishes show the same pattern.

NOTES

1.   D.E.C. Eversley.   'Population History and Local History' in An Introduction to English Historical Demography (edited by E.A. Wrigley (London 1966).), 21-2.

2.   Eversley, op.cit., n.22.

A NOTE ON THE LIFE-TIME MOBILITY OF MARRIED WOMEN IN A PARISH POPULATION IN THE LATER EIGHTEENTH CENTURY

E. A. Wrigley

Although few people still subscribe to the view that parishes in the past were largely closed communities so that most of their inhabitants were born, grew up, married, laboured and died all in the same place, precise knowledge of the frequency and distance of migratory movements is hard to come by. In this matter 1851 marks a great divide. Then for the first time the head of each household was required to record on the census schedule the place of birth of each person resident in his house on census night. With sufficient labour, therefore, the census enumerators books can be made to yield as full a picture as may be required of the patterns of movement from birth to census night of all those alive on that date.[1] Even this leaves much unclear since changes of residence occurring between birth and the census date go unrecorded. For some purposes it is essential to know the life-cycle pattern of migration and not just its end product, so to speak, but compared with what is available to be studied for any date before 1851, the wealth of data for 1851 is striking.

Before 1851 the census-like listings of inhabitants which survive never include information about place of birth, though a few exceptional listings do show place of residence of family members who were no longer living in their parish of birth.[2] Other sources give a comparative wealth of information — for example the apprenticeship records of London companies, or the biographical details included in depositions made in ecclesiastical courts — but in general they cover only select groups within the population. Moreover, they relate either exclusively or primarily to men rather than women.

The only major exception to the rule of partial coverage is to be found in the marriage registers of a small proportion of parishes which indicate the parish of current residence of the bride and groom. This may give an illuminating picture of the part played by marriage in re-shuffling populations.[3] Both sexes are covered but marriage registers do not directly indicate the typical pattern of permanent settlement after marriage because couples often settled in a different parish from that in which the marriage took place.

Something can be done to reduce the uncertainty about the proportion of the adult population of a parish which was born locally by considering the proportion of those married in the parish whose names can be traced in the baptism register. This statistic is a by-product of family reconstitution and serves to underline the absence of closed populations in the past. In the case of brides the percentage whose baptisms can be traced seems rarely to exceed forty and may fall as low as fifteen or twenty even in rural parishes (the comparable figures for men are commonly lower still). But this is a very clumsy measure, both because the problems of record linkage involved are such that the 'true' percentage would normally be higher than the apparent level, and because many brides leave the parish in which they were married soon after the wedding to settle elsewhere.

Occasionally there is more direct and complete evidence to be had from parish registers, and in such cases the female population may be better covered than the male. This is true of a short period in the register of Colyton, Devon. This note is intended to describe the nature of the information available and the evidence it affords about the pattern of life-time migration of married women in the later eighteenth century.

The information is drawn from the baptism register of the parish between 8 April 1765 and the end of 1777. During these dozen years it was normal practice to give the name, occupation and parish of the mother's father in addition to very full details about the father and mother themselves. The form of entry suggests that the incumbent had in mind the maternal grandfather's parish of habitual residence. The register therefore provides direct evidence about the wife's parish of origin.[4] With sufficient labour it would be possible to check this by searching the registers of parishes named for the wife's baptism, but I have not done this. The following is a typical entry of the period:

> 'Mary daughter of James Drewe husbandman by Mary his wife daughter of Joseph Sydenham of the parish of Southleigh yeoman was born the 22[d] of November 1770 and baptized the first of January following'.

Where the maternal grandfather's name and occupation are given but no parish of residence is mentioned I have assumed that the women was a Colytonian. This is more easily checked and appears to be an accurate assumption.[5]

Table 1 shows the number of maternal grandfathers whose names appear in the baptism register and whose place of residence was a parish other than Colyton, together with the number of those presumed to be Colyton men. I assume that it gives a reliable indication of the place of birth of the mothers in question, and thus of the life-time mobility at the time of childbirth of the population of married women of childbearing age. This is a sweeping assumption. In a proportion of cases the maternal grandfather's parish of habitual residence may not have been the place where the daughter in question was born, because the parents did not stay in one parish throughout their early married life but probably the proportion of such cases was small. Reconstitution offers some supporting evidence for this view since a high proportion of all married couples were buried in the parish where they were married when their first child was also baptised there. It should be noted that the Colyton baptism register always names the maternal grandfather and gives supporting detail even though in half or more cases he must have been dead at the time.

Table 1 Origin of Colyton wives from baptism register entries, 1765-1777.

Wife's father's parish of residence		No.
Colyton		164
Parishes wholly or partly within 5 miles of Colyton parish church		
Axminster	15	
Shute*	14	
Stockland	14	
Kilmington	12	
Northleigh*	10	
Southleigh*	10	
Widworthy*	8	
Seaton and Beer*	7	
Sidbury	7	
Combpyne	7	
Axmouth*	4	
Musbury*	4	
Offwell	4	
Honiton	3	
Farway*	2	
Dalwood	2	
Monkton	2	
		125
Other parishes wholly or partly within 10 miles of Colyton parish church		
Upottery	7	
Luppitt	6	
Chard, Som.	5	
Sidmouth	3	
Thorncombe, Som.	2	
Salcombe	2	
Yarcombe	2	
Combe Raleigh	2	
Buckerell	1	
Awliscombe	1	
Newton Poppleford	1	
Dunkeswell	1	
Broadhembury	1	
Payhembury	1	
Whitchurch, Dorset	1	
		36
Other parishes		41
Not stated		4
Total		370

*parish contiguous with Colyton

Baptisms of illegitimate children or of children whose mothers were illegitimate are excluded from the table since there is no information relevant to the table in these cases. Where more than one child from the same family was baptised on the same day, as for example following the birth of twins, the entry has been treated like an entry referring to a single child. The table is based on 370 baptism entries. In four cases there is an incomplete entry in which the wife's father is not named and these appear in table 1 as 'not stated'. The remaining 366 entries either name a parish other than Colyton as the wife's father's residence, or, by omitting reference to a parish of residence, leave it to be assumed that her father was a Colyton man. In 202 of the 366 cases, or 55 per cent, the wife was a 'foreigner'. Most of these wives came from close by. 125 of the 202, or 62 per cent, came from parishes within five miles, and a further 36 or 18 per cent came from an outer tier of parishes between five and ten miles from the Colyton parish church.[6] The remaining forty-one (20 per cent) came from further afield. All these came from Devon, Dorset or Somerset parishes, except for one woman from the Isle of Wight. Almost all were from parishes within a radius of twenty-five miles from Colyton.

The table is not, of course, a reliable guide to the relative importance of **individual** parishes in the overall pattern of migration into Colyton both because the numbers are small and because one wife of high fecundity whose early married life fell within the twelve year period might easily appear half a dozen times in the baptism register, where another of lower fecundity or at a different point in her married life, might appear only once or twice. The relative importance of the successive concentric bands is, however, probably accurately captured by the table. There appear also to have been sectoral differences in the size of migration flows. A narrow belt of parishes immediately to the north of

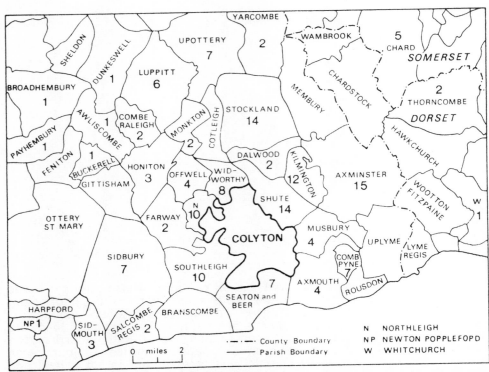

Fig 1 — Origin of Colyton wives from parishes within 10 miles of Colyton parish church (see Table 1).

Colyton (Northleigh, Offwell, Widworthy, Shute, Dalwood, Kilmington, Stockland, Monkton, Luppitt and Upottery) contributed seventy-nine of the 202 baptisms to 'foreign' wives, a much larger number than were to be found in other sectors centred on Colyton.

In about a tenth of the entries used for table 1 the father of the child baptised is recorded as living in a parish other than Colyton and in these cases there is a rather greater likelihood that his wife is also from another parish. The details are set out in table 2. It will be seen that even when such cases are excluded the percentage of 'foreign' wives is not greatly changed.

Table 2 Origin of Colyton wives in mid-eighteenth century

	All entries	%	Husband's residence not Colyton	%	Husband's residence Colyton	%
Colyton	164	45	11	34	153	46
Other	202	55	21	66	181	54

That a significant number of baptism entries related to couples who were not resident in Colyton is an interesting point in its own right. Over the same period covered by table 1, 8.9 per cent of all entries (thirty-three out of 370) concerned a child whose parents lived outside Colyton. I have shown elsewhere that in the early nineteenth century many people had their children baptised in a 'foreign' parish.[7] That study does not yield a directly comparable figure but it suggests, for example, that about 5 per cent of all children born in Colyton at this period were baptised in neighbouring parishes. The baptism register of Colyton in the 1760s and 1770s contains clear evidence that this habit was as widespread in the middle decades of the eighteenth century as it was two generations later. It would be interesting to know whether this is true of the whole parish register period, and therefore any register which was kept in a way which enables the issue to be examined for the sixteenth or seventeenth centuries would be a valuable 'find'.

The mid-eighteenth and mid-nineteenth centuries can also be compared in regard to the mobility of married women in the parish population. The 1851 census enumerators' books show marital status and place of birth so that the information exists to permit the birthplaces of all married women of child-bearing age to be tabulated. Table 3 provides a breakdown of the birthplaces of married women in Colyton who were under forty-five years of age — the group within the married population in the years of child-bearing. This is closely similar in coverage to the mothers appearing in table 1. Comparison of tables 1 and 3 shows how little the pattern of life-cycle mobility of married women had changed over the 80 years before 1851. The relative importance of individual parishes of origin varied somewhat in the two lists though the numbers are too small for any significance to be attached to these changes. The northern sector no longer contributed disproportionately to the migration flow into Colyton, and in the residual list of 'other parishes' there was a larger number of women from a considerable distance (Middlesex 1, Kent 1, Cornwall 1, Ireland 2). But the overall lack of change is much more striking than such minor differences from the earlier pattern. Table 4 may serve to summarise this point. Even the slight fall in the

Table 3 Origin of Colyton wives under 45 from 1851 census enumerator's book

Parish of origin				
Colyton		91		
Within 5 miles[1]			**Within 10 miles[2]**	
Shute*	13		Ottery St. Mary	5
Seaton and Beer*	11		Gittisham	3
Axmouth*	9		Broadhembury	3
Musbury*	9		Sidmouth	2
Axminster	8		Chardstock, Dorset	2
Southleigh*	5		Lyme Regis, Dorset	1
Farway*	5		Chard, Som.	1
Sidbury	4		Salcombe	1
Northleigh*	3		Upottery	1
Branscombe	3		Hawkchurch	1
Offwell*	2		Whitchurch, Dorset	1
Stockland	2		Awliscombe	1
Membury	2		Luppitt	1
Kilmington	1		Yarcombe	1	24
Honiton	1		Other parishes		26
Combpyne	1		Total		221
Uplyme	1	80		

[1] Parishes wholly or partly within 5 miles of Colyton parish church
[2] Other parishes wholly or partly within 10 miles of Colyton parish church
* Parish contiguous with Colyton

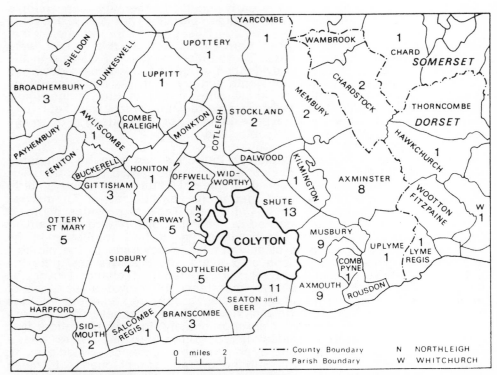

Fig 2 — Origin of Colyton wives under 45 in 1851 from parishes within 10 miles of Colyton parish church (see Table 2).

Table 4 Comparison of origins of Colyton wives between mid-eighteenth century and 1851.

	Baptism register 1765-77		Census 1851	
	No.	%	No.	%
All wives				
Colyton	164	45	91	41
Parishes within 5 miles	125	34	80	36
Parishes within 10 miles	36	10	24	11
Other parishes	41	11	26	12
Total	366	100	221	100
'Foreign' wives				
Parishes within 5 miles	125	62	80	62
Parishes within 10 miles	36	18	24	18
Other parishes	41	20	26	20
Total	202	100	130	100

percentage of local-born wives in the 1851 census may be more apparent than real in that a larger proportion of the children of 'foreign' wives may have been baptised outside the parish, which would have had the effect of inflating the apparent importance of Colyton-born wives in 1765-78.

Within the group of 'foreign' wives the percentage share of parishes within five miles, within ten miles, and at a greater distance, did not change at all.

If in the course of time studies similar to this brief examination of the mobility of married women in Colyton were to be carried out for a substantial number of English parishes, particularly during the early decades of the industrial revolution, we should become much better informed about the degree of stability in local population movements which may have obtained even in periods of great upheaval in some aspects of social, political and economic life. Any great change in the proportion of 'foreign' mothers in a community seems likely to involve major changes in the quality of local life in other respects. Absence of change, on the other hand, given the part played by mothers in the socialisation of their children, may have wider implications for the ways in which the community adapts to the stresses of changing times.

NOTES

1. Far more will be known about these patterns of movement as revealed in the 1851 census when the major study directed by Dr. Michael Anderson of the University of Edinburgh and financed by the SSRC is completed.

2. See R. S. Schofield, 'Age-specific mobility in an eighteenth century rural English parish,' **Annales de démographie historique** (1970), pp. 261-74.

3. For an excellent review of existing knowledge about pre-industrial migration in England see Peter Spufford, 'Population mobility in pre-industrial England,' **Genealogists' Magazine** 17, No. 8 (1973), pp. 420-429; 17, No. 9 (1974), pp. 475-481; and 17, No. 10 (1974), pp. 537-43. See also C. F. Küchemann, A. J. Boyce and G. A. Harrison, 'A demographic and genetic study of a group of Oxfordshire villages' **Human Biology** 39, pp. 251-76, reprinted in M. Drake (ed), **Applied historical studies** (London, 1973), and B. Maltby, 'Parish registers and the problem of mobility,' **LPS** 6 (1971), pp. 32-42.

4. This type of information but covering **both** grandfathers was widely recorded in the 1790s and 1800s in parishes in the Durham diocese. I am indebted to Mrs. W. J. Hodgkiss for this information which suggests that a great opportunity awaits students of social and geographical mobility in this area and period.

5. An earlier exercise designed to check the accuracy of linkages made during family reconstitution provided indirect evidence on this point. I have not made further direct checks.

6. Drawing circles in this fashion is arbitrary and one or two parishes fall partly within each successive concentric circle whose main population centre may be outside the radius of the circle.

7. E. A. Wrigley, 'Baptism coverage in early nineteenth-century England: the Colyton area,' **Population Studies** 29, No. 2 (1975), pp. 299-316.

PERSONAL MOBILITY IN THREE WEST RIDING PARISHES, 1777-1812

Moira Long and Bessie Maltby

The first part of this paper compares personal mobility in three West Riding parishes, Skipton, Addingham and Bolton Abbey, with that in a number of parishes in the Plain of York which were discussed in an article by B. A. Holderness in the **Yorkshire Archaelogical Journal**[1], enquires whether any significant differences are to be found and considers such differences in relation to the economic and occupational structures of the two areas. The second part of the paper is particularly concerned with changes from one occupation to another between the generations.

Introduction

The demographer who discusses the mobility of past generations is well aware of the slenderness of his statistical resources before the census of 1851 when householders were required to give precise details of date and place of birth of all who lived under the same roof. Recent analyses of 'listings' found scattered throughout the country give glimpses into a movement which appeared to be going on everywhere: a static community seems to have been no more common in earlier centuries than it is now. It has been shown that the turnover of population even in long established agricultural communities was remarkably high: for example, in Clayworth (Notts.) 61.8 per cent of the inhabitants in 1688 had not been living there twelve years earlier.[2]

Several methods of using parish registers to give some insight into this movement have been tried with varying success. The change in names recurring over a given period, the provenance of marriage partners, even the complete Family Reconstitution of a sample of families from several adjoining parishes, all do little more than confirm the general impression that a large part of the population moved out of the parish of their birth during their lifetime, but that the movement was, as might be expected, chiefly confined within an easy day's walk.

In the **Yorkshire Archaeological Journal,** Dr. Holderness analyses the figures from nine parishes, chiefly in the Plain of York, in which, between

1777 and 1822, in response to a direction from Archbishop Markham, the baptismal registers record the place of residence of both the paternal and maternal grandfathers of the infant. If these places of residence lie outside the parish where the grandchild is being baptised it is assumed that the baby's parents have emigrated from the villages where their parents lived and settled in the parish where their baby is being baptised. These changes of residence are then analysed and tabulated according to distance travelled and the father's occupation. There will of course be some entries in the registers which do not correspond to this pattern: for example, in some cases the grandparents may also have changed their place of residence[3], but it remains true, as Holderness observed, that "within the small scope offered the evidence is as precise as we are ever likely to obtain" and the detailed residential information which registers of this type afford is of great importance in illuminating the mechanics of population movement. It must also be continually borne in mind that we are dealing only with one segment of the population, those of childbearing age and that it is people of this age-group who, if migration is considered as related to stages in the life cycle, are most likely to have migrated recently.

Three further parishes in Yorkshire, Skipton, Addingham and Bolton Abbey, have registers which contain similar extended baptismal entries for a comparable period and it is these which will be discussed in this article.[4] These parishes differ considerably from the ones considered by Holderness both in their topography and in their occupational structure: their farms were mainly upland, pastoral farms which had different labour requirements from the arable farms on the Plain of York and there was also rapid development of the textile industry in Skipton and Addingham at this time. These three parishes are contiguous, Skipton being close to the River Aire and Bolton Abbey and Addingham on the Wharfe. They are, however, very diverse in character. Skipton is an old-established market town with several large agricultural villages inside its parish boundaries. Bolton Abbey, although technically a chapelry of Skipton, kept separate registers and covered a large agricultural and moorland area with several small settlements on both banks of the Wharfe. Addingham is the smallest of the three parishes and lies chiefly on the west side of the Wharfe. The village, known in the seventeenth century as Long Addingham, straggles along the road towards Skipton and was already very much involved with the woollen trade and worsted manufacture even before the building of its first large mill in 1787.[5]

The position of Skipton in the Aire Gap made it an important centre of communications. Market roads, improved in the eighteenth century, connected it with other markets at Settle, Kirby Malzeard, Masham and Ripon, as well as providing a route through to the west into Lancashire. Turnpike roads, preceding the canal era, passed through Skipton linking Keighley to Kendal and Skipton to Leeds. The construction of the Leeds-Otley-Skipton turnpike was sanctioned in 1758. The Leeds-Liverpool canal was also of great importance to Skipton: this received parliamentary approval in 1770 and, although not fully completed until 1816, gave Skipton links with many other towns on both sides of the Pennines.[6] The availability of water transport stimulated local development and a small feeder canal was built round the base of the castle rock to connect with the main canal which was used from 1774 onwards for carrying limestone from the quarries to Bradford and coal from the Bradford mines on the return journey.[7] The occupation of boatman occurs regularly in the Skipton registers.

We have not attempted to make any estimates of population in the last quarter of the eighteenth century but recent work on mid-Wharfedale indicates that the population and economy of this area grew rapidly from about 1740 to 1770. For a period after 1770 there are indications that the increase in population had outstripped the means of subsistence but after about 1800 improvements in the economy restored the balance. However, it must always be remembered that while we are discussing movement into and within our parishes as shown by the baptism register entries there was also very considerable movement of population out of the area.[8] The recorded populations of our three parishes at the time of the first census were Skipton town 2305, Skipton's rural settlements 1082, Addingham 1157 and Bolton Abbey 492, with 276 persons in Beamsley which was divided between Bolton Abbey and Addingham.[9]

Compared with the Plain of York, the land in the Dales parishes is agriculturally poor: indeed, an observer in 1795 declared that "the whole country westward into Lancashire . . . (from Leeds) . . . does not produce grain or feed sufficient to supply one fifth of its inhabitants."[10] It was, however, rich in water power which, with improved techniques, gave an impetus to the development of textile industries. There had long been a domestic woollen industry but towards the end of the eighteenth century small mills were being opened in the area. Nor were they exclusively woollen mills. High Mill, Skipton, which spun cotton, opened in 1785 and the occupations recorded in the Skipton register show a change, around the turn of the century, from wool to cotton, possibly due to the influence of the flourishing cotton industry in Lancashire and the good communications between Skipton and Lancashire. By 1835 the numbers employed in cotton manufacture in Skipton were 605 and in Addingham 288.[11] There were also other cotton mills in the neighbourhood at Gargrave, Keighley, Haworth and Bingley but none of them employed as many persons as did the two mills at Addingham.

Geographical mobility

The topographical differences between the Dales group of parishes and those in the Plain of York made modifications to Dr. Holderness's methods of analysis necessary. The number of small settlements in each parish and the physical characteristics of our area make it difficult to apply the concept of "adjacent vills" as used by Holderness. This classification implies that the surrounding vills are equally accessible. In practice, of course, this is never exactly so, but the history and topography of the Dales parishes have created large parishes and a settlement pattern so far removed from the ideal hexagons of geographical theory that it was felt better to classify migrations according to distance. For these reasons we have divided migrations into two classes, short range (under 10 miles) and long range (10 miles and over) in order to permit direct comparisons with the Plain of York parishes. Thus the categories of "adjacent vills" and "under 10 miles" used for the Plain of York parishes are combined in order to compare with the Dales figures for short range migration.

In addition, Skipton, the largest of the Dales parishes, has been divided into two parts, the town itself and the rural parish which consists of the other settlements most of which were independent townships and later became civil parishes. This division of the ecclesiastical parish allows migration patterns to be seen more clearly since we can now take account of a move from one of the old-established villages in the parish, such as Embsay, Eastby or Draughton, into Skipton town as a migration.

Since the degree of migration has often been linked to economic opportunity, it may be helpful to consider the occupational composition of the three Dales parishes, as shown in Table 1.

Table 1: Occupational composition of Dales parishes.

	Farmers	Tradesmen	Labourers	N
	%	%	%	
Skipton	1.1	79.5	19.3	616
Skipton parish	18.5	50.0	31.4	254
Addingham	16.6	72.8	10.4	372
Bolton Abbey	43.4	37.2	19.4	226

The overall percentages are shown in Table 2, with the figures from the Plain of York parishes for comparison.

Table 2: Comparison of Dales and Plain of York parishes.

	Farmers	Tradesmen	Labourer	N
	%	%	%	
Dales	14.5	66.2	19.4	1468
Plain of York	25.0	34.7	40.3	1128

The different characteristics of the two areas show clearly in these figures particularly in the far higher proportion of tradesmen in the Dales parishes. Bolton Abbey corresponds most closely to the Plain of York parishes, but the difference in the type of farming practised in the two areas is indicated by the relative proportions of farmers and labourers. The ratio of labourers to land occupiers in Wharfedale is considerably below that for the country as a whole,[12] and reflects the small size of the farms in the Dales area and the fact that the mainly pastoral farming employed fewer day labourers than the arable farming practised on the Plain of York.

The percentage of tradesmen in the Dales parishes was nearly double that in the Plain of York parishes and was highest in the town of Skipton and the mixed industrial/agricultural village of Addingham. The tradesmen fall into two main groups: those concerned with providing goods and services and those engaged in some branch of textile manufacture. In

Addingham, for example, 64.5 per cent of the tradesmen recorded were working in textile manufacture as woolcombers, weavers, cotton spinners and linen weavers. Thus, in this parish, 16.6 per cent of the men who appear as fathers in the registers were farmers, 25.8 per cent were tradesmen providing goods and services, 47.0 per cent were engaged in some branch of textile manufacture and 10.4 per cent were labourers. It can be seen, then, that there were considerable occupational differences between the Dales parishes and the Plain of York parishes, and that the Dales area contained a substantial proportion of textile workers whose migrational patterns might perhaps be different from those of other groups in the community.

The period which the extended registers cover is one of great importance in the transition to industrialisation and in Skipton and Addingham we have two parishes which were undergoing considerable changes. This economic change was accompanied by shifts in the balance of the different groups in the population and these are shown by analysis of the information in the extended registers. We have made comparisons between the Dales area where there was a mixture of industry and agriculture and the predominantly agricultural parishes in the Plain of York and find that although, in each area, almost half the childbearing population was still native to the parish where they lived, the more industrialised parishes had received a higher proportion of long range migrants. The proportion of long range migration was highest amongst the tradesmen and their wives and we would suggest that it was this factor which, from a demographic point of view, distinguished the parishes which were becoming industrialised from those which remained agricultural. Long range however, is a relative term and it must be emphasized that, as will be shown below, Skipton and Addingham were attracting migrants principally from the older-established textile producing areas of the county.

The following table shows the percentages of men in each occupational group who had, respectively, remained in their father's place of residence, migrated less than 10 miles, or migrated 10 miles or more. It can be seen that within each occupational group, the figures follow much the same general pattern in each area though there are some interesting differences.

Table 3: Mobility of occupational groups in relation to parish of origin.

	Same Parish	Under 10 m	10 m and over	Unidentified	N
	%	%	%	%	
Farmers					
Dales	56.5	32.2	11.0	0.0	214
Plain of York	54.1	30.0	14.8	1.1	283
Tradesmen					
Dales	48.4	26.0	25.5	0.0	972
Plain of York	47.7	29.8	17.9	4.6	391
Labourers					
Dales	37.5	38.2	24.0	0.0	282
Plain of York	31.8	42.7	18.1	7.4	454

As might be expected, the farmers were the most stable occupational group and the only one in which more than half had remained in their father's place of residence. The percentage of short range migration is very similar in both areas but the Plain of York parishes attracted more long distance migrants in this group than did the Dales parishes. This runs counter to our general conclusion that the Dales parishes received the higher proportion of long range migrants but it highlights the importance of economic factors in determining individual decisions about migration. A farmer would only move to a new area when he could buy a holding or take up a vacant tenancy and the more fertile land on the Plain of York would undoutedly be more attractive than the upland farming of the Dales area. It should be noticed though that almost half the farmers in the Dales sample were in Bolton Abbey which was part of the Duke of Devonshire's estates so that if the policy of the estate had happened to favour any particular type of tenant at this time this could have a significant effect on the figures.

The tradesmen formed the largest occupational group in the Dales parishes. Here 66 per cent of the men in the registers followed some specific trade as against 35 per cent in the Plain of York parishes (Table 2) and although the percentage of those remaining in their place of origin was about the same in both areas, the Dales parishes, as in the case of the labourers, attracted a higher proportion of long range immigrants. Twenty-five per cent of the tradesmen in the Dales registers had come from places ten miles or more away and amongst the labourers 24 per cent had come from similar distances. In both areas the labourers were the most likely to move away from their original place of residence and they have, in both areas, the highest proportion of short range migrants. Thus, it appears, that a short migration of under ten miles was particularly characteristic of the labourer. It is possible that individual labourers might have made several such moves in the course of their working lives depending on the availability of work and housing.

It must be emphasized that the Dales parishes as a whole did not have a higher proportion of in-migrants than the Vale of York parishes at this period, but they did draw a higher proportion of those in-migrants from a distance of ten miles or more. When the groups are combined and the overall percentages compared it is clear that the Dales parishes received a smaller proportion of short-range migrants, but a larger proportion of long-range migrants, than the Plain of York parishes. Table 4 shows clearly that in the Dales parishes there was less of that short range movement which Holderness has described as a "milling about" of the population, "an ebb and flow across parish boundaries," but more long distance movement.

Table 4: Comparison of mobility.

	Same Parish	Under 10 m	10 m and over	Unidentified	N
	%	%	%	%	
Dales	47.5	29.3	23.2	0.0	1468
Plain of York	42.8	34.9	17.1	5.0	1128

130

The overall comparison of mobility between the two areas demonstrates the greater economic attraction of the Dales parishes. Fewer of those born in the Dales parishes found it necessary to move away from their homes and these parishes attracted a higher proportion of in-migrants from over ten miles. These trends are shown clearly in the figures for the tradesmen and labourers, the two classes most affected by industrial change. In Skipton town, for example, there were actually more long-range migrants in the register than short-range migrants.

It is clear that Skipton as the larger town had a greater attraction for migrants than Addingham, although the proportions of tradesmen in the two samples were fairly similar (see Table 1). In the Skipton register 30.6 per cent of the tradesmen had travelled ten miles or more and 32.7 per cent of the labourers had made similar journeys. Corresponding figures for Addingham are 22.1 per cent and 17 per cent. These figures suggest that even at this relatively early stage in the industrialisation of this area the larger town which had long been important as a market and a route centre drew in a significantly higher proportion of long distance migrants.

Skipton had been a market town since the early medieval period and also held fairs for the sale of horses, cattle and sheep. That these fairs served a wide area of countryside is shown by a charter of 1597 which describes them as 'very useful to those living within forty miles near.' The town became a gathering point for wool from the Craven district and had also some domestic woollen industry. The expansion and industrialisation of Skipton began after the opening of the canal in 1774 so that the extended registers cover the period when the earliest mills were being built, for example, High Mill near the Castle was opened in 1785, and when the gardens of the houses in the High Street were being filled with rows of cottages to accommodate the increasing numbers of workers.[13]

The majority of the long-range migrants who came to Skipton came from areas which already had strong links with the town and this emphasises the great importance of pre-existing contacts and knowledge in determining migrations. Fleeces and animals came into Skipton from Craven and from further north and the Keighley-Skipton-Kendal turnpike road was much used for the transport of wool from Westmorland to the Halifax area. A substantial group of migrants followed this route to Skipton from Settle, Sedbergh, Lancaster, Kirby Lonsdale and Kendal. Contacts made in the distribution of wool throughout the West Riding drew migrants, who probably already had skills in the textile trades, from Halifax, Huddersfield, Wakefield, Leeds and the smaller towns in that area. Also, Skipton's position on the age-old trading route through the Aire gap meant that migrants came from South Lancashire attracted by the establishment of cotton mills in the Skipton area.

These regions provided the majority of the in-migrants between 1777 and 1812. There were also a certain number from North Yorkshire, mainly from Wensleydale and Swaledale and there were, of course, individual migrants who had travelled very far from their parish of origin. For example, there were a woolcomber from Bristol, a whitesmith from Edinburgh and a gardener from Arbroath, as well as a comedian from Westminster who, one may suppose, was not a permanent resident of Skipton but had come to play in the theatre which then existed in the town and where Edmund Keane is said to have appeared in 1803.

An attempt was made to see whether any significant break in the numbers of migrants occurred at ten miles. This was done by plotting as bar graphs the distances travelled by the individual tradesmen and labourers who appear in the Skipton register. In neither case did there appear to be a break at ten miles though there was a break in the tradesmen's graph between 27 and 30 miles and in the labourers' graph between 16 and 20 miles.

The mobility of the womenfolk follows very much the same pattern as that found among the men. Like their husbands, the women in the Dales parishes made a smaller proportion of short range migrations and a larger proportion of long range migrations than the people of the Plain of York parishes. However, as in the Plain of York the overall percentage of wives remaining in their father's place of residence was less than that of the men, while their percentage of short range migration was higher, no doubt due to marriages between men and women of neighbouring villages when it was more likely that the girl would move to the husband's place of residence.

Table 5: Mobility of wives.

	Same Parish	Under 10 m	10 m and over	Unidentified	N
	%	%	%	%	
Dales	41.7	33.6	24.7	0.0	1468
Plain of York	35.3	41.3	18.2	5.2	1128

The mobility of the women in the Dales registers varies to some extent with the occupation of their husbands. The labourers' wives were an exception to the general conclusion that fewer women than men remained in their father's place of residence. In this group 39 per cent of the women remained in their father's place of residence as against 37.5 per cent of the men. The same is true in the Plain of York parishes and this difference between the labourers on the one hand and the tradesmen and farmers is doubtless because among the labourers there were not the same factors of inheritance or occupation to determine male residence.

Short range migration was highest among the farmers' wives (46 per cent) and lowest among the tradesmen's wives (30.6 per cent). The highest percentage of long range migration in the survey was that of the tradesmen's wives (27.3 per cent), higher even that that of their husbands (25.5 per cent). Some couples had obviously travelled together, for example, a cabinet maker and his wife both from Lancaster and a shoemaker and his wife from Hull, but there was only a small number of these and most couples in the register had come from different parishes. If we look at the figures for tradesmen's wives in Skipton itself we find that 34.7 per cent of those in the register had made a migration of ten miles or more compared with 30.6 per cent of their husbands. The relatively small number of long-range migrant parents who were of the same parish of origin shows that most of these women in-migrants had come to Skipton before marriage and one must assume that their decision to migrate was prompted by the same social and economic factors as affected the men.

The textile industry was carried on, to a large extent, by women's labour and the presence of a high proportion of women in-migrants of child bearing age must have had consequences from the demographic point of view beyond the immediate effect of a widening of marriage horizons. This in itself was important genetically but the facts that women's earnings made it easier for couples to marry earlier, that children were also employed at an early age and that migrants 'were freed by movement from the restraints on marriage of their traditional environment'[14] must all have contributed strongly towards population growth.

It is interesting to compare the mobility of women in both the Dales parishes and the Plain of York parishes with similar figures published by Dr. Wrigley for Colyton, Devon.[15] A comparison of Table 5 (Yorkshire) with Table 6 (Devon) shows the greatest difference to be in the amount of long range migration which was significantly smaller in Colyton both in the mid-eighteenth century and in 1851 than in either of the Yorkshire areas in the intervening period.

Table 6: Mobility of wives in Colyton.

	Same Parish	Under 10 m	10 m and over
	%	%	%
1765-77	45	44	11
1851	41	47	12

Short range migration was markedly higher in Colyton than in the Dales parishes and perhaps serves to reinforce the point made earlier that while there was less short range movement in the areas which were changing under the influence of industrialisation there was correspondingly more long range movement into these areas.

Occupational mobility

As well as the geographical mobility of the various groups, farmers, labourers and tradesmen, there was also over the period a considerable change in the occupations of the population.

Straight counts, that is, the number of times an occupation is given in baptismal and/or marriage and burial registers, is the method most frequently used to show the occupations within a parish or group of parishes. It can however be distorted in a small community by large families of certain categories of workers or even the inclusion of a few particularly prolific families. We have been able to count the heads of households rather than the number of entries, as the detailed information regarding grandfathers and grandmothers avoids the difficulties often encountered of distinguishing between men who share a common name.

Addingham is the parish which underwent the greatest change. In a small community the establishment of a mill was not only likely to change the occupational structure among families already living there but also to cause an influx of labour. The first five years (1777-1781) show only 59 child-bearing families, whereas in 1808-12 there are 155. In the earlier period 20.3 per cent were farmers or land-workers, 20.3 per cent labourers, 23.7 per cent textile workers and 35.7 per cent practised various trades, including services such as innkeepers and carriers. In the latter five years the figures were 17.4 per cent farmers, 5.2 per cent labourers (to which we refer later), 50 per cent textile workers and 26.4 per cent tradesmen. This great increase in textile workers indicates Addingham's role as an early textile village.

Skipton shows a similar, though not so striking a pattern. As a market town its trades and industries were more diversified (paper-making, rope-making as well as textiles) and retail shopkeepers make their appearance — bakers and grocers. However, an increase in baptisms over burials between the five years 1777-1781 and 1808-1812 from 375 to 579 (with an insignificant change in the number of burials) indicates some immigration. Skipton shows a great decrease in the farming community, a small fall in the number of labourers, but sizeable increases in general trades and especially in textile workers.

Bolton Abbey is the most stable of the three parishes, continuing to be primarily a farming community, with an increase in textile workers (many of the men employed in the Addingham mill might well have lived in the Bolton Abbey parish). The number of tradesmen remains steady, but the number of labourers shows an increase.

The baptismal registers in the three parishes yield such a wealth of detailed information that many other lines of enquiry might be followed: change of occupation between generations; changes between generation in the same family; changes in social status; tendency of intermarriage between certain categories of workers; and even the possibility of greater occupational change in long-range immigrants.

We have attempted the first three of these enquiries. In comparing the occupations of fathers and grandfathers it must be remembered that the comparison is between younger and older men and includes grandfathers who may not have lived or worked in the Parish.

Out of 1468 heads of families, 1397 entries give relevant information about occupation and residence, and the following tables show the years 1778-1812.

Table 7: Occupations in period 1778-1812.

Combined parishes	Grandfathers		Fathers	
Farmers	417	(29.8%)	210	(15.0%)
Labourers	272	(19.4%)	253	(18.1%)
Textile workers	207	(14.8%)	375	(26.8%)
Tradesmen	477	(34.1%)	540	(38.6%)
Professions and gentry	24	(1.7%)	19	(1.3%)
	1,397		1,397	

Skipton	Grandfathers		Fathers	
Farmers	146	(18.2%)	49	(6.1%)
Labourers	203	(25.3%)	175	(21.8%)
Textile workers	114	(14.2%)	168	(20.9%)
Tradesmen	317	(39.5%)	392	(48.9%)
Professions and gentry	21	(2.6%)	17	(2.1%)
	801		801	

Addingham	Grandfathers		Fathers	
Farmers	143	(37.2%)	68	(17.7%)
Labourers	53	(13.8%)	38	(9.8%)
Textile workers	75	(17.5%)	173	(45.0%)
Tradesmen	110	(28.6%)	103	(26.8%)
Professions and gentry	3	(0.7%)	2	(0.5%)
	384		384	

Bolton Abbey	Grandfathers		Fathers	
Farmers	128	(60.3%)	93	(43.8%)
Labourers	16	(7.5%)	40	(18.4%)
Textile workers	18	(8.0%)	34	(16.0%)
Tradesmen	50	(23.5%)	45	(21.2%)
Professions and gentry	—		—	
	212		212	

The change in the percentage of labourers in the combined parishes is small, but in Addingham and Bolton Abbey it operates in opposite ways and is not easy to explain. In Addingham the fall might be attributed to the overall decline in landworkers — the day labourers being absorbed by the new textile industries and paid weekly as mill employees. The large increase in Bolton Abbey requires a different explanation. Seventeen of the forty Bolton Abbey labourers, however, were sons of husbandmen or farmers, so one might assume that in part the difference is between a younger day-worker on a farm and an established tenant farmer. There is also the possibility that the distinction between labourers and husbandmen in a predominantly rural parish was not always clear: the nomenclature might be the choice of the incumbent.

The following table shows the percentage of men who followed their father's occupation. As might be expected, farming is the most "hereditary" occupation, despite its overall decline in the parishes from 417 families to 210. It is perhaps interesting to note that there were 42 landworkers in the three parishes whose fathers' occupations were other than farmer, husbandman or yeoman. Of these 13 were sons of labourers and 6 of butchers. It does, however, leave 23 (or 10.9 per cent) whose fathers are definitely described as tradesmen of various kinds or textile workers, including a hosier, a tanner and a schoolmaster. Does this indicate that "the land" exerts a pull for certain individuals even in a rapidly industrialising society?

Table 8: Percentage of men following father's occupation.

	Skipton	N	Addingham	N	Bolton Abbey	N
Farmers	79%	39	72%	49	85%	79
Labourers	50%	88	22%	8	32%	13
Textile workers	41%	69	37%	64	32%	11
Tradesmen	42%	165	40%	41	36%	16

Note The percentages are based on the numbers of cases given in Table 7 for the corresponding parish and occupation in the column headed 'father.'

Among the tradesmen in Skipton and Addingham, masons and blacksmiths seemed the most likely to carry on their fathers' trade. In Addingham 50 per cent of masons' and blacksmiths' sons followed their fathers' occupation. In Bolton Abbey the picture is slightly different; six of the ten carpenters were sons of carpenters, but this trade, apart from cordwainers (whose sons' occupations were diverse) was the only one to reach double figures.

No firm conclusoins can be drawn about social status from comparisons of occupation of different generations, based as the latter are on comparisons between younger and older men. Assuming labourer, husbandman, farmer and yeoman are rungs on the social ladder in the farming world, it is frequently noted that the grandfather is one rung above the father. The interchange of trades and country occupations and textile workers seems to indicate little difference in social status. The intermarriage of various groups appeared to throw more light on social mobility, so an analysis was made of the occupation of the father and his father-in-law. Among the farming community the same rule applied generally as between different generations. In Bolton Abbey, nine men who called themselves farmers married daughters of yeomen (only three of them from Bolton Abbey Parish), many husbandmen married farmers' daughters and it seems probable that the eighteen labourers who married daughters of husbandmen or farmers were themselves day workers on the land, who might in course of time inherit their own fathers' farm or that of their father-in-law.

No definite pattern emerged in Addingham, the parish where the greatest change of occupation took place. Approximately half of each group married women from similar backgrounds, and over a third of the tradesmen and textile workers who married farmers' daughters were themselves sons of farmers or husbandmen. The labourers' wives who were not themselves daughters of labourers, came almost equally from tradesmen's (including textile worker's) families and from the farming community.

Skipton, with its greater variety of trades is more complicated. Few of its 181 labourers married farmers' daughters (the farming community was small), but this might show that they were not land workers but labourers in other occupations. Amongst the tradesmen, retail shopkeepers appeared to be slightly higher in the social scale than textile workers since a larger number of them found wives from professional and farmers' families. For example, only one of the 20 innkeepers married a labourer's daughter: one married a gentleman's daughter, one a bailiff's and 8 married farmers' daughters. None of the 27 grocers found wives from labourers' families: 3 married yeomen's daughters and one a ship's officer's. None of the other retail tradesmen found their wives in the labourers' group but their numbers were very small, 4 bakers, 4 mercers and a 'shopkeeper.' The mercers married the daughters of a farmer, an ironmonger, an army captain and an architect, whilst the shopkeeper married a watchmaker's daughter. One chairmaker and one painter married yeomen's daughters and one joiner married into the gentry (his wife's father's residence was Chester-le-Street, Co. Durham).

The impressions given here of social status and mobility are necessarily limited by the small numbers involved but it would be interesting to see whether they would be confirmed by studies of other extended registers. The whole question of population movement at this period and the relationships between migration and industrial development are of considerable interest and the Dales registers afford material for further investigations particularly perhaps into the backgrounds of the textile workers. When general models and theories of migration are proposed it must be remembered that each migration was the result of an individual decision and the special interest attaching to these extended registers is that, for a space of a few decades, we can see something of the origins and family backgrounds of the men and women who made such a decision.

NOTES

1. B. A. Holderness, 'Personal mobility in some rural parishes of Yorkshire, 1777-1822', **Yorkshire Achaeological Society,** pt. 168, vol. xlii, 1970.

2. P. Laslett, **The world we have lost,** 1965, p. 147.

3. This point is discussed by E. A. Wrigley, 'A note on the life-time mobility of married women in a parish population in the late eighteenth century', **L.P.S.,** 18, 1977, p. 23.

4. **Skipton register,** ed. W. J. Stavert, Skipton, 1896.
   Addingham register, ed G. D. Lumb, Yorkshire Parish Register Society, 1920.
   Bolton Abbey register, ed. A. P. Howes, 1895.

5. M. Pickles, 'Mid-Wharfedale 1721-1812', **L.P.S.,** 16, 1976, p. 25.

6. M. Beresford and G. R. J. Jones, (eds.), **Leeds and its region,** 1967, pp. 148-9.

7. G. Firth, 'Early years of the Leeds-Liverpool canal', **Industrial Past,** 1977.

8. M. Pickles, **LPS,** 16, p. 32, table 12.
   (It is not possible to make direct comparisons between, for example, the figures quoted for occupations in this article and here, since the periods of time involved are not exactly the same.)

9. **Victoria County History, Yorks.,** vol. iii.

10. Beresford and Jones, p. 149.

11. E. Baines, **History of cotton manufacture,** 1835, p. 387.

12. For Wharfedale see M. Pickles, **LPS,** 16, note 19, and for the national estimate see J. H. Clapham, 'The growth of an agrarian proletariat, 1688-1832', **Cambridge Historical Journal,** 1923, pp. 93-5.

13. A. Raistrick, **West Riding of Yorkshire,** 1970, pp. 155-159.

14. H. J. Habakkuk, **Population growth and economic development since 1750,** 1971, p.43.

15. E. A. Wrigley, **LPS,** 18, 1977, p. 28.

MOBILITY AND REGISTRATION IN THE NORTH IN THE LATE EIGHTEENTH CENTURY

W. J. Sheils

The exceptional detail contained in some registers of the north of England in the later eighteenth century has often been noted by archivists, genealogists and historians.[1] The problems involved in giving legal proof of identity did not escape the notice of contemporaries either, and one of the purposes of Hardwicke's Marriage Act of 1754 was 'to preserve the evidence of marriages, and to make the proof thereof more certain and easy' whilst a bill for registration of births and deaths at the same time failed to pass the House of Lords.[2] The limitations of the registers, however, were not only apparent to legal minds, but also to the antiquaries who often had recourse to search the registers in compiling their local histories. Ralph Thoresby, in **Ducatus Leodiensis** published as early as 1715, had provided an improved form of registration which included dates of both birth and baptism, father's name and occupation, mother's name, and place of residence for each entry.[3] This was the direct inspiration for the registers of the parish of Husthwaite near Thirsk where an improved version adding the mother's maiden name, was adopted from 1769 in order 'to afford much clearer intelligence to the researches of posterity.'[4] Of course, in line with the interests of the antiquaries, the research in mind was largely genealogical. It was presumably a refinement of this sort of register which Dr. Wrigley was able to exploit recently for his study of the life-time mobility of married women at Colyton in this period.[5] Thoresby was not alone in his concern and another northern antiquary, William Dade of Barmston,[6] who had direct experience of the problems of registration during his time as a curate in the city of York from 1763, devised a form of registration with even fuller information than Thoresby.

A new parish register was purchased for St. Helen's church in Stonegate, York, when Dade became curate in 1770 and on the first page was inscribed a note; 'the following method of ascertaining the births and baptisms, deaths and burials in this parish of St. Helen's, York was introduced in 1770 by William Dade . . . curate of this church. This scheme, if properly put into execution, will afford much clearer intelligence to the researches of posterity than the imperfect method hitherto generally adopted'. The register was divided into columns for the information given; that for baptisms included child's name and surname, father's name, profession, descent and place of residence, mother's name and descent and dates of birth and baptism; the burial information included the deceased's occupation, residence, dates of death and burial, age at death and cause of death. The extent of detail is perhaps best illustrated by the first two full entries in each category:

Thomas, 1st born [child of] Cochran, William, coachmaker, eldest son of William Cochran, coachmaker, and Elizabeth, his wife [and] Martha, 3rd daughter of Mr. John Brooks, coachman, of the Minster Yard, and Sarah Rhodes, his wife, Davygate, born 20 July baptised 24 July 1770.

Daniel Corsican, late of London, a coach trimmer to Mr. Cochran and a married man, of Swinegate died 14 January, buried 16 January 1770 in the new burying ground. Aged 30 years, Consumption

and their value is obvious for studies of both migration and mortality.[7] It is with the former that I am particularly concerned. The detail provided in these baptismal registers, giving information on occupational status and residence for both grandparents and parents, opens up the exciting possibility of linking migration to social mobility through reference to occupational status. Dade, who compiled materials for a history of his native Holderness and was later elected an F.S.A., shared his post at St. Helen's with another curacy at St. Olave's, Marygate where the same policy was also adopted in 1770.[8] His example was followed by one or two of his clerical friends in the city,[9] but what really makes Dade's initiative important is the influence which his principles had on the new archbishop of York in 1777, William Markham. Markham was impressed with the legal difficulties arising from insufficient registration and so, at his primary visitation of 1777, ordered that Dade's scheme be put into practice throughout the diocese 'as great complaints have arisen of the registers of marriages, births, and burials belonging to several parishes, being inaccurately kept and drawn out, so as not to identify and ascertain the persons etc., whereby they have not their due weight in point of evidence'[10]. This confirms D. J. Steel's suggestion that the uniformity of entries could be attributed to episcopal recommendation, but his view that the order was 'largely ineffective', happily needs to be reconsidered.[11] Markham's order gave the new form of register official support which was endorsed in the following year by the Dean and Chapter at the visitation of the parishes within their jurisdiction.[12] The result was that Dade's initiative was copied elsewhere, making the information available of more than local value to both contemporaries and historians. It is as well to examine the effect it had within the area of the present archdeaconry of York which covers an area within a radius of approximately fifteen miles from the city. The parish records of this area are deposited at the Borthwick Institute and, of 161 registers deposited from the archdeaconry, 82 give all details under Dade's scheme whilst others, such as those for Crayke, provide some information, mostly concerning maternal descent or maiden name. Indeed local printers began to print registers arranged in columns with headings necessary for the scheme. The very layout of the registers encouraged better registration and they were purchased by over half the parishes examined.[13] Of course not all parochial officials continued to use the system for the same period of time; as the table below shows there were considerable variations but the figures are still impressive.[14]

Duration	No. of parishes	Percentage of archdeaconry population (1801 census)
0- 4 years	13	8.5
5- 9 years	14	7.5
10-20 years	21	13.5
20 years plus	14	10.2
1778-1812 complete	20	19.0

They are even more so if, as in column three of our table, they are plotted against the 1801 census figures. The total population of the parishes covered by the survey was 86,233 in 1801[15] and the figures in the above table refer to the percentage of that population living in the parishes in each category. Thus, within the archdeaconry, 58.7 per cent of the population were affected by the new order to some extent and we have information for a period of more than ten years from parishes containing 42.7 per cent of the total population of the region. There were of course geographical variations within the archdeaconry, the order being less effective in parishes to the east and north of the city than in those in the city itself and to the west, but the coverage for the whole area remains impressive. Only five parishes with populations greater than 1000 in 1801 failed completely to comply with the order.[16] Individual studies of particular parishes have already been undertaken by students in extra-mural classes or pursuing the applied historical studies course for the Open University,[17] but the material offers scope for that study of inter-generational migration and social mobility in 'an entire, close-knit geographical region during the generation from 1778 to 1812' suggested by Dr. Holderness. This is considerably earlier than similar work based upon Census material, and a start has been made on the project. For York and its hinterland we can thank William Dade and William Markham for providing this opportunity, but did they know of precedents elsewhere, and do similar opportunities exist? I would be grateful for any information.[18]

NOTES

1. See for example, D. J. Steel, **National Index of Parish Registers,** i, 1968, p.44, he says that very full details are given 'from about 1765' in some Lancashire, North Yorkshire and Durham registers, though the examples he gives are taken from the period after 1778. A valuable article by B. A. Holderness, 'Personal mobility in some rural parishes of Yorkshire,' **Yorkshire Archaeological Journal,** vol. 42, 1970 pp. 444-54, exploits this detail using printed registers.

2. 26 Geo. II, cap. 33; W. E. Tate, **The Parish Chest,** 1969, p.49.

3. R. Thoresby, **Ducatus Leodiensis,** 1715, p.163, he gave examples and attributed the method to Thomas Kirke, esquire.

4. B[orthwick] I[nstitute] PR. HUS.2.

5. E. A. Wrigley, 'A Note of the life-time mobility of married women in a parish population in the later eighteenth century.' **Local Population Studies,** 18, pp.22-29.

6. **D.N.B.**

7. B.I., PR. Y/HEL.3.

8. **Ibid.** PR.Y/OL.5.

9. In 1773 at St Mary, Castlegate and St Cuthbert, see **The Parish Register of St Mary Castlegate, York,** ed M. F. M. Mulgrew (Yorkshire Arch. Soc. Parish Register Section, vol. cxxxvi, 1972) and B.I. PR.Y/CUT.3.

10. See **Ibid.** PR.ALN.4; and the note in PR.K/W.4, which mentions the visitation.

11. Steel, p.44.

12. York Minster Library, C/3a, Printed visitation articles of Dean Fountaine, 1778.

13. Some were in fact purchased by parishes which did not comply with the full details of the order. Several parishes did give additional information on descent than had previously been the case, even if they did not always include occupation and place of origin.

14. This table includes only those parishes giving details of **both** occupation and residence for both sets of grandparents for the period given, some continued to give partial details for considerably longer but this is not shown. A few places such as Sherburn in Elmet even operated an index system for descents to avoid writing out repetitive details at length. Six rural parishes within the archdeaconry are excluded from the survey as their records have not yet been deposited.

15. **Census, 1801**

16. New Malton, St Leonard; New Malton, St Michael; Coxwold; Sheriff Hutton and Bubwith.

17. Mr. B. Pace has worked on St Mary Bishophill Senior, York; Miss E. Barton on St Mary Castlegate, York; and Mr. R. Moore on Easingwold. See also the work on marriage registers at Easingwold by Mrs. B. Maltby, 'Easingwold marriage horizons,' **LPS** 2, pp. 36-9 and her 'Marriage registers and the problems of mobility,' **LPS** 6, pp.32-42.

18. Holderness, p.454; see the note in Wrigley p.29 n.4, which suggests that Durham followed York's example.

Anyone with any information please contact me at the Borthwick Institute, St Anthony's Hall, York.

A NEW APPROACH TO THE STUDY OF MARRIAGE HORIZONS

Jeremy Millard

Introduction

There have been relatively few attempts by historical demographers to analyse marriage horizons beyond a simple examination of marriage numbers and percentages. This article aims, by way of a case study of parishes in north Buckinghamshire, to introduce readers of **LPS** to several more powerful techniques which are well within the grasp of the amateur local historian and which are, indeed, introduced in Leslie Bradley's **A Glossary for Local Population Studies.**[1] It must be stressed from the outset, however, that the techniques introduced here are not intended to replace the more traditional historian's descriptive and analytical skills, nor supersede the more straightforward use of percentages. On the contrary, these additional techniques must be seen as complementing the more familiar methods. It is generally true that any technique, if properly used, can throw its own unique light on a subject, but, at the same time, its use inevitably involves a series of assumptions, short cuts or over-generalisations. This is why, in one sense, the more techniques used in analysing a particular topic the better, although in practice techniques will be selected, with both their strengths and weaknesses in mind, to do a particular job or fulfill a specific need. This article is therefore a demonstration of how certain techniques can be used when looking at the topic of marriage horizons. It will also be suggested that they are especially powerful in bringing out the underlying trend in a series of data, in other words, in looking for valid generalisations, as well as seeking to explain particular local situations. The value of these generalisations is that it allows us to make comparisons between different places and times.

The marriage distance

Parochial marriage registers constitute a vast and, as yet, largely untapped source of data for the analysis of **marriage distances,** both spatially and temporally. A marriage distance is defined as the distance between the parish of residence of the groom and the parish of residence of the bride, on the eve of their marriage, as recorded in the register. The site of the parish church is normally used in measuring these distances.

In looking at the marriage distances for a particular parish during a specific time period, it is possible to devise a measure of parish **isolation** by calculating the percentage of extra-parochial marriages (i.e. marriages in which one partner resided outside the parish). The higher this percentage is the less isolated the parish can be said to be. It is also demonstrable that, in general, parishes with large populations tend, for many reasons, including their better developed transport system, to have more, and more extensive, connections with the outside world; i.e. these parishes would, in these terms, exhibit a low degree of isolation. From a study, completed in 1976,[2] however, it is apparent that there is a tendency for parishes with large populations to have **low** percentages of extra-parochial marriages. In other words, parishes with large populations, which we assume are less isolated than those with small populations, in fact come out as more isolated when this is measured by the percentage of extra-parochial marriages. This apparent paradox is a useful illustration of the fact that the use of quantitative techniques requires an awareness of the assumptions being made and the implications involved, and a very careful definition of what precisely is being measured. In fact the contradiction can perhaps be explained by the notion that in parishes with a large population any individual seeking a marriage partner within the parish has a greater chance of finding one **simply** because the population is large. It also tends to be the case that these parishes contain more urbanised populations, and it can be suggested that there is a greater likelihood of intermarriage within this population than with the more 'rural' parishes round about, because any individual tends to seek a mate from amongst the same or similar class or occupational grouping.

It is apparent, therefore, that, when trying to interpret something like the percentage of extra-parochial marriages, it is not possible to do so in any simple cause-and-effect manner, that many other factors also have a greater or lesser impact to make, and that it is constantly necessary to relate any attempt at explanation to the total societal context from which it comes. This lesson is particularly important when using graphical or quantitative techniques to examine an aspect of society, and this is certainly true of the techniques presented in this paper. However, I hope I can demonstrate the analytical value of certain techniques in advancing our understanding of the past, when these problems are borne in mind. Graphical and quantitative techniques are only aids, or tools, to help increase our understanding; they are certainly not panaceas allowing us to circumvent historical problems. In fact their use often throws up a whole new set of problems which must be faced by the historian. If they are faced successfully, however, they can add greatly to our knowledge.

Hypotheses

A study of extra-parochial marriages can also be used to examine **spatial interaction.** In other words, the distance, direction, and intensity of the inter-connections between different places over time. In this context, the marriage distance is a **surrogate** measure for spatial interaction. By a surrogate measure is meant something which will stand in, or approximate, for something else for which there is no direct information. For example, historical demographers often use baptisms as a measure of births, and burials as a measure of deaths. They are not quite the same thing and there are, therefore, problems associated with their use. Nevertheless these surrogates are often the only measures available. In fact extra-parochial marriages are more than mere surrogates, because they are themselves one type of spatial interaction, and, in this sense, they are used as indicators of the general pattern of interaction over time.[3]

Given fairly complete and accessible marriage registers, which also record each individual's parish, a study of marriage distances can commence at an early date. These conditions, however, do not normally prevail before 1754. It was in this year that Lord Hardwicke's 1753 'Act for the prevention of clandestine marriages', making it virtually impossible to contract a valid marriage unless it were carried out in a church according to an Anglican ceremony, came into force. The act also provided printed registration forms for the first time and these made provision for an individual's 'parish' to be recorded. From 1754, therefore, despite problems of under- and mis-registration, we can be reasonably certain that there is a representative picture of the marriage patterns of a particular parish. It was not until 1837 (when civil registration of births, marriages and deaths commenced) that male occupational information was explicitly asked for on the registration form, although it was many years before it was also elicited from the bride. Before this date detailed class and occupational analyses can be carried out on a few registers for limited periods, and it is only possible to examine the gross marriage patterns.

The compilation of marriage distance data must be based on sufficiently large samples, in order to ensure that the resulting interaction patterns are likely to reflect reality. For any one parish, this means aggregating data into time-period groupings. The periods I used in north Buckinghamshire were of forty years' duration, and, over the 160-year period from 1754 to 1913, this allowed four sequential patterns to be compared. As outlined above, it was felt that the accuracy and completeness of data is sufficiently reliable after 1754, whereas the socio-economic context (particularly because of transport possibilities) was significantly changed after 1913, for this data to act as a natural terminus. The four 40-year groupings were allocated because the commencement of the second, in 1794, is close to the appearance of the first relatively reliable population data (1801 Census); shortly after the commencement of the third in 1834 the era of railway construction began; and the last period (1874-1913) coincides nicely with the rapid breakdown of rural isolation first identfied by Perry in his study of rural Dorest,[4] thus facilitating a comparison with his study. Naturally there are many other possible period groupings. The point needs to be made, however, that they should be chosen both to ensure a sufficient sample size and to reflect the needs of particular localities and study objectives.

The study objectives which I pursued were articulated as a series of six hypotheses. These can be stated as follows:

1. Interaction between places is strongly influenced by distance, i.e. the greater the distance from the parish the less interaction there is with that parish. This phenomenon will be called the **distance effect** in this article. (Note in much geographical literature the phrase 'distance decay' is used.)

2. The distance effect itself decreases over time.

3. A sudden decrease in the distance effect is evident in the last quarter of the nineteenth century (as identified by Perry in Dorset).[4]

4. In the context of north Buckinghamshire, there are two distinctive scales of interaction:

   (i) up to about twenty kilometres. This is the supposed maximum walking and, later, cycling distance enabling regular face-to-face contact to be maintained; this normally being necessary for a marriage to take place. This **local** scale of interaction exhibits no directional bias;

   (ii) over twenty kilometres. At this **regional** scale there is strong directional bias to the south-east and the north-west (i.e. to London and the Midlands). An important channel of this movement being Watling Street, later supplemented by the railway.

5. At the local scale of the interaction there is a tendency for urban parishes to interact more strongly with other urban parishes than with rural parishes. Thus, at this scale, the socio-economic character is another variable, in addition to distance, which affects spatial interaction. In this study, parishes were allocated to an **index of agricultural occupation** on the basis of the 1831 Census, taken midway through the study period, which gives nine occupational categories for males over twenty years of age on a parish basis (information which is not available before or after this date at the parish level). Of the categories given the major divisions are between persons employed in agriculture, those employed in manufacturing, in retailing and crafts, as capitalists, bankers, professional and other educated men, non-agricultural labourers, others, and servants. Ideally we need to identify 'urban' occupations in order to identify 'urban' parishes, but there are great problems in doing this. If the aim is to define 'urban' in terms of a 'service' centre, and not as a location for manufacturing or crafts (which, in any case, often took place within a rural environment in the early nineteenth century), the only occupation listed which we could use would be retailing. Unfortunately, retailing is grouped together with crafts. It appears intuitively sounder, however, to identify agricultural occupations with a 'rural' location, and to assume that 'rural' and 'urban' characteristics are the inverse of one another, so that as one increases the other falls. Thus, I decided to use what I have called the index of agricultural occupation as a surrogate for allocating parishes to either a 'rural' or an 'urban' category.

The index was obtained by ascertaining the numbers employed as farmers or labourers in agriculture, and dividing this total by the numbers of those known **not** to have been employed as such. Those employed as servants or others were completely excluded from the calculation as we do not know whether or not they were employed in an agricultural context. The index thus obtained for each parish, within the local scale of interaction, was used to allocate it to either a 'rural' or an 'urban' category. Parishes with an endex of 0.4 or above were categorised as 'rural', and those with less than 0.4 as 'urban'. This figure is, of course, arbitrary, but it was in fact arrived at in this study by plotting the index for all parishes within the local field (as shown in figure 1b) and finding that, inter alia, the figure of 0.4 did clearly separate out what could be called an 'urban group' of parishes from the others.

6. There is some sort of negative relationship between the population size of a parish and the distance of interaction in a **relative** sense — i.e. the larger the population of a parish, the lower the **proportion** of marriage contacts over, say, twenty kilometres. In terms of **absolute** numbers (as opposed to proportions) of marriage distances, however, the larger the parish population, the greater is the contact over, say, twenty kilometres. (This hypothesis is in line with the discussion in the opening paragraphs of this article.)

Techniques

The graphical and quantitative techniques now introduced allow a progressive analysis of the above hypotheses to be undertaken, and are of four main types:

- (i) marriage contact fields;
- (ii) chi-square analysis;
- (iii) average marriage distances;
- (iv) regression analysis.

(i) Marriage contact fields

These can be constructed by placing a grid, centred on the parish under study, over the area of interaction. Examples are shown in figures 1 and 2 where grids have been centred on the parish of Stony Stratford in north Buckinghamshire. This visual method specifically brings out any directional bias in spatial interaction and is probably the easiest method of summarising and analysing the data. Figure 1a shows the case study area divided into 25 grid cells, representing the 'regional field' discussed in hypothesis 4, and figure 1b shows the detail of the 'local field', divided, in this case, into sixty-four cells. Figures 2a and 2b show the number of marriage contacts falling in each of the grid cells, derived from figures 1a and 1b. In figure 2a note the strong north-west to south-east directional bias and the absence of any definite bias in the local field. This relates back to hypothesis 4, which could be said to be confirmed in this particular example. (A technique which can more objectively test this conclusion will be discussed in (ii) below.) Relating the numbers of marriage con-

146

tacts back to maps in this way is a useful reminder that the data being manipulated are, in fact, derived from a particular locality. Although the overall aim here has been stated as a search for generalisations, which can then be compared with similar results from other parts of the country, the detail of the analysis, especially when trying to explain specific anomalies, needs to be referred to the real world if any sense is to be made of the results. For example, the regional directional bias identified here may be readily understood by referring to the location of London and the urbanising Midlands, as well as by the orientation of the major lines of communication. Similarly, the general density and distribution of population in an area, particularly in upland Britain where physical features form barriers to movement, as well as channelling it, may have a pervasive influence on the pattern of spatial interaction.

Marriage contact fields, like those in figure 2, can be produced for successive periods in order to examine how this spatial interaction changes over time.

Figure 1a. Sketch map of the 'regional field', centred on Stony Stratford, showing the main settlements, Watling Street and the London and North-Western Railway (constructed in the 1830s).

147

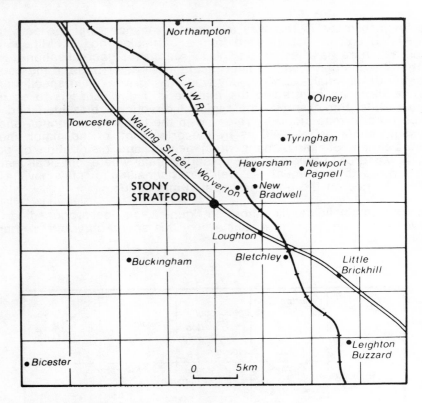

Figure 1b. Sketch map of the 'local field'.

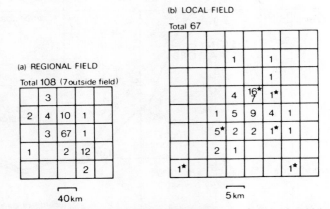

Figure 2. Observed marriage contact fields for Stony Stratford, 1834-1873. The figures in each grid cell indicate the number of marriage contacts from places in that cell with Stony Stratford. The local field shows the detail of the central grid cell of the regional field. Stony Stratford was identified as an 'urban' parish (see text) and its contacts with other 'urban' parishes are marked with an asterisk in the local field.

(II) Chi-square analysis

Hypothesis 5 proposed that socio-economic factors, as well as distance, would be important in influencing spatial interaction, especially when measured by marriage distances. Ideally, of course, we would wish to examine the socio-economic characteristics of the individual bride and groom, normally by recording their employment or social status, but this information, for **both** partners, is rarely available in the marriage registers. (Although it may be possible to discover it through the technique of **nominal linkage;** i.e. by cross-checking individual names from other sources, such as the census, where the required information may be found.)

An alternative method is to classify parishes into socio-economic types (see hypothesis 5 above) and to measure the interaction between both similar and dissimilar types. This is legitimate as long as the analysis undertaken uses aggregated interaction data; it would not be acceptable to analyse specific marriages in this way or to use very small samples, because they may not be representative of the parish as a whole.

Figure 2b uses the grid derived from figure 1b, with its centre positioned over Stony Stratford. It shows that Stony Stratford (which is identified as an 'urban' parish) had twenty-five contacts with other 'urban' parishes and forty-two contacts with 'rural' parishes within the local field. On the face of it, these figures show that Stony Stratford has more contact with 'rural' parishes than with 'urban' ones, but this would be to ignore the **proportion** of these two types of parish present, both in terms of their number and the population they contain. This could be taken into account by enumerating the number and population size of all 'urban' and 'rural' parishes within the area of the local field. However, an easier method, which does not require this detailed information because it remains constant (or 'given') no matter which parish's contact pattern is being analysed, is to examine interaction data for a number of parishes. I set out below the extra-parochial marriage data for six parishes in north Buckinghamshire,[5] located at a maximum distance of fifteen kilometres from each other (see figure 1b), and with 'urban' and 'rural' types spatially mixed, in order to reduce any impact that distance may have on the data. This is important because we are attempting to isolate the socio-economic factors from the geographic ones.

OBSERVED DATA

		extra-parochial marriage type		
		urban	rural	total
parish type	urban	52	120	172
where marriage took place	rural	9	94	103
	total	61	214	275

A visual examination of these figures seems to show that, indeed, parishes of the same socio-economic type do interact more with each other than with parishes of other types. It is possible, however, to be much more precise in analysing this data by using a simple technique known as chi-square.[4] Basically, chi-square compares an observed situation (as, for

149

example, the data given above) with one which we would **expect** if there were no association between the variables being investigated. The two variables in this case are, firstly (as shown in each row above), the socio-economic character of the parish in which the marriage took place (and where one of the marriage partners resided), and, secondly (as shown in each column) the socio-economic character of the parish from which the extra-parochial marriage partner came. We are interested in whether or not there is any association between these two variables.

We now need to compare this **observed** distribution with the **expected** distribution which can be easily calculated. For a given observed figure, its expected counterpart is derived by multiplying the row total by the column total and dividing by the grand total. Thus, the first observed figure of 52 has an equivalent expected figure of $\frac{172 \times 61}{275} = 38.2$.

This calculation produces expected values based on the assumption that there is no association between the two variables. Given the total number of marriages taking place in 'urban' parishes (i.e. 172) and the total number of marriages with 'urban' extra-parochial marriage partners (i.e. 61), a figure is calculated (i.e. 38.2) purely on the basis of the proportions of the 'urban' categories available within each of the two variables. Each of the expected values is calculated in the same manner, thus:

EXPECTED DATA

		extra-parochial marriage type		
		urban	rural	total
parish type	urban	38.2	133.8	172
where marriage took place	rural	22.8	80.2	103
	total	61	214	275

It should be noted that an important limitation of chi-square is that not more than one-fifth of the expected values should be five or less. Clearly there is no problem in this case, but if the criterion is not met it would be necessary to combine two or more of the categories within each variable until it is. In this example there are only two categories (i.e. 'urban' and 'rural') so combination could not, in any case, be undertaken. It would have been quite possible, however, to have devised a socio-economic classification by allocating parishes not just into a broad or urban-rural dichotomy but into three, or more, categories. For example, where sample sizes are large enough, an 'urban' type could be defined as having an index of rurality of 0.3 or less (as in this study), an 'intermediate' type of between, say, 0.3 and 0.7, and a 'rural' type of over 0.7. Finer or different categories could of course be devised. Again it should be stressed that any classification needs to reflect the particular needs of the study. The categories within each of the variables used in chi-square should therefore be large enough not to contravene this one-fifth rule, but also numerous enough to examine characteristics thought important. It will be readily appreciated that the bigger the difference between the observed and expected values, the more likely it is that they are significantly different from each other, and therefore the more likely that our initial hypothesis will be upheld. The chi-square technique involves calculating this difference then squaring it (i.e. multiplying it by itself) in order to get rid of any negative values, dividing it by the expected value so that the difference calculated is expressed as a proportion of the expected value, and then summing all the values obtained to give a composite chi-square statistic. This procedure is given by the formula:

$$\text{chi-square} = \sum \frac{(0-E)^2}{E}$$

where $\sum$ simply means add up the individual items that follow,

$$0 = \text{observed value}$$

$$E = \text{expected value.}$$

The calculation is normally effected by constructing a table:

0	E	(0 — E)	(0 — E)^2	(0 — E)^2 ÷ E
52	38.2	13.8	190.4	5.0
120	133.8	—13.8	190.4	1.4
9	22.8	—13.8	190.4	8.4
94	80.2	13.8	190.4	2.4

$$\sum \quad 17.2$$

(Note: The apparent symmetry in the above table, giving the same (0-E) and thus (0-E)^2 values, is due to the fact that each of the two variables only has two categories: 'urban' and 'rural'. If more categories were to be used this would be unlikely to happen.)

The next step is to work out a figure called the **degrees of freedom**. This is simply a measure of how many chances for variation exists in the observed table of figures we started with. If we accept that the row and column totals are fixed, then the only chance for variation in terms of the columns is one, since once a value is entered in the first column the value in the second column is pre-determined. Similarly, if we examine the two rows, there is again only one chance of variation, since after the first value is entered the second is fixed. If, however, there had been, say, five rows, then the chance for variation would have been four, as the first four figures would be free to vary (assuming they did not exceed the total), leaving the fifth as pre-determined. Thus the degrees of freedom (or the total chances for variation which have called it) equals the number of columns minus one, multiplied by the number of rows minus one. In our case this is $(2-1) \times (2-1) = 1$. In order to assess the significance of the result, it is necessary to refer to either a chi-square table or graph (found in the standard textbooks). This will show that a figure of 17.2 with 1 degree of freedom falls well below the 0.1% 'critical value' of chi-square. This means that this could only be produced by chance less than 0.1% of the time (or one time in a thousand).

By convention, the observed distribution of data between any two variables is taken as being 'significant' (i.e. that there is an association between them) if the chance or random element could be responsible 5% or less of the time. You should note, however, that this is only a convention, and that the 'critical value' of any chi-square statistic you calculate should always be quoted. In this case, we note that chance has not been eliminated (i.e. it is possible, though unlikely, that the figures were produced by chance), and that even if the 'critical' value had been, say 10%, this would still mean that chance plays a 'small' role even though, by convention, we say it plays 'too big' a role. The point is that the value of a technique like chi-square is that it enables words like 'small' or 'big' to be discarded in favour of a numerical value; it does not allow us to definitely 'prove' or 'disprove' a hypothesis. In fact, even though by using statistical jargon, we could say our result was 'very significant', all we have really done is to show that within the constraints of the table of data we have constructed, it is unlikely that the figures we have observed are randomly determined. We can only conclude that extra-parochial marriages are not randomly distributed between 'urban' and 'rural' parishes. The notion we have that it is 'urban-urban' and 'rural-rural' links which are over-represented (as compared with 'urban-rural' and 'rural-urban' links) is only added by inspection of the observed table. In other words, it is where the numbers fall that leads us to surmise this, not the value of the chi-square statistic itself. The latter can only indicate the strength, not the form, of a relationship.

Despite these important caveats, however, a technique like chi-square is more powerful than a simple visual inspection of the figures. This is because it allows us to quantify the relationship between two variables, to be precise in allocating the influence of chance, and, thereby, to be able to make direct comparisons with other chi-square results calculated with different data or by different researchers.

The chi-square test is a very valuable and simple technique which has many uses. It can, for example, test the significance of the directional bias observed in marriage contacts at the regional level, discussed in (i) above. If the data presented in figure 2a are taken as a display of observed values, we can proceed to calculate expected values. First of all, however, it will be apparent that, because so many of the cells in fig. 2a have nil values and many others are under 5, it is very likely that the expected values will not meet the one-fifth criterion discussed above. A check would confirm this to be correct. It is necessary, therefore, to combine cells so as to boost the value of each resulting group of cells. Bearing in mind that we wish to test for directional bias in a north-west to south-east direction, the 25 cells can be amalgamated into 4 cell groups, so that there is a north-west, north-east, south-east and south-west group. Ignoring the central cell (which is disregarded because it has no effect on directional bias) it will be seen that each of the 4 cell groups contains 4 whole cells and 4 half cells. This is because the 8 central vertical and horizontal cells each fall into 2 of the 4 cell groups. Thus, the total number of marriage contacts in the north-west cell group is $3 + 2 + 4 + (10 \div 2) + (3 \div 2) = 15.5$. Producing cell groups in this way also removes the distance variable from the analysis, since each of the 4 groups is equidistant from the centre, thus the test will focus exclusively on directional bias.

Proceeding on these lines, the following observed values are obtained:

north-west cell group	15.5
north-east cell group	6.5
south-east cell group	15.5
south-west cell group	3.5
	41

The calculation of expected values in this instance cannot be achieved by using row, column and grand totals as in the previous example, because the data we have is not in this sense cumulative. Simply using common sense, however, we would expect, if there was no directional bias, that each of the 4 cell groups would have an equal share of the total number of marriage contacts available; in other words, each would have 41 divided by 4, or 10.25.

A chi-square calculation table is constructed in precisely the same manner as above and a result of 11.2 is obtained. Similarly, we cannot calculate the degrees of freedom on the basis of number of rows and number of columns. In this case, we simply subtract 1 from the total number of variables. Therefore degrees of freedom equals 3. This makes sense if we consider that, if the total is fixed, in this case at 41, then the first 3 cell-groups are free to vary, but once they are determined the fourth is fixed.

Reference to a chi-square graph or table reveals that the difference between the observed and expected values is between the 0.1% and the 1% critical value of chi-square. In other words, there is by convention a significant difference between the two and the visual impression of directional bias obtained from fig. 2a is supplemented by a more objective piece of evidence. As noted above, however, we should remember that all we have really done is to show that the scatter of Stony Stratford's extra-parochial marriage contacts is unlikely to be the result of random processes. The notion that there is a north-west to south-east orientation to the pattern is one which is added by looking at the data; the chi-square statistic does not tell us this. All we can do is to rule out the idea that the distribution is random, and we must articulate further hypotheses if we are to try to discover the reason for this. For example, reference to fig. 1a will show that Birmingham is situated in the north-west sector and London in the south-east. The directional bias **may** have been due to these two large towns, and we could test this possibility by doing the analysis once again, excluding them. If the directional bias were thereby removed, we may be strengthened in the notion that it was Birmingham and London 'causing' it, although we should still not rule out the possibility of other 'causes' which we had not thought of.

Using chi-square with geographical data of this kind, where the grid, as the unit of measurement, is arbitrary, does require care. Our expected distribution of values, for example, was produced on the assumption that there was an equal number of potential contacts (or population) in each cell, or cell group. Clearly this is not the case, and we must refine our reasoning, and hence our conclusion, by constant reference to the realities of the geography of the area.

Table 1. Marriage distance data for Stony Stratford, 1754-1913.

| | (1)
total
marriages | (2)
total
extra-
parochial
marriages | (3)
extra-
parochial
marriage
% | (4)
mean
extra-
parochial
marriage
distance
(kilo-
metres) | (5) (6) (7)
median and quartile
extra-parochial
marriage distances
(kilometres) | | |
					lower quartile	median	upper quartile
1754- 1793	370	108	29.2%	29.8	4.1	11.8	34.2
1794- 1833	509	164	32.2%	23.9	2.1	11.3	31.5
1834- 1873	381	115	30.2%	34.7	2.1	11.3	60.3
1874- 1913	361	156	43.2%	49.0	2.2	21.2	80.9

	(8) mean census popul- ation	(9) extra- paro- chial annual marriage rate (per 1000)	(10) annual marriage rate (per 1000)	(11) gradient of re- gression line	(12) correl- ation coeffic- ient (r)	(13) coeffic- ient of determin- ation (100r²)	(14) % of extra- parochial marriages used in regression
1754- 1793	—	—	—	—2.19	—0.93	86.6%	94.4%
1794- 1833	1564.7	2.6	8.9	—2.39	—0.94	88.6%	98.2%
1834- 1873	1873.7	1.5	5.1	—2.03	—0.92	84.3%	93.0%
1874- 1913	2070.7	1.9	4.4	—1.87	—0.86	74.4%	82.7%

(III) Average marriage distances

In addition to the examination of successive marriage contact fields, the changing nature of spatial interaction can also be analysed by reference to marriage distance data which has been manipulated in certain ways. For example, it is possible to compare the four periods by looking in turn at the following data in Table 1:

Column 3 percentage of extra-parochial marriages.

Column 4 the mean extra-parochial marriage distance. The mean is what we normally term the average. It is simply arrived at by adding each individual marriage distance and dividing the total by the number of distances used.[7]

Columns 5, 6, 7 the mean and quartile extra-parochial marriage distances. The mean, as shown in column 4, gives no indication of the range of spread of values about it and is badly affected by extreme values. The median,[7] on the other hand, is not so affected, as it is simply the central number, below which, and above which, fifty per cent of all the numbers fall. For example, if there are twenty-three distances arrayed in ascending order. the median is the twelfth distance. Similarly, the upper quartile is the median between the actual median and the highest value, and the lower quartile is the median between the actual median and the lowest value.[8] The calculation of median and quartile distances gives some indication of the spread of values, and is, therefore, probably more suitable than the mean for comparing marriage distances.

Columns 8, 9, 10 the marriage rate[9] is the number of marriages in a given year expressed as a rate per thousand of the total population. In the example, only the last three periods have rates calculated for them because of the unreliability of population data before the Census commenced. Marriage rates have been used because they tell us, for a given population, how many marriages there were (according to the registers). This may have an effect, although this is speculation, on the marriage distance patterns produced, both as a result of socio-economic or cultural factors and also as a result of the geographical availability of suitable marriage partners, which may be particularly problematic in a small parish.[10]

When using marriage rates, however, it must not be forgotten that an important factor is the age structure of the population to which it refers. For example, if there were a higher than average proportion of persons in the 20-30 age group we would expect, regardless of any socio-economic, cultural or geographic influences on marriage, that the marriage rate would be boosted. This is not a factor that has been directly taken into account in this case study, although it would have been possible to do so using the published Census, from 1821 onwards, when information about age is first included. It is, however, a factor which should not be overlooked.

(Iv) Regression analysis

Regression analysis[11] involves the comparison of two variables in such a way that we can see how a change in one variable results in, or is the result of, a change in the other. The two variables of concern here are distance and the number of marriage contacts. For every extra-parochial marriage we can, of course, calculate its marriage distance, but every marriage distance is a unique and specific measurement. In order to see the effect of distance on the **number** of marriages, we need to **group** the marriages in a certain way. This is done by allocating each marriage to a **distance band,** by drawing a series of concentric circles, around the parish church under study, in such a way that each successive circle has the same increase in radius as the last. In this case study a series of distance bands were chosen, each with a width of five kilometres. Kilometres were used, rather than miles, simply because the marriage distance was not measured directly on the map, but calculated from the six figure National Grid Reference (based on kilometres) for the two parish churches, using the Pythagoras theorem.[12] Five kilometre distance bands were chosen because any smaller distance did not allow at least one marriage contact to fall within each band, up to a one hundred kilometre limit, beyond which bands containing no contacts start to appear.[13] Column 14 of Table 1 shows the percentage of extra-parochial marriages included as a result of imposing this limit.

Another important decision which had to be made was whether or not to include the number of intra-parochial marriages in the first distance band (i.e 0 to 5 kilometres). On the one hand it could be argued that because, in 1834 to 1873 for example, 266 marriages took place in Stony Stratford between people who had a 'zero' marriage distance, this is just as crucial in measuring the distance effect on the selection of marriage partners as the fact that eleven marriages took place with people from another parish. On the other hand, one could argue that because we are only concerned to examine interaction between **different** places, we can ignore the number of intra-parochial marriages. Obviously, whichever way the decision is made will have a dramatic effect on the analysis of data, simply because the number of intra-parochial marriages is so large. In this case study, I chose to use only extra-parochial marriages, mainly because it seems that the majority of earlier studies do the same, and comparison between findings is a very important aim of any work of this nature.[14]

The way in which all these problems are perceived and confronted must, of course, depend upon the preferences, aims, and difficulties encountered by each researcher. It is important to remember, however, that such decisions can have a pervasive effect on the results obtained and they must therefore be only considered with a full realisation of the implications involved.

These problems are a good example of the additional difficulties thrown up by the use of new techniques which are, nevertheless, worth tackling because of the additional understanding we are able to gain.

Some results of these procedures are shown in Table 2. Column 1 indicates the distance band, and column 3 the number of marriages falling in that band. Notice that column 4 is labelled **standardised** number of marriages. This is because the number of marriages at any given distance must be standardised for area. The reason is that, as distance increases away from the study parish, there are potentially a greater number of parishes supplying marriage partners. As described above, when a series of concentric rings is drawn outward from the study parish, the area of

Table 2. Number of extra-parochial marriage contacts by distance bands, Stony Stratford, 1834-1873.

(1) Distance band order (km.)	(1) Distance band order	(2) ratio of area to first distance band	(3) number of marriage contacts	(4) standardised number of marriage contacts	(5) logarithm of column 4 (y axis)	(6) logarithm of column 1 (x axis)
(0-5)	1	1	11	11.0000	1.0414	0.0000
(6-10)	2	3	34	11.3333	1.0543	0.3010
(11-15)	3	5	16	3.2000	0.5052	0.4771
(16-20)	4	7	4	0.5714	—0.2431	0.6021
(21-25)	5	9	6	0.6667	—0.1761	0.6990
(26-30)	6	11	6	0.5454	—0.2633	0.7782
(31-35)	7	13	2	0.1538	—0.8130	0.8451
(36-40)	8	15	1	0.0667	—1.1759	0.9031
(41-45)	9	17	2	0.1176	—0.9296	0.9542
(46-50)	10	19	2	0.1053	—0.9776	1.0000
(51-55)	11	21	1	0.0476	—1.3224	1.0414
(56-60)	12	23	3	0.1304	—0.8847	1.0792
(61-65)	13	25	1	0.0400	—1.3979	1.1139
(66-70)	14	27	1	0.0741	—1.1302	1.1461
(71-75)	15	29	1	0.0370	—1.4318	1.1761
(76-80)	16	31	2	0.0968	—1.0141	1.2041
(81-85)	17	33	8	0.2424	—0.6155	1.2304
(86-90)	18	35	3	0.0857	—1.0670	1.2553
(91-95)	19	37	1	0.0270	—1.5686	1.2788
(96-100)	20	39	2	0.0513	—1.2899	1.3010

each successive ring is greater than the inner ring. The greater the area the higher the population it can potentially contain and therefore the more marriage partners it could supply. The number of marriage contacts each ring provides is therefore standardised so that it is expressed as the number of marriages per unit area. This is, in fact, less complicated than it sounds, as the unit of area used is that contained in the innermost ring. If this inner ring is said to have an area of one, then, by using the formula πr^2 for the area of a circle, it can be shown that the second ring has an area of three, the third of five, the fourth of seven, the fifth of nine etc.[15] The number of marriage contacts in the second ring are therefore divided by three, the number in the third by five, and so on, to give the standardised number of marriages for each successive distance band away from the study parish. The ratios to be used in each case are shown in column 2.

It is obvious that this standardisation procedure would be more reliable if it were based on the actual population in each ring rather than the area of the ring. The difficulty here is, of course, that we do not have reliable population statistics for parishes falling within each ring until the 1801 Census, and, even after this date, the population figures may hide much inter-decennial variation in actual numbers. The distribution of population in north Buckinghamshire and adjacent areas, was, throughout the study period, relatively uniform in the sense that there were no areas of sparse population. But in parts of the country where this is likely to be a problem, population figures, rather than land area, should be used if possible. Whether or not this can be done, constant reference to the realities of the local geography of an area (for example, figures 1a and 1b) should guide the interpretation of the results. It can be noted, for instance, that the number of marriages (column 3 of Table 2) in the 81-85 kilometre distance band goes dramatically against the trend of decreasing marriages with increasing distance, probably London and Birmingham are included within this band. If we were able to standardise on the basis of population in this case study it is likely that this band would conform more closely to the trend.

Once the data have been prepared in a suitable form, they can be used to construct a **scatter graph**. Most graphs, such as those shown in figures 3 and 4, are made up of two axes: a horizontal (or x axis) and a vertical (or y axis). These two axes represent the two variables which are being compared. We want to see how a change in one variable (called the independent or x variable) affects the other variable (called the dependent or y variable). In our example, the independent variable is distance, and the dependent variable is the standardised number of marriage contacts. To produce a scatter graph each point is located with reference to these two axes; for example, if there were fifteen marriages at five kilometres, the point representing this would be level with fifteen on the number of marriages axis and with five on the distance axis. Each point is plotted in the same way on the graph.

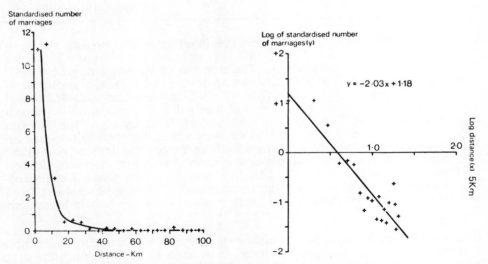

Figure 3. Graph showing the relationship between standardised number of marriages and distance in Stony Stratford, 1834-1873.

Figure 4. Double-log graph showing the relationship between standardised number of marriages and distance in Stony Stratford, 1834-1873.

Now, it has been hypothesised (see hypothesis 1) that, as distance increases, the number of marriage contacts decreases (i.e. a distance effect). We therefore expect to see a series of points which **trend** from the top left-hand side of the graph to the bottom right-hand side. Reference to fig. 3 (based on data from columns 1 and 4 of Table 2) will show that this does, in fact, happen, although the trend is not regular but seems to indicate that, with increasing distance, the **rate** in the reduction of marriage contacts decreases. Figure 3 also shows the **best-fit** line, (i.e. that which best summarises the trend of the points), as a steep curve.

Regression analysis involves the construction of a best-fit line mathematically, to produce a **regression line** which can be expressed as a mathematical equation. It is this equation which specifically defines the relationship between the two variables. Although curves are susceptible to mathematical expression, the calculations are complex. One way of getting around this problem is, rather than have two axes with uniform scales, to construct scales based on logarithmic numbers. This produces an axis which increases **proportionately** rather than in absolute terms, as shown in figure 4 (based on data from columns 5 and 6 of Table 2). When this double-log graph (as it is called) is used with most data which analyses the distance effect, a straight line is produced; **i.e.** the trend of the points approximates to a linear, or straight-line, relationship. This linear regression line has a relatively simple mathematical equation[17]

$$y = ax + b$$

where y (as the dependent variable) is the standardised number of extra-parochial marriage contacts

x (as the independent variable) is distance

a is the slope, or **gradient,** of the line (i.e. the greater a is the steeper is the line)

and b is the value of y where the line crosses the y (vertical) axis.

The gradient of the regression line, 'a', in distance effect equations invariably slopes from top left to bottom right, and, by convention, this is termed a 'negative' slope, with 'a' being given as a negative value. If the regression line sloped from bottom left to top right the value of 'a' would be positive. In figure 4, 'a' has a value of — 2.03, and reference to Table 1 will show how this value changes for each of the four time periods (column 11). If the distance effect decreases over time, therefore, we would expect the value of 'a' to also decrease.

The regression line equation, therefore, mathematically describes the trend of the data. However, it does not indicate how close the fit is between the line and the points scattered around it on the graph. To measure this, the **correlation coefficient** is used,[18] which ranges from + 1, through 0, to — 1. Zero indicates no correlation at all; i.e. the points are randomly distributed right across the graph in such a way that there is absolutely no trend. A value of one indicates perfect correlation; i.e. every point is exactly on the regression line. The coefficient is either positive or negative, depending on whether the gradient of the regression line is positive or negative as described above.

The correlation coefficient of the regression line shown in figure 4 is — 0.92, which indicates that all the points are very close to the line. In fact, the regression lines for each of the four periods in this example exhibit very high correlation coefficients, which tends to mean that a great deal of faith can be invested in the ability of these regression analyses to describe the marriage distance data. This is further supported by another necessary statistical technique, which we must carry out, called the **standard error** of the coefficient.[19] This indicates how 'significant' the correlation coefficient is, i.e. how probable is it that the data was not generated by a random process. In general, the larger the sample size (i.e. the greater the number of points) together with a high correlation coefficient, the more 'significant' the correlation can be said to be. In the example, all the correlation coefficients produced were highly significant; i.e. all had less than 1 time in 1000 of being chance results. The correlation coefficients do, in fact, seem to vary in relation to the percentage of extra-parochial marriage data used in the regression analysis (column 14 of Table 1). This is, arguably, to be expected, and shows that the results are influenced by the decisions taken in regard to the width of the distance bands and their outer limit.

One further useful technique is termed the **coefficient of determination** which is calculated in column 13 of Table 1. It is quite simply derived by squaring the correlation coefficient and multiplying the result by 100. Its usefulness is that it tells us how much of the total variation in the dependent variable is associated with, or 'explained' by, the variation in the independent variable. In other words, we can say that, using the 1834-1873 data, 84.3% of the variation in the standardised number of extra-parochial marriages is 'explained' by the distance between the parish of residence of the groom and that of the bride.

Conclusion

The techniques described above were used to analyse spatial interaction in six parishes in north Buckinghamshire from 1754-1913. All six of the hypotheses stated were supported with one important aberration.

A distance effect was found in the data for all six parishes, and the strength of this effect generally decreased over time. However, in three[20] of the six parishes the second period (1794-1833) was marked by an increase of the distance effect (see column 11 of Table 1 which shows the Stony Stratford figures). The same three parishes also showed relatively high marriage rates (both extra-parochial and total) in this period (see columns 9 and 10). The distance effect in the other three parishes steadily decreased in strength over time, and there was not this variation in the marriage rates. There seems to be, therefore, some sort of relationship between a steadily decreasing distance effect and stable marriage rates on the one hand, and high marriage rates and an increasing distance effect on the other.

Reference to the mean and median distances (as for example in columns

4-7 of Table 1) also seems to indicate a lowering of marriage distances between 1794 and 1833. In addition, the extra-parochial percentages (column 3) show an increase at this time a little above that expected from the overall trend throughout the period, and this seems to confirm the evidence of the marriage rates that, although there were a higher proportion of extra-parochial marriages, the distances which they mark out are less than expected.[21]

Are there any reasons why spatial interaction was more resricted than expected, and marriage rates abnormally high in this period? (Note, however, that because we do not have reliable population data before this period, we cannot, with certainty, state that the rates had risen at this time; although see Note 22.) The very fact that we begin to ask questions such as these, which arise directly out of the application of the techniques demonstrated, forges the essential link between a perhaps mechanical and pedestrian exercise and the focus of historical and intellectual interest which is the real objective of our endeavours. In the same way that we noticed one figure in particular on Table 2 as being a deviant against the overall trend of decreasing numbers of marriages with increasing distance (i.e. in the 81-85 kilometre band), asked why, and we discovered London and Birmingham fell in that band, we can ask questions about the overall thrust of the results; particularly if they are not what we expected. These questions must include, of course, a realisation that the particular technique employed and a particular procedure followed may themselves, and not the historical reality, be responsible for the pattern of the results. But when we find that a combination of different techniques point to a similar conclusion, we can have a lot more faith that our results are genuinely indicating something of interest.

It is beyond the scope of this article to discuss any possible historical reasons for this apparent retrenchment of marriage horizons, in the last decade of the eighteenth century and first decades of the nineteenth century, beyond suggesting that the reasons may include the level of wage rates and the operation of the Poor Law at the time. I have instead been concerned with means rather than with ends, and have therefore tried to show how a series of techniques of increasing complexity, but not beyond the reach of the amateur local historian, can be used in the analysis of spatial interaction based on marriage distance data. The techniques demonstrated here do not, by any means, constitute an exhaustive list, but they do enable, with diligent and careful use, a greater degree of understanding to be brought to bear upon a particular historical topic.

NOTES

1. L. Bradley, **A glossary for Local Population Studies,** second edition, 1978.
2. J. Millard, **Marriage distances and spatial interaction in north Buckinghamshire, 1754-1913,** unpublished M.Sc. thesis, Birbeck College, University of London, 1976.
3. The most important historical, geographic, and demographic studies using marriage distances to examine spatial interaction and mobility are:—
   A. Constant, 'The geographical background of inter-village population movements in Northamptonshire and Huntingdonshire. 1754-1943', **Geography,** Vol. 33, 1948.
   C. F. Kuchemann, A. J. Boyce, G. A. Harrison, 'A demographic and genetic study of a group of Oxfordshire villages', **Human Biology.** Vol. 39, 1967 (reprinted M. Drake, (Ed.) **Applied Historical Studies: an introductory reader,** London, 1973).
   B. Maltby, 'Easingwold marriage horizons', **Local Population Studies,** No. 2, 1969, pp. 36-9.
   B. Maltby, 'Parish registers and the problem of mobility', **Local Population Studies,** No. 6, 1971, pp. 32-42.
   R. F. Peel, 'Local intermarriage and the stability of rural population in the English Midlands', **Geography,** Vol. 27, 1942.
   P. J. Perry, 'Working-class isolation and mobility in rural Dorset, 1837-1936: a study of marriage distances', **Transactions of the Institute of British Geographers.** Vol. 46, 1969.
   P. E. Ogden, 'Marriage patterns and population mobility: a study in rural France', **University of Oxford School of Geography Research Paper 7,** 1973.
4. Perry, pp. 131-2.
5. The six parishes incorporated into the 'parish type where marriage took place' variable are Stony Stratford (urban), Newport Pagnall (urban), Haversham (rural), Little Brickhill (rural), Loughton (rural). Tyringham (rural). Parishes incorporated into the 'extra-parochial parish type' are, of course, all the parishes within the local field.
6. Bradley, pp. 34-5.
7. Bradley, p. 26 and p. 45.
8. Bradley, p. 28.
9. Bradley, pp. 14-15.
10. D. Mills, 'Aspects of Marriage: an example of Applied Historical Studies', a Social Science publication, The Open University. 1980. Mills contrasts market towns in lowland England with parishes, such as those in Wharfedale, with a large land area but small scattered population (pp. 8-10).
11. Bradley, pp. 53-4.
12. The Pythagoras theorem simply states that the square of the hypotenuse (the side of a right-angled triangle which is opposite the right angle) equals the sum of the square of the other two sides. Thus. if we wish to work out the straight line distance between two parish churches using the National Grid Reference, we first have to ascertain the six figure grid reference for each church. This is done either by reading it from an Ordnance Survey map, or by reference to a suitable gazetteer. The first three figures of the grid reference refer to the 'easting' of a church from the National Grid's origin, and the second three figures refer to its 'northing'. Each of these pairs of three figures will locate the church to the nearest 0.1 kilometre. In order to work out the grid reference of the third point of the triangle, the point which makes the right angle, we simply take the lowest 'easting' of the pair of parishes and the lowest 'northing', to make a composite six figure grid reference. For example, if the two parish churches are located at 415370 and 455340 respectively, the grid reference of the right-angled point of the triangle is 415340. It is now a simple matter to calculate the 'easting' distance and the 'northing' distance of the two parish churches from this right-angled point, the former being:
$$45.5 - 41.5 = 4.0 \text{ kilometres}$$
and the latter:
$$37.0 - 34.0 = 3.0 \text{ kilometres.}$$
The distance between the parish churches is the hypotenuse of the triangle and is found as described above:
$$(\text{hypotenuse})^2 = 4^2 + 3^2$$
$$= 16 + 9$$
$$= 25$$
$$\text{hypotenuse} = \sqrt{25} = 5 \text{ kilometres.}$$

This method is particularly useful for the calculation of longer distances, because it is not affected by the inaccuracies which inevitably result from directly measuring the distance on the map using a ruler.

13. The reason it is necessary to avoid zero marriage contacts falling in any distance band is because the regression analysis undertaken involves using the logarithm of the number of marriage contacts (as described below) and, as the log of zero does not exist, their inclusion would make a nonsense of the procedure.
14. Few studies discuss these sorts of problems openly, but it is usually apparent from the data presented that the decision has been taken to exclude intra-parochial marriages. For example, compare Table 1 (page 124) with figs 3 (p. 130) and 6 (p. 137) of Perry (1969).
15. See R. Watson, 'Measuring Migration' **Local Population Studies,** No. 21, 1978, p. 61, for a detailed description of how these ratios are calculated.
16. Bradley, pp. 43-4. If you are unsure how to obtain the logarithm of a number, consult a standard textbook. Nowadays, of course, logs are also available as a function on many pocket calculators. You should particularly note, however, that the convention of giving the logarithms of numbers less than 1.0 as 'bar' logs is misleading when used in regression analysis. For example, the log of 0.5714 is normally given as 1.7569. What this means mathematically, however, is $-1 + 0.7569 = -0.2431$. It is this latter figure which must be used to plot figures on the graph. Similarly, the log of 0.0513 is usually given as 2.7101, whereas mathematically this means $-2 + 0.7101 = -1.2899$.

    You should also note that the use of logarithms in this way, to 'transform' the data so that they approximate to a straight line, produces what is called double-log graph. There are some problems involved in using these graphs which mean that you should only use them as **indicative** of the distance effect and in conjunction with other techniques, as in this paper. However, the graph gives a very succinct description of the distance effect, thus enabling comparisons to be made between sets of data, and it is relatively easy to fit and interpret. See P. J. Taylor, 'Distance Decay in Spatial Interaction', **Concepts and Techniques in Modern Geography,** No. 2, 1975.
17. Bradley, pp. 53-4.
18. Bradley, pp. 36-9. Notes, that the particular measure used in this article is the product-moment correlation coefficient, and, as Bradley states (p. 39) the method is given in the standard textbooks.
19. Bradley, p. 39.
20. Stony Stratford, Newport Pagnell and Tyringham.
21. An examination of the evidence presented in Peel, Constant, and Kuchemann, **et al.,** (see Note 3) also gives some very tentative support to this observation, although the way the data are presented in these papers does not allow any firm conclusions to be drawn.
22. J. T. Krause, 'Some neglected factors in the English Industrial Revolution', **Journal of Economic History,** Vol. 19, 1959 (reprinted in M. Drake, **Population in Industrialisation,** London, 1969): '... in England it is relatively certain that the marriage rate rose sharply in the late eighteenth and early nineteenth centuries and then fell in the 1830s. The suggested causes of this development are many: early industrialisation, with its child labour, the Poor Laws, enclosure, and mining.' (p. 106). See also page 109, which mentions 'cultural disorganisation' as a probable cause.

THE POPULATION OF STEPNEY IN THE EARLY SEVENTEENTH CENTURY;

a report on an analysis of the parish registers of Stepney, 1606-1610, by the East London History Group, Population Study Group (Mr. A.H. French, Miss Marybel Moore, Miss Jocelyn Oatley, Mr. M.J. Power, Mrs. D. Summers, Mr. S.C. Tongue).

Introduction

Parish registers are one of the most important sources for local history. East London is fortunate in having a particularly good series of registers for the parish of St. Dunstan, Stepney. Baptisms, marriages and burials all begin in 1568, and continue with few breaks to the present day. All these registers, except the most recent, are kept in the Greater London County Record Office at County Hall and can be easily consulted on application to the archivist.

Historians can use registers in two ways. In the past, registers have been searched to find biographical and genealogical information about famous inhabitants of a parish. More recently historians have begun to count the entries in registers to try to learn something about the population of England before the nineteenth century. By recording the names of all the baptised and tracing them among the marriages 15 - 50 years later, and among the burials up to 105 years after baptism, it is possible to build up a figure of the number of people alive in a parish at a particular date, the size and extent of families, at what age people married, died, and so on. This exercise is termed 'family reconstitution'.

Such an exercise takes a great deal of time. There is a simpler method of collecting information from the registers involving a count of all the entries. This exercise is termed 'aggregative analysis'. It does not tell us as much about the population as family reconstitution can. but the study group thought it should be tried first because it is simple to undertake.

We chose a five year period, 1606-1610, for analysis. In collecting information from the register we noted the sex of each person baptised and buried, the hamlet of each person baptised, married and buried. and the occupation of the father of each child baptised. The results of the analysis are set out in the sections below. Most of the conclusions are tentative because of the nature of aggregative analysis. We are attempting to learn about the total population of

Stepney from a source which tells only about baptisms, marriages and burials. Our conclusions should not be accepted uncritically. That said, we hope that this Report may indicate what the population of Stepney was like at the beginning of the seventeenth century. And, equally important, it will give an example of the technique of aggregative analysis and the difficulties of the exercise.

1. The total population of Stepney

In order to estimate the total population of Stepney we counted the burials in each year. The average number of burials per year was about 525. If we omit the number of burials due to plague, the average number of burials per year falls to about 415. Seventeenth century demographers suggest burial ratios by which this figure can be multiplied to a population figure. John Graunt, writing in the 1660's stated that one burial represented 32 living people (1). Sir William Petty gives a similar figure. He thought, in 1682, that one burial represented 30 living people (2).

$$\text{Graunt:} \quad 32 \times 415 = 13,280$$
$$\text{Petty:} \quad 30 \times 415 = 12,450$$

Thus the total population of Stepney was probably about 12,000 to 13,000 at the beginning of the seventeenth century. This assumes that the burial ratios of Graunt and Petty give accurate population figures for Stepney. We have no more reliable way of estimating the population.

2. The relative size of the population in the hamlets of Stepney

Stepney was a large parish in the early seventeenth century. It extended from Whitechapel on the west, to the river Lea on the east, and from Hackney on the north, to the river Thames on the south. A large number of hamlets made up the parish; Wapping, Shadwell, Ratcliff, Limehouse, Poplar and Blackwell lay by the river; Spitalfields adjoined Whitechapel and Shoreditch; and three inland hamlets, Mile End, Bethnal Green and Bow, filled the centre and north of the parish. Inhabitants of all these hamlets, except Bow, are mentioned in the registers of Stepney. Bow is excluded from this Report because it has its own church and kept its own registers, although it was still a hamlet of Stepney parish at this date. The size of Stepney prompts us to ask where its population was concentrated.

The registers note the area lived in by most of those baptised and buried in the church of St. Dunstan between 1606 and 1610. By counting the register entries by hamlet, we hoped to gain an idea of the relative size of the population in each hamlet. This analysis was complicated because the area given in the register entries was sometimes only a street or an alleyway, not a hamlet. The number of entries in the register which could not be assigned to a hamlet was very small, never exceeding 5% in any year. Such a small percentage is not sufficient to invalidate the hamlet analysis. We assumed that the total of baptisms and burials for the five year period would indicate the relative size of the population in the hamlets. The totals are set out in the table below:

Hamlet	Baptisms 1606-10	% of total baptisms (approx)	Burials 1606-10	% of total burials (approx.)
Bethnal Green	74	4%	106	4%
Limehouse	423	24%	444	17%
Mile End	86	5%	162	6%
Poplar and Blackwall	166	10%	229	9%
Ratcliff	576	33%	664	25%
Shadwell	171	10%	353	13%
Spitalfields	58	3%	227	9%
Wapping	157	9%	338	13%
unplaced	41	3%	97	4%
TOTAL	1,752	100%	2,620	100%

Two hamlets, Ratcliff and Limehouse, have very large baptism and burial figures. They account for 57% of the total baptisms and 42% of the total burials in Stepney. Shadwell, the third most populous hamlet, has figures which are much smaller than those of Ratcliff or Limehouse. The two remaining riverside hamlets, Poplar and Blackwall, and Wapping, have figures a little smaller than Shadwell. The hamlet of Poplar and Blackwall was larger than Wapping, judging by the baptism figures, but smaller than Wapping, judging by the burial figures. The five riverside hamlets claim 85.5% of the total baptisms and 77% of the total burials. Clearly the population was heavily concentrated along the riverside. The three inland hamlets, Bethnal Green, Mile End, and Spitalfields, have comparatively small baptism and burial figures. Bethnal Green and Mile End have similar figures. They account for 9% of the total baptisms and 10% of the total burials. The Spitalfields figures pose a problem, also met with in the Wapping figures. The burial figures make both hamlets seem more populous than the baptism figures do. The Spitalfields burial figure suggests that it had a population almost as large as Poplar and larger than Bethnal Green or Mile End; but the baptism figure suggests that it had the smallest population of the eight hamlets. Which figure, the baptism or the burial, should be used as an indication of the size of the population?

To answer this question the baptism and burial figures of the hamlets must be looked at more closely. In all eight hamlets there are more burials than baptisms. In Limehouse, Poplar and Blackwall, and Ratcliff, the discrepancy is not great; in two hamlets, Shadwell and Wapping, there are over twice as many burials as baptisms, and in Spitalfields there are over four times as many. A great excess of burials over baptisms suggests an unhealthy area where there was an unusually high death rate. Spitalfields, Shadwell and Wapping seem to have been particularly unhealthy hamlets judging by the heavy incidence of plague in them. Between 1606 and 1610 27.3% of the burials in Spitalfields were of plague victims; in Shadwell the percentage was 28, in Wapping 27.8. In the other hamlets the percentage of plague deaths was much lower, 18.2% in Limehouse, 15.5% in Ratcliff, 11.7% in Poplar, 17.9% in Bethnal Green, and 17.2% in Mile End. Since a burial figure inflated by plague deaths gives an inflated idea of the population in each hamlet, it would be wiser to trust the baptism totals as indicative of the relative populousness of the hamlets. Baptisms tend to fluctuate less than burials under the influence of disease. We can conclude that Spitalfields, with the smallest number of baptisms, was the least populous hamlet.

3. The fluctuation of baptism, marriage and burial statistics

The graph shows these three sets of figures. The preponderance of burials is striking. There were 2,620 burials compared with 1,752 baptisms in the five years. This discrepancy indicates a natural decrease of population. It was particularly marked in 1608, 1609 and 1610, when burial figures were abnormally high due to plague. In 1606 and 1607, when burials were not unduly inflated by plague, baptisms sometimes outnumbered burials, notably in winter 1606 and spring 1607.

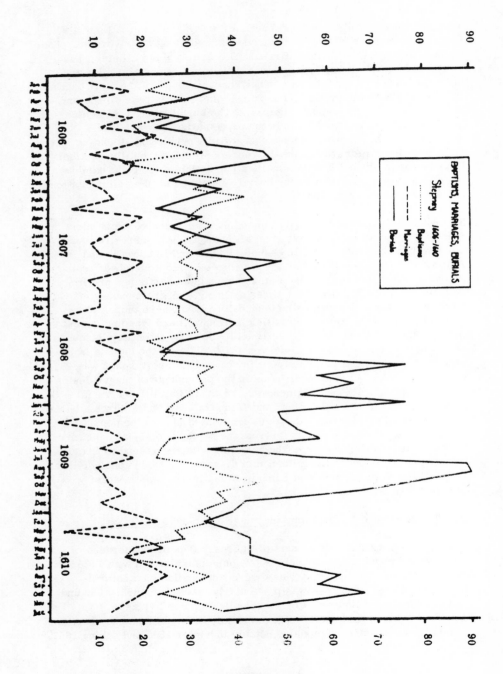

BAPTISMS, MARRIAGES, BURIALS
Stepney 1606-1640

Baptisms
Marriages
Burials

But even discounting plague burials there were more burials than baptisms.
A total of 2,078 people, who died from causes other than plague, were
buried, compared with 1,752 who were baptised.

Also obvious are the seasonal fluctuations.   Each summer and autumn
the burial figures rise spectacularly to a peak, due to plague.   The
number of plague burials each month is shown on the following table:-

	1606	1607	1608	1609	1610
January			1	25	8
February				20	2
March	1	1		16	
April	1	3	1	15	5
May		1	1	24	5
June		2		3	3
July	1	12	9	13	11
August	1	10	25	36	13
September	2	25	25	37	16
October	10	14	13	23	11
November	2	13	29	16	4
December	3	2	14	8	6
TOTAL	21	83	118	236	84

The attacks of plague in summer had several possible causes, most
important the spreading of infection by the increased breeding activity
of the plague carrying fleas (Xenopsylla Cheopis) which normally lived
on rats.   In winter, plague normally died out and burials slumped.
There is one exception to this trend.   The burials remained
abnormally high in the winter of 1608/9, possibly because the winter
was a particularly severe one (3).   But another reason, as the table
shows, was the continuance of plague, which may well have entered a
pneumonic phase, which occurs in colder weather when people crowd
together in ill-ventilated rooms and spread the disease through
airborne infection.

How plague spreads is a problem which deserves further study.
Sometimes it struck only scattered individuals, as in the springs of
1606 and 1608.   At other times the disease spread more quickly,
among people living closely together.   One example of the spread of
disease within a family is provided by the unfortunate Clements
family of Limehouse.   In February 1609, the wife and daughter of

Thomas Clements, a schoolmaster, died of plague; in March two sons died; and in May a second daughter died, all of plague.

The annual plague and its effects, and the influence of Lent upon marriages, are some more obvious explanations of fluctuations in the statistics plotted upon the graph. It would be unwise to interpret other minor monthly fluctuations too closely. All kinds of unknown factors might have caused them.

4. The Structure of the Population

Aggregative analysis cannot tell us much about how the population was composed but certain characteristics of the population are hinted at by analysing baptisms and burial entries by sex and status:-

Baptisms:	Male	Female	Total	Sex Ratio (Male: Female)
	887	865	1,752	102:100

Burials:	Infant/ Child	Man	Son	Woman	Daughter	Widow	Total
	224	626	605	467	591	107	2,620

	(Male total) 1231	(Female total) 1165

The first interesting fact is that there were more men than women, shown by the preponderance of males being born and dying. A second striking fact is that only about 42% of the population was married at the time of death; about 8.5% of those buried were described as 'child' or 'infant' (the majority being 'infant'), about 45% were described as 'son' or 'daughter', and about 4% were widows. We cannot conclude from these figures that these were the proportions of married and unmarried people in the population for they include only those who died, not those who remained alive. But we can learn something about the cross-section of the population that died. 'Infants', 'sons' and 'daughters' account for almost 54% of those dying. These three categories combined represent the younger section of the community. The 'sons' and 'daughters' would be either still dependent upon their parents, or young people not yet married. Few of them should have been old people described as son or daughter since their parents would probably be dead by then. It seems that the younger section of the community was either a majority of the population or had a particularly high death rate, highest of all among infants. Infant mortality cannot be measured precisely, using our statistics, but a rough idea of its severity can be gained by comparing the number of infant deaths with the number of baptisms during the period. The number of infants and young children who died between 1606 and 1610 amounted to between 12 and 13% of those born during the same period. One other point deserves mention, the small proportion of widows that died. There is no doubt that there were a considerable number of widows in the population. No less than 41% of the women marrying between 1606 and 1610 were widows. But it seems that women rarely died widows. The great number of widows remarrying indicates that women did not remain widows for long. It is probable that the men they married would be younger and thus tend to outlive their wives. The erstwhile widow would thus die a wife.

5. Immigration

(i) Evidence from the baptism and burial registers

We have noted that Stepney suffered a natural decrease in population in the early seventeenth century, i.e. more-people died than were born. The population should have grown smaller. Instead it increased. This increase was due to large scale immigration from surrounding areas, a phenomenon which affected the whole of London at this time. We hoped that the registers would shed some light on this movement. In fact, evidence of immigration in the baptism register is meagre. In only 13 of the 1752 entries in the five years are the baptised or their parents noted as strangers to Stepney. Six were from the London area; five were from nearby counties; one was from 'Gaunte'; and one was a vagrant, origin unknown. Two of the infants baptised, from London, were illegitimate. This suggests a possible reason for the parents leaving their own parishes to have the infant baptised in Stepney.

The burial register yields more information. Of the 2620 entries in the five years, 84 relate to people who were strangers to Stepney. These 84 burials do not give the number of immigrants to Stepney between 1605 and 1610, but only how many immigrants the register records as having died in these years. They do, however, indicate where these strangers came from. This information is set out in the table overleaf.

Not all the deceased were actual immigrants to Stepney. Two were described as, 'the daughter of a Mercer of London', and 'a Draper of London'. In both cases it is possible that the deceased lived in

Area	Number of burials	Approximate % of immigrant burials
London city and suburban parishes	43	51%
Home counties(i.e. within a 50 mile radius of London)	17 (including Essex 6 Kent 6)	20%
Distant counties (i.e. outside a 50 mile radius)	9	11%
Aliens Scotland 8) Ireland 1) Guernsey 1) France 4)	14	17%
Unplaced	1	

London, and had a country house in Stepney.   These entries would
then refer not to immigrants but to occasional inhabitants.   In some
cases the strangers were merely visiting Stepney when unforeseen
accidents ended their life.   For example, plague accounted for a man
from Cumberland, one from Lancashire, and two Scots.   Often it is
quite clear that the buried stranger had not intended to settle in
Stepney.   One of the Scots died on his ship.   And a west country
man had been hanged for piracy at Wapping.   The number of
immigrants who died in Stepney was thus less than 84.

Nevertheless, the figures indicate the most common origins of
immigrants who died and may be taken as a rough guide to where most
of the immigrants came from.   Of the total number of immigrants
or visitors buried, 71% came from London and the home counties.
This indicates that the majority of immigrants did not move far from
their original home to settle in Stepney.

A second kind of immigrant is noted in the burial register, the vagrant.
Fifty-five vagrants died in Stepney between 1606 and 1610.   In only
five cases is the place of origin mentioned, Essex, Herefordshire,
Cambridgeshire, Hampshire, and Scotland.   The register is more
informative about the place of death.   A significant number, 26 of
the 55, died in Spitalfields.   Was Spitalfields already assuming its
role as the last refuge of the social misfit?   Of the remaining
vagrants, seven died in Wapping, three each in Limehouse, Mile End,

Poplar, Bethnal Green and 'the fields', and one in Shadwell.   From
this scanty information it seems that most immigrants came from a
relatively small area around Stepney, and that there was a large
number of vagrants among them.

(ii)   Evidence from the marriage register

Marriage often causes people to move home.   The Stepney
marriage register gives the place of origin of most marriage partners
and by studying these we can learn who moved into Stepney and
married, and how far they moved.   In our five year period there
were 841 marriages.   Of this total 63%, 527 marriages, were
between partners from the same hamlet in Stepney, and 16%, 134,
were between partners from different hamlets within the parish.
Over three-quarters of the people married in Stepney thus found
partners within the parish.   The tendency of East London people to
marry locally existed in the seventeenth century, as the studies of
Willmott and Young have shown that it exists today.   Only 180
marriages, about 21% of the total, involved partners from outside
Stepney.   Of these 180 marriages, 87 involved one stranger and one
local partner; in 74 cases the stranger was the groom and only in 13
was the stranger the bride.   There are two possible reasons for
this imbalance.   More men than women might have migrated to
Stepney to seek employment and thus there would be more chance of
marriage between immigrant men and local girls.   Or, it may be
that marriages usually took place in the bride's parish.   In this case
Stepney registers will record marriages of Stepney girls to men from
other parishes.   But the marriages of Stepney men to girls from
other parishes would take place in other parishes and will be recorded
elsewhere.   In 83 of the 180 marriages both partners were
strangers to Stepney; in five other marriages the place of origin of
one partner was unknown or unstated and the other partner was a
stranger; in two marriages the place of origin of neither partner was
known or stated: and three marriages were between Negroes.

The number of strangers and immigrants whose place of origin was
stated, was 259.   The areas they came from are as follows:-

Area	Number of marriage partners	Approximate % of strangers whose origin is known
London city and suburban parishes	194	75%
Home counties (i.e. within a 50 mile radius of London)	48 (including:-	18%
	Essex 18	
	Kent 15	
	Middlesex 6	
Distant counties (i.e. outside a 50 mile radius)	16	6%
East Indies	1 (a negro)	
	259	

It seems that people did not usually move far to marry, just as they did not move far before they died. Of the total strangers marrying, 93% came from London and the home counties.

It is impossible to assess the reliability of these statistics for measuring immigration to Stepney. There is no guarantee that the strangers who married in Stepney stayed in the parish after marriage. What we can say with certainty is that many people came into Stepney and were married and that few of them came from outside a 50 mile radius.

6. The occupations of Stepney people

From about 1600 the Stepney baptism register records the occupations of the fathers of baptised children; the burial register notes the occupations of the deceased from about 1605. We analysed the occupations mentioned in the baptism register because its record of occupations was more complete than in the burial register. Five half-year periods, each January to June, 1606 to 1610, were analysed and the occupations divided into seven groups shown in 'The Table of Occupations'. The percentages show how important each occupation group was within each hamlet.

If we look first at the total figures for Stepney the varying importance of the occupation groups can be seen. The river and sea occupation

TABLE OF OCCUPATIONS

	Bethnal Green No.	%	Mile End No.	%	Spital-fields No.	%	Poplar No.	%	Lime-house No.	%	Ratcliff No.	%	Shadwell No.	%	Wapping No.	%	Total No.	%
Agricultural	12	32	1	3			9	11	2	1	2	1					26	3
River and Sea	1	3	1	3			41	50	100	53	119	46	48	72	35	44	345	45
Shipbuilding					1	6	4	5	23	12	29	11	6	9	12	15	75	10
Land Crafts	8	22	19	54	11	65	12	15	29	15	51	20	8	12	18	23	156	20
Provisioners	1	3	4	11			9	11	14	7	32	12	4	6	5	6	69	9
Middle Class	3	8	4	11			4	5	9	5	7	3			1	1	28	4
Miscellaneous	12	32	6	17	5	29	3	4	13	7	19	7	1	2	8	10	67	9
TOTAL	37	100	35	100	17	100	82	100	190	100	259	100	67	100	79	100	766	100

is by far the largest. Of the 345 in this group, 320 were mariners; there were a few watermen and lightermen, and a small number of fishermen from Poplar. The second largest group is the land crafts, which includes 36 tailors and shoemakers, 29 carpenters, 27 weavers and 15 smiths. The shipbuilding group comprised 51 shipbuilders, and various other associated craftsmen, ropemakers, sailmakers, pulley-makers and so on. The other occupation groups are small by comparison. Provisioners, most of whom were suppliers of food and drink, bakers, butchers, grocers, victuallers, vintners, and so on, account for 9% of the total. The 27 middle class people include knights, gentlemen, members of London companies, and professional men, lawyers, ministers and so on. Agricultural occupations include yeomen and husbandmen. Occupations which could not be easily categorised were included in the miscellaneous section. The large percentage of this group in Bethnal Green included five labourers, two porters, two 'moniers', a player, a gardener and a hackneyman.

The occupation structures of the hamlets vary considerably. The three inland hamlets stand out because they have scarcely any river and sea occupations. Bethnal Green has a higher percentage of agricultural occupations than any other hamlet. Mile End has the highest percentage of middle class people, and a high percentage of provisioners, perhaps explained by middle class demand. One feature which all three inland hamlets share is the size of their land craft groups. In Bethnal Green and Mile End this is explained by the number of weavers: five of the eight land craftsmen in the former were weavers, and six of the nineteen in the latter, more than any other single occupation in the group, were weavers. In Spitalfields the land crafts were more diverse; the eleven in this group included two weavers, two basketmakers, two threadmakers, two carpenters, a bricklayer, a brickmaker and a smith. Of the five miscellaneous occupations in Spitalfields which make up the only other substantial group in the hamlet, four were labourers. Clearly Spitalfields was, at this date, dominated by craftsmen and unskilled labourers, and was not the stronghold of a weaving industry it was later to become.

The five riverside hamlets are all dominated by their river and sea occupation groups. This dominance is marked in Shadwell, which has a particularly one-sided occupation structure. Limehouse and Ratcliff, the two most populous hamlets have similar percentages of river and sea, shipbuilding, and land craft occupations. Limehouse, in addition, has a higher percentage of middle class people than any other riverside hamlet except Poplar. And Ratcliff has a higher percentage of provisioners than any other hamlet. The supplying of ships probably accounts for some of the 32 provisioners; eight were victuallers and five were chandlers. Six bakers, three millers and four brewers probably also shared in the ship supply trade. Wapping is notable for having the highest percentage of shipbuilders and a higher percentage of land crafts than any other riverside hamlet. But Poplar has the most remarkable occupation structure of all the hamlets. It has a high percentage of river and sea occupations in common with its riverside neighbours. It also has an agricultural group second only to Bethnal Green. And, in addition, it has substantial percentages of land crafts and provisioners, and not inconsiderable percentages of middle class people and shipbuilders. It was a hybrid hamlet, having an occupation structure which was amalgam of a riverside and an inland hamlet.

Conclusion

The sections of this report have shown some methods of analysing statistics from a parish register. We have been able to make an estimate of the total population, compare the relative populousness of the hamlets of Stepney, learn something about the behaviour of baptism, marriage and burial statistics and the structure of the population, learn a little about immigration, and compare the occupations in different hamlets. But our picture of the population is a very imperfect one. Most of our conclusions are tentative because our figures are not of the population as it was during the five years which was studied, but of a certain section of the population, those being married, having children and dying. At best our figures give only an indication of the size and nature of the population in the early seventeenth century. Even so, the parish registers give an insight, however imperfect, into the population, which no other source would provide.

NOTES

1. <u>Natural and Political Observations on the Bills of Mortality.</u> 3rd edn. 1665. 141.

2. <u>Another Essay in Political Arithmetick Concerning the Growth of the City of London.</u> 1682. Reprinted in C.H. Hull, <u>The Economic Writings of Sir William Petty.</u> 1899. ii, 459.

3. Information of Dr. D.J. Schove.

MID-WHARFEDALE 1721-1812: ECONOMIC AND DEMOGRAPHIC CHANGE IN A PENNINE DALE[1]

May F. Pickles

The connection between economic and demographic change in England in the eighteenth century is easily recognized but the nature of the causal relationship is obscure. This is partly due to a lack of reliable statistical evidence on a national scale. Although there is now available considerable economic data on a national scale, information on national population trends, at least before 1801, is both scanty and imprecise.[2] This will gradually improve as more local statistics are centrally assembled.[3] Meanwhile progress is likely to be made in a series of detailed studies which reveal the mechanisms of change operating at local level.

The partial industrialization of mid-Wharfedale in the eighteenth century is a subject well suited for research into economic and social history. As a subject for study mid-Wharfedale has the advantage that the region comprises two contrasting parts, a market town area and an area of rural hinterland.[4] Moreover, the valley settlements are exceptionally well documented in the eighteenth century making it possible to examine and survey many important problems in detail.

For convenience the two areas are identified on the basis of ecclesiastical parishes recognized in census material for 1801.[5] Thus the ecclesiastical parish of Otley represents the market town area and eight ecclesiastical parishes and chapelries, namely Conistone, Rylstone, Burnsall, Linton, Bolton Abbey, Addingham, Ilkley and Weston constitute the area of hinterland. In all, the region selected for study occupies approximately 150 square miles of land of which just over one fifth belongs to Otley parish.[6] A map (fig. 1) illustrates the administrative boundaries and the physiographical characteristics of the region.

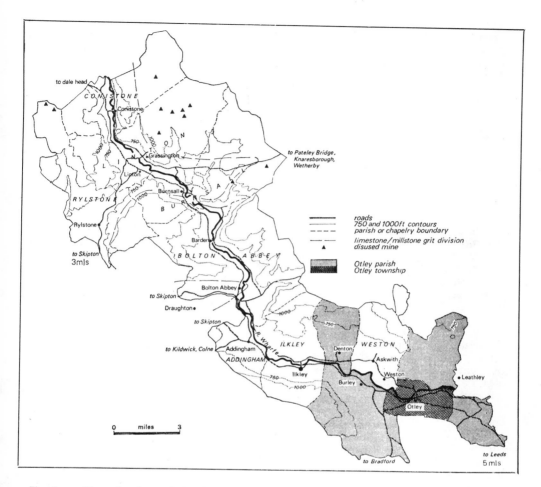

Fig 1 — Map showing administrative boundaries and physiographical characteristics of the region. Note. The unnamed township to the north of Weston parish is part of Otley parish.

The study is based mainly on information derived from parish registers.[7] These provide evidence for occupational change during most of the eighteenth and early nineteenth centuries. In our case they are used to show evidence of demographic trends over a slightly longer period. In addition limited use is made of probate inventories[8] and six contemporary surveys originating either at regional or national level: two hearth tax assessments (one for 1664[9] and one for 1672[10]), three archiepiscopal surveys (that of Compton in 1676,[11] that of Herring in 1743[12] and that of Drummond in 1764 [13]) and the national census dated 1811[14].

Taken together these various sources indicate that economic and demographic change within the region of mid-Wharfedale formed a recognizable pattern of growth falling into four main phases. The first, between

179

1721 and 1740, is one in which economy and population are almost stagnant with some overall emigration in the rural parishes leading to a population decline there. The second, between 1740 and 1770, witnesses rapid growth both in population and the economy. In the period after 1770 the situation begins to change. For some years it looks as though population is growing faster than the technology of the day could easily support. It is a Malthusian-type situation in which for a short time at least population growth has outstripped the means of its own subsistence. By 1800, however, the equilibrium is restored. New technological advance provides the means by which the population is carried. The lead mines begin to prosper, textile mills proliferate, new industries emerge. Mid-Wharfedale is set on a period of further expansion.

i) Occupational change

Our first task is to examine the extent to which occupational change occurred within the selected region. Several of the books of parish registers of mid-Wharfedale provide material for study in the period 1721-1812. In the marriage books the occupation of the groom is generally given, in the baptism and burial books it is that of the head of the family in which the birth or death occurs. Occasionally occupation is recorded in all three series though usually in only one or two, being found most often in the baptisms register. Thus the baptism books for Rylstone and Conistone regularly record occupation for periods of more than eighty years, in Ilkley for an unbroken period of almost seventy years, in Linton and Burnsall for periods of more than forty years and in none is it recorded for a period of less than twenty years. There is, therefore, a vast body of evidence suitable for research into occupational change during the eighteenth and nineteenth centuries; the problem is how to extract this without giving rise to distortion.

Basically the extraction can be done in two ways. The first is to count the number of individuals occuring in, say, a twenty year period and after-wards to tabulate the results into suitable groupings. In this way it is possible to observe the frequency with which men changed their occupa-tion or held dual occupations or again, in times of economic stress, which section of the population is in receipt of parish relief. The second, is to make a simple count of the frequency with which different types of occupation appear in the register, ignoring the frequency with which any one head of family might appear, on the assumption that this evens out in a large number of entries. With the first method there are two problems: common names sometimes make it difficult to decide how many individuals are involved, and a person resident in a parish for a year or two would count as heavily, provided he appeared at least once in the register, as a man who had lived his whole working life there. The main drawback to the second stems from the fact of differential fertility as between the different occupational groups in the population. It has been found for instance that industrial workers in some areas tend to have the largest families.[15] For the present study, however, in which it is desirable to know the strength of each occupational group, a simple frequency count probably yields the best results. The number of events counted in this way should be roughtly proportionate to the number of working man-years spent in a parish over a given period.

A further difficulty is due to uneven recording of occupation. At best occupations are given in 90% of all the entries where they might be expected,[16] and in most registers the rate does not drop below 75% though there are exceptions. In Linton, for instance, between 1721 and 1740 and again in Otley between 1801 and 1812 registration is less than 70%. In the case of Linton it was possible to increase the rate by searching for another entry relating to the same individual and in this way supplementing information already recovered. For Otley, however, this procedure was deemed unsafe. Owing to the large size of the parish and the consequent number of entries involved, the difficulty of duplication made this exercise too hazardous. It is possible, therefore, that uneven recording may have led to under-registration of some kinds of occupation in this period. There appears to be no way in which this deficiency can be rectified.

Another difficulty in extracting this information is that individual parish registers do not always record occupation for the same years. Nevertheless it is possible to devise an occupational structure for two periods, namely 1721-40 and 1761-80 or in the case of Otley 1721-40 and 1801-12, by making certain adjustments (Table 1(a), 1(b), 2(a), 2(b)). For instance in the Addingham register occupation is not recorded until 1766. However, from other sources[17] and from a general knowledge of the district it seems clear that Addingham in the early part of the century was in many ways similar to Ilkley. I have, therefore, modelled the occupational structure for Addingham for the period 1721-40 on that for Ilkley adjusting the total number of entries to comply with the approximate size of Addingham's population at the time. In the case of Bolton Abbey, occupation is not recorded until 1778. At this time Bolton Abbey parish is the most rural of any and it seems inconceivable that its occupational structure could have varied significantly over the preceding half century. I have, therefore, simply taken the number of entries in the period 1781-1800 and reduced them to comply with the approximate size of the population in 1721-40. In Weston, occupation is not recorded in connection with baptisms in the period 1761-80. In this instance use has been made of occupational recordings found in the marriage series omitting grooms who after marriage do not appear to reside within the parish. Again the result is adjusted in order to conform with the approximate population size at the time.

In parish registers for which occupational information is available for periods of unequal numbers of years, there are further difficulties. When comparing occupational frequencies for periods of unequal numbers of years distorting results can follow. This is resolved by adjusting the number of occupational recordings for a given period of years to the number of occupational recordings for a decade. Thus it becomes very easy to compare the figures for, say, the twenty year period 1721-40 with the twelve year period 1801-12. This is the method we have adopted when considering the question of industrial change in several Wharfedale parishes.

These, then, are the main adjustments we have made in order to extract occupational information from parish registers. Any further adjustments are explicit in the tables and need no comment here.

TABLE 1 (a) Occupational analysis of eight rural parishes 1721-40

Occupation	Conistone	Rylstone (1723-40)	Burnsall	Linton	Bolton Abbey	Addingham (1718-35)	Ilkley	Weston (1721-39)	All Parishes No.	All Parishes %
1. Land	42	126	140	141	153	80	104	61	847	40
2. Landless labour	40	19	28	10	92	42	55	59	345	16
3. Leadmining	19	11	8	55	1				94	4
4. Textiles	1	52	28	5	37	4	5	7	139	7
5. Clothing and footwear	5	7	29	57	22	17	22	9	168	8
6. Food and drink	2	4	6	21	11	14	18	4	80	4
7. Building	6	25	28	47	28	21	28	9	192	9
8. Rural trades and minor industries	3	24	32	36	7	23	30	16	171	8
9. Services		1			1	6	7		14	<1
10. Professions			8	4				1	15	<1
11. Gentry	8	2	5	14		2	2	2	35	2
12. Servants			2	4		1	2	1	10	<1
13. Militia				1	1				2	<1
14. Pensioner										
15. Lodger						2	2	1	5	<1
16. Traveller										<1
TOTAL	126	272	314	395	353	212	275	170	2117	100

Bracketed percentage groupings (All Parishes %): rows 3–4 } 11; rows 5–8 } 29; rows 9–12 } 4.

Notes: Figures in italics conjectural. It is possible that a few unspecified coal miners are included in group 3.

Table 1 (b)   Occupational analysis of Otley parish 1721-40

Occupation	Town	Rural part of town parish	All parish	
			No.	%
1. Land	8	421	429	26
2. Landless labour	125	154	279	17
3. Leadmining				
4. Textiles	44	145	189	11
5. Clothing and footwear	55	79	134	8
6. Food and drink	61	39	100	6
7. Building	92	89	181	11
8. Rural trades and minor industries	122	98	220	13
9. Services	10	8	18	1
10. Professions	19	10	29	2
11. Gentry	15	20	35	2
12. Servants	20	26	46	3
13. Militia				
14. Pensioner				
15. Lodger				
16. Traveller		19	19	1
TOTAL	571	1108	1679	101

(Rows 5–8 bracketed as 38; rows 9–16 bracketed as 9)

Looking first of all at the years between 1721 and 1740. (Tables 1(a) and 1(b)) we can see that land employments (group 1) provide the dominant group in each part of the valley. In the rural parishes the combined total of husbandmen, yeomen and farmers accounts for 40% of the working population there and in Otley for 26%. Land employment in this period usually means sheep-raising, dairying or stock breeding, though cropping influenced by soil-type is found in several places. Cropping in limestone villages usually means barley and oats, the occasional pulse, often peas. On the claylands of the lower valley these crops are supplemented with a little wheat, a few potatoes (possibly a garden crop) and occasionally beans. In the later eighteenth and early nineteenth centuries a very few experiments seem to have been made with clover and turnips.[18]

The number of labourers (group 2) in mid-Wharfedale is, as we should expect, relatively small because of the type of farming practised and because of the small size of most farms.[19] It could, of course, be argued that terminology is responsible for the small number of labourers encountered in parish registers. But since the number varies so little from one parish to another and from one period to another it seems likely that these figures accurately reflect the situation.

There are two main industries in mid-Wharfedale, leadmining and textiles (groups 3 and 4). Leadmining, which accounts for 4% of working populations in rural parishes, is confined to the upland parishes of Linton, Conistone and Burnsall. Textiles, on the other hand, which at this time include linens, woollens and worsteds, provide employment for a few people in every parish (7% in the rural parishes and 11% in Otley).[20] There is no certain evidence for a woollen industry in the rural parishes after c. 1740 but this branch of the trade continued in Otley and in some of its dependent settlements throughout the century.

All tertiary occupations (groups 5 to 8) are found to be more numerous in Otley parish. Here, this group forms 38% of the recorded total as against 29% in rural parishes. In fact very few of the trades represented by these occupations are exclusive to Otley parish, though the division of labour in some trades there is different. In the building trade (group 7), which includes a relatively large number of persons everywhere, plasterers are confined to Otley parish, mainly to the town itself, while masons predominate over carpenters in the town but not elsewhere. A division of labour which might suggest that timber framed houses continued longer in country districts, though it must be remembered that carpenters may have included furniture and farm implements among their products, since occasionally they are described as joiners. A slightly different situation obtains in the case of clothing and footwear trades (group 5). Hatters, glovers and hosiers are few everywhere, while in the market town parish shoemakers and cloggers outnumber tailors but in rural parishes the position is reversed. As between the food and drinks trades (group 6), which in the early part of the century mainly comprised butchers, millers, brewers, alehouse-keepers and maltsters, there is an equal division of labour everywhere. But in food alone butchers predominate over millers in the town but not elsewhere. Otley parish had at this time the only fishmonger and the town the only grocer, though grocers began to appear in other places soon afterwards. The wide range of rural trades and minor industries (group 8) emphasises the self-supporting nature of rural communities at the time. In this group references to blacksmiths are found most often. This is to be expected since horses played such a vital role in most branches of rural economies.[21] Leather workers form the next largest group since hides were a major product of pastoral economies. Shoemakers have already been mentioned but in addition there are skinners and tanners, and most particularly in Otley saddlers, curriers and fellmongers. Other occupations listed under trades and minor industries are potters, whitesmiths, coopers, ropemakers, dishturners, papermakers, stirrupmakers, tallow chandlers, millwrights, and less often clockmakers, nailmakers and tobacconists. All these are common to both town and country. The market town, however, had a monopoly of ironmongers, soap boilers, chairmakers and drapers.

Men belonging to the professions and specialized services (groups 9 and 10) are relatively more frequent in Otley though they appear in small numbers in several parishes. Each parish had its priest but a few schoolmasters, some apothecaries, surgeons, excisemen, one architect, an occasional sexton, parish clerk, barber, limeburner and surprisingly one jockey appear over the whole region.

The gentry (group 11), most of whom were 'parish gentry' for titles were rare, occur in equal numbers in each part of the valley. Some indication of the wealth and status enjoyed by the gentlemen is provided by hearth tax assessments for the seventeenth century. According to a return made in Wharfedale in 1664, fifteen gentlemen's houses were assessed at five to ten hearths, four at sixteen to eighteen hearths, three at twenty-one to twenty-four hearths and, exceptionally, a sixteenth century hunting lodge at twenty-nine hearths. These figures may be compared with the 1,471 houses, or 90% of the total, which were assessed at two hearths or less.[22]

Table 2 (a)   Occupational analysis of eight rural parishes 1761-80

Occupation	Conistone	Rylstone	Burnsall (1740-61)	Linton	Bolton Abbey (1781-1800)	Addingham (1767-80)	Ilkley	Weston	All Parishes No.	%	
1. Land	35	117	103	132	224	89	118	*106*	924	30	
2. Landless labour	39	63	29	1	136	56	68	*11*	403	13	
3. Leadmining	28	17	69	464	1				579	19	⎫ 30
4. Textiles		52	11	5	54	85	106	23	336	11	⎭
5. Clothing and footwear	10	16	36	70	33	41	39	*16*	261	8	⎫
6. Food and drink	3	12	14	30	16	23	25	*13*	136	4	⎪ 24
7. Building	3	14	27	48	42	28	7	*13*	182	6	⎬
8. Rural trades and minor industries	1	32	21	65	10	22	24	*12*	187	6	⎭
9. Services			3	10		1	3		17	<1	⎫
10. Professions		1	1	11	2	2			20	<1	⎪
11. Gentry		3		6		6		3	23	<1	⎪
12. Servants		2	3	10			5	3	17	<1	⎬ 3
13. Militia			1		2		2		3	<1	⎪
14. Pensioner			1						1	<1	⎪
15. Lodger			1						1	<1	⎪
16. Traveller				1					1	<1	⎭
TOTAL	119	329	320	853	520	353	397	200	3091	100	

Notes: Figures in italics conjectural. It is possible that a few unspecified coal miners are included in group 3.

185

The size of the servant class (group 12) is exceptionally small when compared with what has been found in several places.[23] To some extent this is explained on the grounds of poverty but also it is due to the fact that occupations of this kind tend to go unrecorded in parish registers. Male servants perhaps more than any other occupational group tended to be unmarried persons remaining in the parish for only a short time 'and thus escaping notice in the registers'.[24]

In sum, the parish registers of mid-Wharfedale show a division of labour such as we should expect to find in rural areas during the first part of the eighteenth century.

Table 2 (b)   Occupational analysis of Otley parish 1801-12

Occupation	Town	Rural part of town parish	Whole parish		
			No.	%	
1. Land	28	142	170	15	
2. Landless labour	56	56	112	10	
3. Leadmining					
4. Textiles	75	78	153	14	
5. Clothing and footwear	120	23	143	13	
6. Food and drink	93	13	106	10	54
7. Building	117	40	157	14	
8. Rural trades and minor industries	118	69	187	17	
9. Services	11	3	14	1	
10. Professions	14	3	17	2	
11. Gentry	1	17	18	2	
12. Servants	5	14	19	2	7
13. Militia	5	1	6	< 1	
14. Pensioner					
15. Lodger					
16. Traveller	4		4	< 1	
TOTAL	647	459	1106	100	

By the later eighteenth and nineteenth centuries, however, these traditional arrangements disappear completely (Tables 2(a), 2(b)). By 1761-80 in the rural parishes, and possibly by then but certainly by 1801-12 in Otley,[25] the figure for land employment drops by at least 10%. Also landless labour which includes agricultural labour drops from 16% to 13% in rural parishes and in Otley from 17% to 10%. Industry by contrast, particularly in rural parishes, makes substantial gains. Here, occupations in leadmining and textiles increase in strength from 11% to 30% and in Otley (textiles only) from 11% to 14%. There are changes too in the distribution of working populations among the different types of tertiary employments (groups 5 to 8) though the emphasis in each part of the dale is different. Tertiary employments in rural parishes decrease in strength from 29% to 24% but in Otley they increase from 38% to 54%.

This overall view of occupational change can be illuminated further from a consideration of aggregate totals. From the increase by 974 in the total number of occupational recordings in rural parish registers it can be inferred that there was an increase in the total number of persons employed. This increase is made up of seventy-seven yeomen and husband-men, fifty-eight labourers, 485 miners, 197 textile workers, 155 tertiary occupations and two sundry occupations.[26] From these figures it would appear that practically all additional labour that accrued after c.1740 eschewed land work for other types of employment, particularly industrial employment.[27] Although no similar figure can be produced for Otley parish, owing to the small number of years included in the second period, the general trend is clear enough. Here, most additional labour appearing after c.1740 found employment in tertiary activities rather than in industry.

It is unfortunate that only five of the eight registers belonging to the rural parishes record occupation consistently after 1780. It seems likely, how-ever, that these registers indicate general trends and accordingly an analysis of their occupational content is produced in Tables 3(a) and 3(b). These figures show that between c.1761 and c.1812 textile employ-ments increased from 17% to 33% but that agriculture remained relatively unchanged, 34% as against 35%; employments in landless labour dropped (21% to 9%); tertiary employments continued to decline (23% to 20%) and mining fell a little (3% to <1%).

Table 3 (a)   Occupational analysis of five rural parishes 1761-80

Occupation	Conistone	Rylstone	Bolton Abbey (1781-1800)	Addingham (1767-80)	Ilkley	All parishes No.	%
1. Land	35	117	224	89	118	583	34
2. Landless labour	39	63	136	56	68	362	21
3. Leadmining	28	17	1			46	3} 20
4. Textiles		52	54	85	106	297	17}
5. Clothing and footwear	10	16	33	41	39	139	8
6. Food and drink	3	8	16	23	25	75	4
7. Building	3	14	42	28	7	94	5} 23
8. Rural trades and minor industries	1	36	10	22	24	93	5
9. Services				1	3	4	<1
10. Professions		1	2	2		5	<1
11. Gentry		3		6	5	14	1
12. Servants		2			2	4	<1
13. Militia			2			2	<1} 2
14. Pensioner							
15. Lodger							
16. Traveller							
TOTAL	119	329	520	353	397	1718	100

Table 3 (b) Occupational analysis of five rural parishes 1801-12

Occupation	Conistone	Rylstone	Bolton Abbey	Addingham	Ilkley	All parishes No.	%
1. Land	25	103	149	103	89	469	35
2. Landless labour	23	2	64	21	12	122	9
3. Leadmining	1	4				5	<1 } 33
4. Textiles		31	75	274	60	440	33 }
5. Clothing and footwear	3	7	20	32	9	71	5)
6. Food and drink	6	9	13	21	13	62	5 } 20
7. Building	8	22	17	39	8	94	7
8. Rural trades and minor industries		5	8	21	10	44	3)
9. Services		4	2	6		12	1
10. Professions				4		4	<1
11. Gentry		3		4	1	8	<1
12. Servants			5	1		6	<1 } 3
13. Militia				1	4	5	<1
14. Pensioner							
15. Lodger							
16. Traveller							
TOTAL	66	190	353	527	206	1342	100

From these figures it is quite clear that industrial activity in the rural parishes increased substantially after c.1780. The rapid rise in textiles easily off-sets the decline in leadmining. In which case we may assume a division of labour in this part of the valley in the early nineteenth century as follows: industry 35% to 40%, agriculture 30% or less, landless labour some 11%, tertiary employments some 22% and sundry others 2%.

Thus information derived from parish registers can show the scale and direction of occupational change in the period studied. Agricultural employments decline almost everywhere, at the same time employments in industry grow sensationally in the fural parishes, while employments in trades and minor industries rise only in the market town. The cause of these changes and the external forces which appear to have influenced them must now be examined.

ii) Agricultural change

It is often argued that there could have been no industrial revolution in England without a preceding revolution in agriculture; that until agricultural productivity per head had risen sufficiently to permit a diversity of occupation, the additional labour necessary for industrial development could not be made available.[28] The Wharfedale registers provide evidence which conforms well with this hypothesis.

The fall in land employments which occurred between the first and second halves of the eighteenth century cannot in fact be explained in terms of more efficient farming solely at a local level. Meat output apparently increased within the region, partly through an extension to the cultivated area through enclosure of waste, moors and common pasture,[29] and also through a more intensive use of lime spread on the fields as manure.[30] Crop yields on the other hand hardly increased since enclosure came early and was virtually complete in several places by c.1720.[31] In this connection too, the new root crops and grasses, as we noted earlier, were hardly used at all. In order, therefore, to ensure against food shortages, particularly at a time when population was rising fast, it seems likely that provisions came into the valley from outside, most probably from the East and North Ridings. Such imports would demand an improvement in communications and this can be shown to have occurred.

Several roads were raised to turnpike status from the mid-eighteenth century onwards. The road from Leeds to Otley and thence by way of Addingham to Skipton was improved by Turnpike act in 1755.[32] Otley benefitted as well when a road running east to Tadcaster was re-made in 1753.[33] Another road leaving Grassington (Linton parish) for Pateley Bridge and thence by way of Knaresborough to Wetherby was repaired and widened in 1758.[34] And again a road leading from Addingham to Kildwick and thence passing into Lancashire was improved in 1755.[35] Moreover, the Leeds and Liverpool canal completed its link between Leeds and Skipton in June, 1777.[36]

These improvements, effected in the mid-eighteenth century, gave new patterns of employment which were different in each part of the valley. Generally, new labour in the rural parishes found employment in one or other of the two major industries, and in Otley sometimes in industry though most often in trades or services.

iii) The development of industry

The transition from agriculture to industry shows itself most conspicuously in Linton parish. Here, land employments fell between the first and second halves of the century from 36% to 15%, while leadmining rose from 14% to 54%. The narrative of events which led up to this remarkable achievement is part of the subject of Dr Raistrick's book, *Leadmining in the mid-Pennines*.[37]

During the eighteenth century leadership in the industry came from men whose primary interests were often quite different from mining. Such men, some of them traders, merchants, yeomen, lawyers as well as scions of landed families 'took out many leases in the name of small partnerships, and had the mines worked either by miner-partners or by wage labour'.[38] Such was the success of these venturers, assisted as they were by an acceptance of new invention,[39] that lead output figures from all the mines reached unprecedented levels within a very short space of time. At the Grassington mill (Linton parish) output of refined lead at the beginning of the century was around one hundred tons a year. By 1736, when continuous figures become available, output was in the region of 150 tons; 'in 1742 300 tons was reached; in 1752, 450 tons was exceeded, and there was then a rapid rise to 1765, when the average fluctuated for many years between 500 and 700 tons'.[40] Figures for Burnsall parish mines, though discontinuous, show similar trends. Following a major development in 1752 at one mine a record output figure of 400 tons a year was reached in c.1782. Unfortunately there are no early figures available for Conistone parish mines; such information as exists, however, suggests a period of high activity in the 1740s and again in the 1760s, with output of around eighty tons a year being recorded in the 1780s.

These years of high activity, however, were not destined to last. There followed a period of serious decline in which lead output from the Grassington mill had fallen to less than 300 tons a year by 1790. The natural running out of mines, some of which had known continuous working for more than 200 years, together with drainage problems encountered in depth were chief among the causes. It was a situation that called for a drastic reorganization of the whole working system and for a capital investment programme of a type and on a scale such as only mineral royalty owners — in this instance principally the Duke of Devonshire — could provide.

The improvements that followed were elaborate and costly. At Grassington they were marked by two vast undertakings one of which, known as the Duke's level, had cost the owner on completion £33,000. Among the innovations introduced at Grassington was a reverberatory furnace installed there in 1792. About this time too several processes were improved and speeded up through mechanization. Ore dressing was mechanized, so was pumping and to some extent winding. Moreover, new capital which allowed for the sinking of several deep shafts revealed new veins. These and many other alterations to working arrangements, some of which took place over several decades, led to a maximum lead output figure in the six years 1850 to 1855 of 6,000 tons. But in 1812, the year that concerns this study most, output is not likely to have been in excess of 300 tons for the year.[41]

Leadmining was the main industrial activity found in villages situated in the north of our region. In the south it was clothmaking. As with leadmining, textiles too entered upon a period of rapid expansion from about 1740. Initially this was due to a revival of interest in the manufacture of worsted cloth. As in many parts of the Riding local manufacturers turned their attention from woollens to worsteds and either 'forsook woollens entirely, or ran both manufactures together in double harness.'[42]

No continuous information about the worsted trade has survived for the valley as a whole. Nevertheless occupational recordings recovered from the registers of Ilkley and Otley provide evidence of general trends in each area (Table 4). In Ilkley, occupational recordings derived from parish registers indicate a period of rapid expansion in the period c.1740-1800, but a slight decline thereafter. In Otley, the relatively large number of occupational recordings in the period 1721-40 suggests an earlier change from woollens to worsteds than occurred in the valley generally. In Otley, however, the presence of fulling mills together with the recording of several persons described in parish registers as clothmakers and clothiers (who it is felt could just as easily be associated with the making of woollens as with worsteds) renders it virtually impossible to express the relative size of the industry in terms of numbers of persons employed. The figures in Table 4, therefore, are minimal figures only.

The working arrangements of any branch of textiles when compared with those for leadmining are ill-documented. Nevertheless there is in Addingham sufficient documentary evidence to enable us to build up a fairly comprehensive picture of the worsted trade in the latter half of the eighteenth century.[44]

Table 4.   Growth of the worsted trade in mid-Wharfedale.

Dates	Ilkley parish		Otley parish[43]	
	Nos. recorded	Decadal equivalent	Nos. recorded	Decadal equivalent
1721-40 (1718-35 for Ilkley)	1	c.1	34	17
1745-60	72	45	?	?
1761-80	100	50	?	?
1781-1800	115	58	?	?
1801-12	57	48	42	35

It seems that two Addingham men, John Cunliffe a wool-stapler and John Cockshott a stuff manufacturer, went into partnership. As a stapler, John Cunliffe probably bought and collected up parcels of raw wool from various sources near and far. The new wool was then washed and combed and sold to John Cockshott. He in turn put out the combed wool to be spun into yarn by hand. After collection Cockshott supplied the spun yarn to domestic weavers or had the material woven up into cloth in his own loomshops. The loom or weaving shops were a common feature of the industry and in Addingham John Cockshott owned three. Two rooms in the 'Rookery' contained twelve pairs of looms, another house nine pairs, and his large weaving shop sixty pairs. A pair of looms is in fact one hand loom.[45]

At this stage in the process of clothmaking the ways of worsteds and woollens part company. The kerseys, broad cloths and other woollens, some of which were almost certainly made in Otley, still had to go through the process of milling, fulling and tenting, whereas the worsted cloth was ready for market. The nearest markets were Leeds (woollens), Bradford (worsteds) and Colne (worsteds). Such was the importance of Addingham, however, that it possessed its own warehouse or piece hall to which lengths of locally handwoven cloth were regularly brought. This building and two of the three loomshops are still standing in the village, readily recognizeable by their distinctive architecture.

The 'putting out' system clearly made the carriage of wool a prominent feature of clothmaking in the eighteenth century. The following example demonstrates the kinds of distances over which wool or cloth was sometimes carried. An Askwith clothier purchased his wool at York or Wakefield and brought it by pack horse 'along the worst of roads' to Askwith near Otley. Here it was sorted and washed, given out to be combed and returned to the clothier's headquarters; it then went to Cheshire and the adjoining dales of Derbyshire to be spun, was returned to Askwith, and again handed out to be woven. Finally, the woven pieces of cloth went to Colne market to be sold.[46]

The various inventions connected with clothmaking seem to have solved one problem but created another. Kay's flying shuttle solved the difficulty of weaving cloth, particularly broad cloths;[47] but its speed of yarn consumption was such that even when spinning had been accelerated by the use of hand jennies in the latter part of the century it still required four spinners to supply sufficient warp and weft to employ one weaver.[48] The problem was not finally overcome until the 'water frame,' already in use in Lancashire for spinning cotton, was successfully applied to wool.[49] In Wharfedale this happened when the same John Cockshott and John Cunliffe built their spinning mill on the banks of the river Wharfe at Addingham in 1787.[50] This mill (probably the second worsted spinning mill to appear in England) produced the yarn for the first mill-spun worsted cloth ever seen in the district at Piece Hall in Bradford.

It has already been indicated that firm figures for the woollen industry are difficult to obtain. In order, therefore, to resolve the problem posed by ambiguous occupational descriptions we have adopted the expedient of producing alternative sets of figures. In Table 5 the figures in the first four columns represent occupational recordings known to be connected with the manufacture of woollen cloth while those in fifth and sixth columns represent the clothmakers and clothiers whose precise occupations are in doubt. The figures set out in this way make it quite clear that the woollen industry experienced serious decline in our period. Moreover, the downward trend in the number of clothiers and clothmakers which mirrors the downward trend in woollen workers generally may suggest that most were engaged in the manufacture of woollens as opposed to worsteds. Also it is worth noting that the single reference to a woollen worker in the Otley register in the period 1801-12 is in fact to a scribbling miller. This may indicate that Arkwright's power-driven carding engine, which at the end of the eighteenth century was being adapted to scribble wool, had been installed in a mill in the Otley district.[51]

Table 5. **Progress of the woollen industry in mid Wharfedale**[52]

Dates	Nos. recorded	Decadal equivalent	Otley parish Nos. recorded	Decadal equivalent	Clothiers etc.	Decadal equivalent
1721-40	7	4	23	12	67	34
1801-12	0	0	1	c.1	5	4

In the late 1780s, just at the time when leadmining was experiencing serious decline, the textile trade entered upon a period of further expansion. Cotton spinning made its appearance in several Wharfedale villages almost simultaneously. Its appearance is not difficult to explain since, as with worsteds, it reflects a national pattern. It has been said that until c.1775 the cotton industry 'was little more than a subsidiary occupation for a few thousand agriculturalists.'[53] This picture began to alter when in the 1770s, or in some parts of the country a little later, the new inventions of Hargreaves, Arkwright and Crompton effected permanent change From this time onwards cotton manufacture spread out from the Lancashire towns and villages into surrounding districts.

Once again parish registers can give some indication of industrial change in the Wharfedale parishes. Before the mid-1780s rural parish registers make no mention of a cotton worker of any kind. Cotton spinners begin to appear about 1786-7 and these are followed a few years later by weavers and other occupations connected with the manufacture of cotton cloth. In Otley, where industrial progress was usually rather slow, cotton manufacture in the period 1801-12 appears to have outstripped all other types of local clothmaking.[54]

Table 6. Growth of the cotton trade in mid-Wharfedale

Dates	Five rural parishes		Otley parish	
	Nos. recorded	Decadal equivalent	Nos. recorded	Decadal equivalent
1781-1800	50	25	?	?
1801-12	133	111	77	64

It is noticeable that in the 1780s spinners are encountered in parish registers for the first time. This is because cotton spinning was essentially a mechanized process. Cotton mills began to appear in the valley from the late 1780s onwards. In some instances old corn mills were converted, in others new mills were erected in order to take part in this and in other branches of the trade.[55] In Ilkley for example we find that William Middleton leased land to Thomas Hauxworth of Ilkley, gentleman, Jonathan Curtis of Bingley, worsted man and Joseph Hartley of Keighley, engineer, for the erection of a 'cotton mill or other mill fit and proper for manufacturing cotton wool into yarn or for spinning or manufacturing linen, wool or worsted.'[56] A sad reminder of the fact that young children were employed in the mills is preserved for us in the records of several registers. In Bolton Abbey for instance we find that Thomas son of William Phillip of Halton was killed in the cotton manufactury at Draughton in 1802, aged thirteen.[57]

Finally, the linen industry, always of negligible importance in mid-Wharfedale, is seen to decline in our period. Eight references to linen workers are found in the registers for Rylstone, Conistone and Ilkley in the period 1721-40 but in the period 1801-12 there are no references to linen workers at all. In Linton and Burnsall there are thirteen references to linen workers between 1721 and 1740 and five between 1761 and 1780 (incorporating Burnsall figures for 1741-60 as the nearest ones available).[58] In Otley linen workers are found on fifty-five occasions in the period 1721-40 and on nine in the period 1801-12. Unfortunately no local information has survived which might help to explain these figures.

Industrialization in mid-Wharfedale, then, reflects many of the 'contemporary currents' of economic change in the period. The essential ingredients seem to be, capital outlay, reorganization of labour, an acceptance of new invention, diversification of agriculture combined with transport development and finally a capital investment programme of a type, and on a scale, of quite unprecedented proportions. In all these several respects Wharfedale's two major industries run a parallel course.

iv) The development of trades, services and minor industries

We have already seen that in mid-Wharfedale the development of trades, services and minor industries was confined almost exclusively to the market town. In rural areas expansion in these types of activities after c.1740 was quite negligible. This is evidence of a comparatively easy access to Otley from most of the rest of the dale. A concentration of tertiary employments in a single centre in this fashion must itself be presumptive evidence of a relatively well integrated economy which has overcome local transport difficulties.

If, however, we look a little more closely at the occupational structure of tertiary employments, several significant changes are apparent. In the clothing and footwear trades, it is evident that the relative importance of tailors decreases everywhere while that of shoemakers and cloggers increases (Table 7). This raises two possibilities. First, that specialization in at least one branch of the clothing trade had by this time by-passed country districts in favour of larger urban centres; and secondly, that local shoemakers were producing goods for places outside the region.

Table 7. Distribution of shoemakers and tailors

Dates	Rural parish shoemkrs.	tailors	Rural part of Otley shoemkrs.	tailors	Otley town shoemkrs.	tailors
1721-40	55 (44%)	70 (56%)	44 (56%)	34 (44%)	29 (53%)	26 (47%)
1761-80	149 (61%)	94 (39%)				
1801-12	60 (85%)	11 (15%)	19 (83%)	4 (17%)	91 (80%)	23 (20%)

Note — (100 % = total occupational recordings in these two groups in each period).

In the case of the building trades, changes are less than might be expected. While it is true that generally there are a few more plumbers, glaziers and plasterers, the balance between carpenters and masons is almost unchanged (Table 8). In the town, masons always predominate over carpenters; and in the rural part of the town parish as well as in the rural parishes the reverse is always true. A result which might suggest that methods of housing construction during this period remained constant in each area.

Table 8. Distribution of carpenters and masons[59]

Dates	Rural parishes carpenters	masons	Rural part of Otley carpenters	masons	Otley town carpenters	masons
1721-40	56 (52%)	51 (48%)	30 (60%)	20 (40%)	11 (18%)	50 (82%)
1761-80	83 (61%)	53 (39%)				
1801-12	42 (57%)	32 (43%)	16 (62%)	10 (38%)	23 (29%)	56 (71%)

Note — (100% = total occupational recordings in these two groups in each period).

Changes encountered in the food and drinks trades are more complex (Table 9). On the one hand it is noticeable that the relative importance of butchers increases everywhere while that of brewers and other members of the drink trade decreases. The presence of millers on the other hand declines in the rural parishes but rises slightly elsewhere. This is further evidence of the fact that although meat output rose substantially in the latter part of the century, cereals by contrast remained relatively stagnant and in some instances actually declined (see above).

Table 9 Distribution of butchers, millers, brewers etc.

Dates	Rural parishes			Rural part of Otley		
	butchers	millers	brewers etc.	butchers	millers	brewers etc.
1721-40	9 (17%)	18 (35%)	25 (48%)	2 (5%)	15 (40%)	21 (55%)
1761-80	50 (43%)	22 (19%)	44 (38%)			
1801-12	24 (43%)	10 (18%)	22 (39%)	2 (15%)	7 (54%)	4 (31%)

Dates	butchers	millers	Otley town brewers etc.
1721-40	20 (35%)	5 (9%)	32 (56%)
1801-12	36 (51%)	11 (15%)	24 (34%)

Note — (100% = total occupational recordings in these three groups in each period).

An example of the tendency towards specialization, particularly in town areas, is seen in the decline in blacksmiths (Table 10). Whereas formerly blacksmiths would include among their crafts, nailmaking, stirrupmaking and bitmaking, in the period after c.1780 these occupations were fundamentally different, being largely concentrated in the market town.

Table 10. Distribution of blacksmiths, nailmakers, etc.

Dates	Rural parishes		Rural part of Otley		Otley town	
	b'smiths	nailmkrs. etc.	b'smiths	nailmkrs. etc.	b'smiths	nailmkrs. etc.
1721-40	71 (100%)		41 (98%)	1 (2%)	26 (87%)	4 (13%)
1761-80	72 (92%)	6 (8%)				
1801-12	23 (100%)		8 (100%)		3 (9%)	31 (91%)

Note — (100 % = total occupational recordings in these two groups in each period).

Predictably, most of the new trades that appeared in the later period are found only in the market town. These include perukemakers, bucklemakers, gunsmiths, pattenmakers, dyers, staymakers, bacon factors, wine and spirit merchants and silver platers. Exceptionally there are two new trades in rural areas, brass founders and machine makers (the machine was probably a Crompton mule).

Among the professions and specialized services (groups 9 and 10) there is a greater variety in Otley parish in this period than earlier. In addition to those already mentioned there is a banker, a banker's clerk, a bookkeeper, a hairdresser as distinct from a barber, a hardwareman and a stationer.

Evidence of improved methods of transport is seen generally in the increase in the number of carriers, the occasional waggoner and, in Otley, a turnpike man.

It is a truism that urbanization is a necessary adjunct to industrialism usually preceding it, but the relationship between the two aspects of the economy in mid-Wharfedale is perhaps worthy of further comment. For it would appear that in spite of industrialization, trades and services did not expand outside the town.

v) Population and the supply of labour

No amount of capital outlay, new invention or farming innovation could expand trade and industry on a scale such as we have described unless accompanied by some rise in the number of hands. How then did this happen? Where did the numbers come from? There are two possible sources, natural growth and immigration. We must look at both.

It has long been recognized that parish registers provide material for study of population trends in pre-census periods. Moreover, it is generally agreed that from the point of view of accuracy the exploitation of parish registers on the basis of family reconstitution cannot be excelled. This method, however, is a long and laborious business: a single register may take as long as two years to analyse. For this study which utilises material drawn from nine registers I have, therefore, used the faster though less accurate method of aggregative analysis.[60]

Neither method, however, can solve the problem of migration. Not infrequently aggregative material lends itself to two or more interpretations either one of which will fit the relevant data equally well. For example a simultaneous decline in the number of baptisms, burials and marriages could mean that changes in vital rates had occurred or alternatively that mass emigration had taken place. This problem can be solved to some extent where there are available for use two or more estimates of population size. Where this is so it is possible to calculate whether the natural increase achieved between the dates of any two estimates is more or less than the difference between the estimates. If it is more, there has been emigration and conversely, if it is less, immigration.

The four surveys available for use in mid-Wharfedale enumerate population in terms of either family or household units.[61] In order, therefore, to convert this data into terms consistent with that of parish registers I have assumed an average of 4.5 persons per family or household size.[62] It is unfortunate that no reliable survey exists between 1664 and 1743[63] since this means that one must use figures for a date considerably earlier than the period we are studying. Neither do many registers concerned give reliable information before 1672; no attempt has been made to interpolate figures in order to fill the gap caused by this lack of evidence. In the event, however, an omission of eight years from aggregative totals is not likely to prejudice results sufficiently to alter general conclusions. One register, that of Bolton Abbey, does not start until 1689 and in this instance estimates have been inserted into the material between 1672 and 1689 so that all aggregations can begin at the same time.[64]

The presence of nonconformity in the region gives little cause for concern in the period studied. Methodists, though numerous in several parishes after c.1750, continued to make use of Anglican sacraments until well into the nineteenth century. In Otley where Methodists in 1764 are reported as being 300 strong,[65] we find that John Wesley officiated at a wedding in the parish church there in 1788.[66] In fact most Methodists in this period were Wesleyan Methodists. Wesleyan chapels were erected at Otley in 1771, at Addingham in 1778 though not at Ilkley until 1869. Besides Methodists there is one other group of nonconformists that merits consideration here. Quakers, though relatively few in our period, had three licensed meeting houses all of which had burial grounds attached. Mr Hodgson, in his work on Yorkshire Quarterly Meeting records, reports fifty burials for Askwith (Weston parish) between 1671 and 1826 and twenty-nine for Rylstone between 1677 and 1785.[67] Other denominations which in this period continued to make use of Anglican sacraments are Independents (Otley, Addingham and Grassington), Anabaptists (Rylstone and Weston), Presbyterians (Rylstone) and Roman Catholics (Ilkley).[68] The following Table gives some indication of the influence of nonconformity in the region at various times in the seventeenth and eighteenth centuries.

Table 11.   Evidence of nonconformity in mid-Wharfedale

Source	Recusants	Other dissenters	Total of all parishioners	Meeting house
Compton, 1676 (communicants)	29	69	2630	no information
Herring, 1743 (families)	36 (+1 person)	20	1486	3 Quaker
Drummond, 1764 (families)	23 (+2 persons)	15 (+5 persons)	1813	3 Quaker 1 Methodist 1 Roman Catholic

Even if these figures have been somewhat depressed by failure of the incumbent to record the fact of nonconformity it is clear that no serious distortion is involved.

Table 12. Quantitative change of population in mid-Wharfedale

Parish	Population estimate 1664 (1)	Population estimate 1743 (2)	Difference 1664-1743 (2)-(1) (3)	Nat. inc. 1672-1743 (baps-burs) (4)	Inferred emigration 1672-1743 (4)-(3) (5)	% of natural increase lost (5)÷(4)×100 (6)
Rural parishes	4658	3987	−671	1280	1951	152
Otley parish	2520	2700	+180	1129	949	84

Parish	Population estimate 1743 (1)	Population estimate 1764 (2)	Difference 1743-1764 (2)-(1) (3)	Nat. inc. 1744-1764 (baps-burs) (4)	Inferred emigration 1744-1764 (4)-(3) (5)	% of natural increase lost (5)÷(4)×100 (6)
Rural parishes	3987	4928	+941	1229	288	23
Otley parish	2700	3231	+531	531	nil	nil

Parish	Population estimate 1764 (1)	Population estimate 1811 (2)	Difference 1764-1811 (2)-(1) (3)	Nat. inc. 1765-1811 (baps-burs) (4)	Inferred emigration 1765-1811 (4)-(3) (5)	% of natural increase lost (5)÷(4)×100 (6)
Rural parishes	4928	7251	+2323	3127	804	26
Otley parish	3231	5225	+1994	2220	226	10

Given that the sources used are sufficiently accurate to indicate general trends, two points in Wharfedale's demographic history are at once apparent (Table 12). The first is that the annual rate of natural increase achieved between 1744 and 1764 and again between 1765 and 1811 is substantially greater than between 1672 and 1743. This is due to variations in the birth and death rates and will be discussed at a later stage in the study. The second is that population growth was a consequence of natural increase alone. It owed nothing whatsoever to the fact of net in-migration. On the contrary, since in this period many persons left the valley permanently, the population was robbed of numbers that otherwise it might have had. In the rural parishes the number of emigrant persons between 1664 and 1743 was actually in excess of natural increase so that the population here is seen to have fallen (14%). In Otley emigration in this period is substantial; it reduced potential growth by 84%. In the middle period (1744-64), when emigration was at its lowest, potential growth in the rural parishes was depleted to the extent of 23% and in Otley, by sheer coincidence of numbers used, by nothing at all. In the final period (1765-1811) emigration was again on the increase. It reduced potential growth in the rural parishes by 26% and in Otley by 10%.

Even if these figures are somewhat inaccurate by reason of uncertainty about total numbers it is nevertheless abundantly clear that no immigration is involved. This means that populations in mid-Wharfedale grew either as a result of a decline in mortality or a rise in fertility. To determine which of these two factors was at any time the dominant force we must observe the trends in baptisms, burials and marriages in the registers. These events are plotted in the form of nine-year moving averages, using a semi-logarithmic scale, in Figures 2(a) and 2(b).

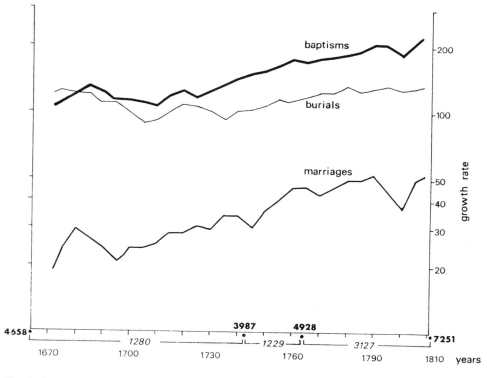

Fig 2 (a) — Eight rural parishes: nine year moving averages of baptisms, burials and marriages.

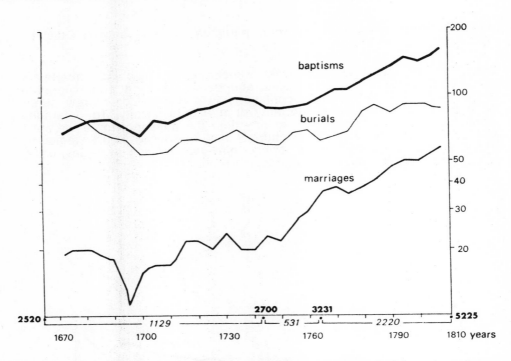

Fig. 2 (b) — Otley parish: nine moving averages of baptisms, burials and marriages.
Note: the darker figures along the horizontal axis in Figs. 2 (a) and 2(b) are population estimates and the lighter figures represent natural increase.

In many respects the two sets of graphs are similar and can, therefore, be considered together. Looking first of all at the trends in marriages, these fall steeply between 1680 and 1695 and again in the rural parishes between 1790 and 1800. This could be due to selective emigration of young people, possibly going into West Riding towns. Alternatively, and this applies most particularly to the later period, it could be the result of postponement of marriage consequent upon the country's economic upsets around the turn of the century. But in view of the estimates and especially since in each case burials and baptisms fall steeply too, it is likely that emigration is the correct interpretation. Conversely, when emigration is at its least, about the mid-century, marriages rise steeply suggesting a high concentration of young people, perhaps staying in the valley in order to take up work in the developing industries. As for the overall pattern in marriages, the level is comparatively rather low in the 1670s and again in the 1690s, a pattern which has been found in several other places[69], it seems to rise faster than the population is rising during most of the eighteenth century and this would, we suggest, be consistent with a falling average age of marriage at this period.

In the light of this marriage pattern the trend in baptisms is a little surprising. Baptisms seem to be rather low at the start of the century

200

but after about 1710 they rise steeply and in general keep pace with marriages until about 1750. The rate of growth of baptisms seems to have lagged behind that of marriages between 1750 and 1790 or in the case of Otley between 1750 and 1800, so that families in these periods would probably be slightly smaller than in the previous half century. It is of course possible that this result is illusory and that emigration is responsible for the smallness of the ratios between marriages and baptisms. If young married couples moved out of the parish before completing their families then the effect on the ratios would be exactly the same. However, in view of earlier trends and especially since excessive emigration occurred in rural parishes only, and there not until c.1790, this seems an unlikely explanation. In this context too the possibility of defective registration cannot be overlooked. Until the passing of Lord Hardwicke's Marriage Act in 1753 there was nothing to prevent any man and woman from establishing a union, recognized as valid in ecclesiastical law, simply by exchanging vows in front of witnesses. In these circumstances therefore it is possible to have a situation in which baptisms were added to the registers but where the corresponding marriage was not. In which case the difference in ratios which occurred could reflect the frequency with which intending marriage partners in the period up to 1753 chose to forego any church ceremony.[70]

The shape of the burial curve up to c.1750 is most revealing. Unless there is serious under-registration of burials the figures imply complete freedom from the heavy mortality which affected other parts of the North and Midlands during the 1720s and 1740s. In Warwickshire for example, out of a group of seventeen parishes for which information is available, six suffered severe mortality as a result of epidemics covering the years 1727-30; in the North and East Ridings out of twelve parishes, two suffered severe mortality in the same period, and in the West Riding out of thirty-one parishes only one suffered similarly. In mid-Wharfedale, however, none of the nine parishes with which this study is concerned suffered mortality of comparable intensity. A similar pattern is to be observed for the two periods 1740-42 and 1745-47. For the Warwickshire parishes the figure is six; for the North and East Riding parishes, three; for the West Riding parishes, three, and for parishes in mid-Wharfedale, one, that being Weston the smallest parish of any.[71] It is possible, therefore, that the Wharfedale parishes may have been exceptionally free of 'crisis' mortality, even by West Riding standards. Although the number of burials continued to rise in mid-Wharfedale during the rest of the century it did not rise quite so fast as the population so there seems to have been a steady improvement in mortality over the period. In general the trend in burials in mid-Wharfedale seems to be consistent with an earlier decline in mortality than is normally postulated for the eighteenth century.

If this interpretation is anywhere near the mark, it follows that the population started to grow in earnest from about 1740. From this time onwards, and in some instances a little earlier, emigration slowed down (in Otley it came to a complete halt) and mortality started to decline. These two factors together produced a favourable base from which an increase in population would follow, so that even if family sizes decreased over time, and even if in some parishes emigration began later to accelerate, the population, because in 'each generation new parents were more numerous than the last,' was bound to grow.

vi) Population, society and the economy

Some of the results obtained from this study of aggregate totals are easy to understand but others are difficult and admit of no simple explanation.

With regard to emigration, found to be high in every parish until at least 1740, this can be ascribed to the custom of inheritance practised within the region. From an examination of many local wills it would seem that in the later seventeenth and early eighteenth centuries a custom of impartible inheritance operated throughout the region. This would mean that unless younger sons were taken on as labourers, or became apprentices in trade, they were compelled to look for work in places outside the region, most probably in the industrial towns of the West Riding.[72] In these circumstances we should expect to find that emigration was at its lowest where there were alternatives to agriculture, as in Otley. Much of the emigration apparent in the later century stems from Linton, the most obvious reason for which is unemployment in the mines.

Several explanations for a decline in eighteenth century mortality have been advanced in recent years but none is found to have much bearing on the situation in mid-Wharfedale.

Inoculation against smallpox, held in some quarters to be an effective weapon in reducing mortality,[73] was not practised locally until c.1780. The earliest evidence for its use in this district comes in fact from Leeds, where in 1781 385 persons were inoculated, of whom four died. A second and more general inoculation appears to have been carried out in the town some time previous to 1788.[74] Besides inoculation there is, of course, the whole field of preventive and therapeutic measures said to have been employed by doctors during the eighteenth century. How far some of these measures were actually harmful, as McKeown and Brown would have us believe,[75] we have no means of knowing since there are no local records available. According to the registers, surgeons and apothecaries were no more numerous in the region at the end of the period than at the beginning.

Apart from medical possibilities, many arguments centre on general advantages due to improved environment and better standards of living. Among these attention has been drawn to the availability of more and better food, to 'raised standards of personal hygiene as a result of the freer use of soap and the coming of cheap cotton clothing',[76] and also to improved building techniques which, it is said, led to the construction of houses better able to keep out the damp and cold.

Since reliable information concerning eating habits in past centuries is so hard to find it is difficult to understand how it is that diet is so often quoted as being one of the more important factors leading to improved health. There is, however, one source, so far little used, which might shed some light on the matter and that is the probate inventory. Probate inventories for Wharfedale parishes are plentiful between c.1680 and c.1750. For our purposes, the contents of some 250 inventories covering the 1680s, 1730s and early 1750s were examined and analysed. Such information on food as these documents contain suggests that Wharfedale parishioners enjoyed 'a typical northern diet' which changed little over a long period of time. On the face of it the most important change was in salt meat. Bacon flitches, which in the seventeenth century are noted on nineteen occasions, disappear completely by the eighteenth century, and beef, which occurs in fifteen of the early documents is found in only three of the later ones. In this connection too it is noticeable that the number of kimlins (tubs used for the preservation of salt meat) are similarly reduced being thirty-four in the first series and seventeen in the later one. Whether this absence of salt meat from later inventories can be ascribed to changes in eating habits or changes in the fashion of inventories is difficult to decide. Certainly much meat or possibly fowl was eaten fresh (and this is before the big increase in animal populations). Articles such as jacks, spitts and dripping tins are found in inventories at all times and at all social levels. Predictably, butter and cheese make their appearance from time to time and from the frequency of pails, kitts and other wooden vessels we may suppose that milk consumption was relatively high. There is of course beer; this was brewed in farms and cottages in every period, being made from either barley or oats. Oats were also the principal cereal, often made into porridge and again part of everybody's diet. References to wheaten flour are extremely rare at any time. By the eighteenth century the only noticeable additions to this list of common food stuffs are potatoes, mentioned three times, cauliflower, inferred from the presence of one caulipot, and tea, again inferred from the very occasional mention of a teapot.

Clearly probate inventories cannot tell us all we should like to know about the eating habits of our ancestors. Perhaps their main contribution in this context lies in their ability to document the differences found to exist between one part of the country and another before transport development blurred such differences. For obviously until new roads and waterways made food transport economically possible, the variety of food in the households of ordinary people is likely to have remained substantially unaltered over several centuries. In these circumstances it seems likely that the probate inventories used here, since they cover a period before the general improvement in transport, accurately reflect the nature if not the quality of people's diet.

As for the freer use of soap, certainly national output figures doubled during the eighteenth century.[77] Whether this happened within the region of mid-Wharfedale itself, however, is open to question. Here, soap boiling was an occupation confined to the market town where it occurs in parish registers twice between 1721 and 1740 and once only between 1801 and

1812. But in any case an increase in soap output does not necessarily reflect an increase in its personal use; the product was much in demand from textile trades and increasingly so after c.1775.[78]

It is difficult to reconcile what we know about the cotton industry with, an improvement in health at least before the late eighteenth century. If it is true that cotton manufacture until c.1775 was in 'the hands of a few agriculturalists' then it seems extremely unlikely that the product was widespread before this. It is possible, of course, that hand-made goods from Lancashire spilled over into West Riding towns and villages before the arrival there of the industry itself. Again probate inventories might have helped, but a perusal of these documents yielded not one article of any kind described as cotton, though the description of 'linin' was frequently applied to bedding and tableware. Also 'course' and 'hempen' sheets were found from time to time.

This brings us to the question of how far better health was due to better housing. And here, the evidence is not entirely clear cut. On the one hand many houses in the valley were re-built. Some 127 dated doorheads have been located in the district belonging to the seventeenth and eighteenth centuries. These fall into two distinct periods each of which belongs to a different area. Fifty-two stones are dated to the period 1650 to 1690 and are found on houses in rural areas; and twenty stones dated to the period 1720 to 1760 are found on town houses.[79] The fifty-five remaining range over the selected period (1600-1800) nowhere in a concentrated block. But against this evidence, which suggests considerable improvement in housing construction (a second re-build being indicated in the market town), there is something to be put on the other side. First, there is the predominance of carpenters in parish registers which suggests that at least in rural areas timber framed houses were still in evidence at the end of the century. Also, glebe terriers,[80] which often describe parsonage houses, indicate considerable backwardness at a social level which might be expected to be somewhat above the norm. The glebe terrier for Weston, dated 1770, describes the parsonage there, despite the fact that it had recently been repaired, as 'part built of stone and part of lath and plaster, the North End slated and the South one part slate, the other thatch'. Neither is Weston an isolated example of the backwardness of the district. At Leathley, two miles downstream from Otley, the vicarage house is 'an old house built of timber laths and lime and the kitchen of rough hewn stone part slated and part thatched'.[81] Moreover, several vicarage houses in the district still had earthen floors in their downstairs rooms. It looks, then, as though improvements to houses in the period with which this study is concerned were far too limited to account for a radical change in public health.

Another and more speculative theory aimed at explaining a fall in mortality in the later eighteenth century is that of the compensatory cycle.[82] It is held that the fall in the death rate which occurred, reflects a degree of immunity in surviving populations following high mortality rates in the previous half century. In a general sense this theory may go some way towards explaining the situation in mid-Wharfedale. For while it is true that there was no epidemic crisis early in the century, the general level of mortality may have been high. In which case the fall in the death rate after c.1740 could reflect an increasing degree of immunity in the surviving population, not to epidemic disease recurring from time to time, but to endemic disease present at all times. In these circumstances the decline in mortality would be compensatory in a general sense rather than in the more usual sense of a compensatory swing.

It would seem, therefore, that until much more is known about eighteenth century mortality, particularly its relationship to economic and social conditions, any explanation of a decline in terms of either disease or resistance to disease should not be discarded.

It is tempting to suppose that the early decline in mortality was responsible for the early decline in fertility through what is known in Malthusian language as prudential restraint or the preventive check. To substantiate such an argument, however, would require the use of family reconstitution, a demographic technique more refined in its method than those used in the present study. We shall, therefore, concentrate on the period 1770-1800 in which there are many valid reasons for supposing that the fall in the birth rate is genuine.

Considered in the long term neither age at first marriage nor size of family necessarily reflect economic circumstance.[83] This, however, is not at all true when considering short periods. In every generation rising unemployment or cuts in wage rates might cause either postponement of marriage or 'family limitation' within it. In eighteenth century mid-Wharfedale economic upsets of this kind frequently occurred. Failure at the mines, dating in some places to around 1770, reduced many miners to pauperism (see below note 89). Many left the district, though a few of the more fortunate were able to transfer their activity to other working areas not so far away.[84] Also in the 1770s, when war with America drastically reduced cloth exports, wages in textile trades suddenly fell. According to one witness 'the decline in wages was 12½% for the relatively well-paid woolcomber, 16½% for the weavers, 20%-27% for the spinners near Halifax, and 30%-40% for those at a distance—often twenty to forty miles away from Halifax.' Commenting on these figures Professor Ashton says, 'cuts in pay of the order mentioned above must have meant destitution: it is little wonder that the poor-rates rose sharply in many towns of the West Riding and east Lancashire, as elsewhere.'[85] Even after the war, wages of textile workers showed little tendency towards improvement. James gives an example of a Bradford weaver who 'by extraordinary exertion' could earn ten shillings a week, but to accomplish this he had to work over-hours one whole night in the week. James concludes that weavers' wages were extremely low at this time.[86] But apart from textile trades, wages in the West Riding generally seem to have been unstable. According to Mrs Gilboy's charts,[87] day rates of craftsmen in Ripon declined from 2/- around 1770 to 1/6 around 1782, returning to their previous level in c.1786. Labourers' wages started to fall a little later and are quoted in the West Riding as being 1/6 a day in c.1775 dropping to 1/- in c.1782; there was then a partial recovery to 1/2 in c.1786. No wage rates for the West Riding are available for the

1790s. In Lancashire, however, wage rates of both labourers and crafts-men show sharp fluctuations early in the decade. From Lancashire too there is some information about real wages.[88] In the three years 1792, 1794 and 1795 real wages of labourers reached their lowest level for almost twenty years, the exception being 1783 when they were very low indeed. It is of course possible that wage rates in the West Riding did not follow these trends; but in view of the general depression of these years it seems likely that wage patterns, if not actual wage rates, were similar on both sides of the Pennines.

The notion that adverse economic conditions seriously affected popula-tions can be demonstrated in another way. Paupers, who until c.1770 make infrequent appearances in the registers, suddenly appear in great profusion.[89] In Addingham, where it will be remembered the economy was most geared to clothmaking, paupers are found in burial records on fifteen occasions between 1770 and 1780. In all registers except Adding-ham paupers are encountered 459 times between 1783 and 1794. There-after their appearance is as infrequent as it was earlier in the century. Generally, paupers are either labourers or persons employed in trade and industry; farmers seldom become paupers.

Given these mining closures, wage cuts and the increasing incidence of pauperism, it is probable that the smaller sized families noted in the later century are an accurate reflection of current economic trends.

vii) Summary

By putting together a variety of local records it has been suggested that the great change in mid-Wharfedale started about 1740. New capital came into the region to stimulate the development of industry at just the time when population was beginning to rise. It is not at all clear why either development should have occurred, though the check to emigration suggests that they were inter-related. Population, however, continued to expand beyond the point at which it could be assimilated at that phase of economic development. The increase, it has been suggested, was due more to a decline in mortality than to an increase in fertility. Its effect was to produce over-population in the valley. Not until the expansion of industry, induced by the infusion of more capital at the end of the century, was a balance restored and the way open for future prosperity.

This is the picture that emerges from the sources and methods we have used. It is possible that refinement of technique in the future may modify our conclusions, but it seems unlikely that they will require fundamental revision.

NOTES

1. I am indebted to Dr E. A. Wrigley and Dr R. S. Schofield who have assisted me with advice and criticism throughout the preparation of this paper. The responsibility for the final version, however, is mine alone. I would like to express my gratitude to Mrs Jean Le Patourel for reading the draft and helping me with the presentation. For help and encouragement during the initial stages of the article my thanks are due to Mr G. C. F. Forster. Finally I would like to thank the Open University Art department for preparing the maps and charts for printing.

2. The first official census of England and Wales was taken in 1801.

3. This is part of the work currently being undertaken by the SSRC Cambridge Group for the History of Population and Social Structure.

4. The relationship between market town and village in the Pennine area is extremely complex. Frequently villages are served not by market towns within the same valley but by one or more in an adjacent dale. And although Otley market (see below) served most settlements included in this study it did not serve those in the upper part of the region. The market town parish is included in the study in order to demonstrate the difference in function between town and village during this stage of their respective developments.

5. **The Victoria history of the County of York,** vol. III, 1913, pp. 531-9.

6. **ibid.**

7. With the exception of Otley all registers used in this study are in print, and details can be found in the index to parish registers at the Yorkshire Archaeological Society, Leeds. The Otley register is in manuscript form after 1753 and is held in several places. The baptism book for the chapelry of Burley (1774-1812) is kept in the church there. The baptism and burial books for the chapelry of Denton (baptisms 1766-1812, burials 1772-1812) are deposited at the Leeds City Archives, the register for the rest of the parish covering the period 1753-1812 is kept in the church at Otley. I would like to thank Canon Clayton and the Rev. D. B. Aldred for allowing me to work on the unpublished registers.

8. Borthwick Institute of Historical Research, University of York. Wharfedale inventories are located in the deaneries of Ainstie and Craven.

9. P.R.O. E179/210/393, membranes 25-35 mm. 71-80 and mm. 1-24. I am grateful to Mr David Purdy who kindly made these figures available to me.

10. P.R.O. E179/210/400, E179/210/417, E179/210/418. Although the return for 1664 generally is the most complete for this region there are a few villages for which the return for 1672 contains more details. In these few cases I have, therefore, taken figures from the later return.

11. Bodleian Library, Oxford, Tanner Ms. 150, ff 27 **et seq.** I owe this information to Mr G. C. F. Forster.

12. 'Archbishop Herring's visitation returns, 1743', 2 vols., ed. S. L. Ollard & P. C. Walker, **Yorks, Archaeolog. Soc. Record Ser.,** LXXI, 1928 & LXXII, 1929.

13. Borthwick Institute, York, Archbishop Drummond's visitation return, 1764.

14. **V.C.H., York,** vol. iii, pp. 531-9.

15. See J. D. Chambers, 'The Vale of Trent, 1670-1800: A regional study of economic change', **Economic History Review,** supplement no. 3, 1957, pp. 52-3.

16. For example no occupation could be expected where only the mother is named.

17. Probate inventories, see note 8 above.

18. Information derived from probate inventories but also from a survey of land use written in the register for Denton dated 1801: acreage, wheat 44, barley 8½, oats 195½, potatoes 8, peas 10¾, beans 20, turnip and rape 12½, rye 0.

19. The ratio of landless labourers to land occupiers in Wharfedale works out at about one to two or less (see below). This is considerably below that for the country as a whole which according to one estimate is put in the region of two landless to every land occupier. J. H. Clapham, 'The growth of an agrarian proletariat, 1688-1832', **Cambridge Historical Journal,** 1, 1923, pp. 93-5. Cited by J. D. Chambers and G. E. Mingay in **The agricultural revolution 1750-1880,** 1966, p. 103. A count of individual labourers made over a period of years suggests that approximately half are associated

with land, the remainder being connected with some kind of trade or industry. In Otley town, as might be expected labourers are found most often in trade and industry.

20. In putting forward these figures it should be remembered that much of the spinning, perhaps most of it before the process was mechanized, was done by women and children.

21. Horses were not only used in farming but were vital for the transport of food, wool and lead as well as for power in the mines. It is clear from the inventories that relatively poor people frequently counted a mare among their possessions.

22. Hearth tax assessments, see notes 9 and 10 above.

23. P. Laslett, **The world we have lost,** 1965, pp. 65, 254.

24. D. Avery, 'Male occupations in a rural Middlesex parish (1574-92)' **Local Population Studies,** No. 2, 1969, p. 31.

25. Occupation is not reliably recorded in the Otley register between 1740 and 1801.

26. If the figures inserted into the material for the parishes of Bolton Abbey, Addingham and Weston are omitted some trends shown in the tables are even more pronounced. In agriculture for example the number of references drops from 553 to 505. On the question of a decline in the number of agricultural workers during the first half of the eighteenth century see P. Deane & W. A. Cole, **British economic growth 1688-1959,** 1969, p. 75.

27. It will be noticed that the increase in the number of labourers is mainly confined to parishes whose population increases but where industry is not yet established, as in Rylstone.

28. See E. A. Wrigley, 'A simple model of London's importance in changing English society and economy 1650-1750', **Past and Present,** No. 37, 1967, pp. 56-8.

29. On the subject of late enclosure in the West Riding see, A. Raistrick, **West Riding of Yorkshire,** 1970, pp. 74-80.

30. For a discussion on land improvement through the application of lime see A. Raistrick, **Old Yorkshire dales,** 1967, pp. 73-89.

31. This is deduced from a study of many local documents including deeds, wills, rentals, court rolls, estate maps and Parliamentary Enclosure Acts both private and general.

32. Leeds Central Library, 28G2/60.

33. Leeds Central Library, 26G2/64.

34. J. F. Goodchild, 'West Riding turnpike trusts', **Wakefield Museum of Local History and Archives,** No. 1, 1961, 32G2/71.

35. **Ibid.,** 28G2/59, 43G3/51. West end not a turnpike road later.

36. C. Hadfield & G. Biddle, **The canals of north west England,** vol. 1, 1970, pp. 74-5.

37. A. Raistrick, **Lead mining in the mid-Pennines,** 1973. See also A. Raistrick, 'The lead mines of upper Wharfedale', **Yorkshire Bulletin of Economic and Social Research,** vol. 5, No. 1, 1953.

38. Raistrick, **Lead mining,** pp. 94, 98.

39. An important innovation was the 'whim' or horse gin. Introduced into Wharfedale around 1750 these contraptions replaced the hand operated jack-rollers. Raistrick, **Yorkshire dales,** pp. 106-8.

40. Raistrick, 'The Lead mines', p. 10.

41. No figures are available for this year. In 1821 the figure was 310 tons, in 1825 666 tons and in 1828 1,042 tons. Raistrick, **Lead mining,** p. 116.

42. H. Heaton, **The Yorkshire woollen and worsted industries,** 1965, p. 267. Woollen and worsted processes use raw wool of different staple lengths, which are respectively carded and combed. Also woollen cloth when woven is fulled, that is to say it is beaten under water until it produces a felt-like appearance; worsted cloth requires no such treatment.

43. In considering the figures for Otley parish it should be remembered that occupations tended to be under-recorded in the nineteenth century.

44. I am grateful to Miss Hilda Holmes for allowing me to look at her collection of local material among which are several essays by Mr W. Lemmon. See also **Ilkley Gazette** for 25th August, 1967, in which an article appears based on the writings of Mr Wade Hustwick, the Bradford historian. This article appears in the **Lister Magazine, 1964.**

45. **The English dialect dictionary,** ed. J. Wright, 1923.

46. J. James, **History of the worsted manufacture in England,** 1857 p. 292.

47. Heaton, p. 340.

48. **ibid.,** p. 338.

49. E. Baines, **Account of the woollen manufacture of England,** 1875, (1970 reprint) p. 43. See also **Ilkley Gazette,** as in n. 44.

50. James, pp. 327-8.

51. I owe this suggestion to Mr Roger Fieldhouse.

52. These figures and those in Tables 6, 7, 8, 9 and 10 are extracted from Tables 1(a), 1(b), 2(a), 2(b), 3(a), (3(a) for Table 6 only) and 3(b), omitting figures which are conjectural. There is, of course, no reason why the two sets of figures should necessarily agree.

53. Dean & Cole, p. 183.

54. For comparison with the Otley decadal figure for cotton (64) in Table 6, the decadal number of occupational recordings for linen was 8, for worsteds 35, for woollens 1, for clothiers etc. 4, for miscellaneous workers as, for example, threadmakers, framework knitters and unspecified weavers 16.

55. Mills were established at Grassington, Linton and for a short time at Rylstone, see Raistrick, **Yorkshire dales,** pp. 39, 175. Also a mill seems to have been established at Burley (Otley parish) about the same time, H. Speight, **Upper Wharfedale,** 1900, p. 139.

56. Yorkshire Archaeological Society Library, Leeds, MD/59/25.

57. **The parish register of Bolton Abbey, 1689-1812,** ed. A. P. Howes, 1895, p. 189.

58. References to linen workers in the two registers of Addingham and Bolton Abbey in the period 1801-12 amount to a total of 14. There is, however, no means of comparing this figure with that for an earlier period.

59. Any carpenter who on occasion is described as a joiner is omitted from these figures.

60. See D. E. C. Eversley, 'Exploitation of anglican parish registers by aggregative analysis', and E. A. Wrigley, 'Family reconstitution', in **An introduction to English historical demography,** ed. E. A. Wrigley, 1966, pp. 44-159.

61. These are, the hearth tax return for 1664, Herring's visitation 1743, Drummond's visitation 1764 and the national census for 1811, details in notes 9, 12, 13 and 14.

62. The choice of 4.5 as a multiplier is quite arbitrary, had the figure been fractionally different it would in no way alter the argument that follows.

63. The two following returns were considered unsuitable for this purpose for the reasons given. The hearth tax return for 1672 usually excludes exempt households; Compton's visitation dated 1676 includes communicants only.

64. The number of events in the Bolton Abbey register for 1689 accounts for 10% of the total of all recorded events in the rural parishes for that year. Accordingly figures for the period 1672-89 have been inflated to this extent.

65. Drummond's visitation as in note 13.

66. Otley parish register, but see Speight, p. 74. Canon Clayton of the Otley parish church and the Rev. W. S. Rose of the Otley Methodist Circuit assure me that Methodists continued to make use of Anglican sacraments long after Methodist churches were established in the valley.

67. H. R. Hodgson, **The Society of Friends in Bradford,** 1926, pp. 74, 81-2.

68. A search in the **Lists of non-parochial registers and records in the custody of the Registrar-General of births, deaths, and marriages,** 1859 revealed deposited registers for Addingham (Independent from 1829), Otley (Salem Chapel, Bridge Street, Independent from 1821), Grassington (Independent from 1811, Wesleyan from 1810), Rylstone (Society of Friends, 1661-1790). Other denominations mentioned in the text are found in parish registers.

69. E. A. Wrigley, 'Baptism/marriage Ratios in late 17th century England', **Local Population Studies,** No. 3, 1969, pp. 15-17.

70. It seems probable that the worst period of under-registration ended early in the eighteenth century. See E. A. Wrigley, 'Clandestine marriage in Tetbury in the late 17th century', **Local Population Studies,** No. 10, 1973, pp. 15-21.

71. These details were kindly given to me by Dr Schofield. Severe mortality in this context means twice the current 11-year moving average of burials.

72. For example, the population of Leeds in-township in 1664 was between 4,600 and 6,000; by 1754 it had reached 14,000, **Leeds and its region,** ed. M. W. Beresford & G. R J. Jones, 1967, pp. 144, 189. Since this was not achieved through a process of natural increase we may assume it occurred through immigration. See also Minoru Yasumoto, 'Urbanization and population in an English town', **Keio Economic Studies,** vol. x, No. 2, 1973, pp. 63-5.

73. P. E. Razzell, 'Population change in eighteenth-century England: a re-appraisal', in **Population in industrialization,** ed. M. Drake 1969, pp. 128-156. P. E. Razzell & L. Bradley, 'Smallpox: a difference of opinion', **Local Population Studies,** No. 10, 1973, pp. 65-70. P. E. Razzell, 'The smallpox controversy', **Local Population Studies,** No. 12, 1974, pp. 42-4.

74. C. Creighton, **A history of epidemics in Britain,** vol. 2, 1965, p. 510.

75. T. McKeown & R. G. Brown, 'Medical evidence related to English population changes in the eighteenth century', in **Population in industrialization** ed. M. Drake, 1969, pp. 40-72.

76. M. W. Flinn, **British population growth 1700-1850,** 1970, p. 40.

77. T. S. Ashton, **An economic history of England: The 18th century,** 1969, pp. 60, 247.

78. **Ibid.,** p. 60. For an indication of the amount of soap used in local textile trades see James, p. 369.

79. I am grateful to Miss Enid Sheldon for letting me have her information on Otley date stones.

80. Borthwick Institute, York, Ter. C. (Old Ainstie D). The year 1770 or in some instances 1764 is the first year in which glebe terriers in this collection describe the parsonage house.

81. The terrier goes on to say that the house has been supported at great expense yearly but has not been inhabited by rector or curate for thirty years.

82. G. S. L. Tucker, 'English pre-industrial population trends', **Economic History Review,** sec. series vol. XVI, No. 2, 1963.

83. E. A. Wrigley, 'Family limitation in pre-industrial England', **Economic History Review,** sec. series, vol. XIX, 1966.

84. Raistrick, **Lead mining,** p. 125.

85. T. S. Ashton, **Economic fluctuations in England 1700-1800,** 1959, p. 159.

86. James, pp. 329-30.

87. E. W. Gilboy, **Wages in eighteenth century England,** 1934, pp. 178-83.

88. B. R. Mitchell with the collaboration of P. Deane, **Abstract of British historical statistics,** 1971, p. 347.

89. Exceptionally in Linton paupers occur approximately 64 times between 1721-40, 31 times between 1741-60, but 152 times between 1782-94.

CONTRIBUTORS

Leslie Bradley
A mathematician by training and headmaster by profession, Leslie Bradley has spent much of his retirement in local demographic studies both on his own and as a member of the Matlock Population Study Group: a Nottingham University extra-mural class. For many years he was the Business Manager of **Local Population Studies.** He is the author of **A Glossary for Local Population Studies.**

W. J. Edwards
Dr Edwards is a lecturer in geography at the University College of Wales, Aberystwyth. His doctorate explored the relationship between marriage and mobility in the Welsh border county of Shropshire in the later eighteenth century.

M. Massey
Margaret Massey, an infants teacher before marriage has been a member of the Burton Joyce and Bulcote Local History Study Group since its beginning and has contributed to both the books they have published **Burton Joyce and Bulcote Studies in the History of Two Trentside Villages** and **Burton Joyce and Bulcote Remembered.**

Dennis R. Mills
Dr Mills is a staff tutor in the social sciences in the South Region of the Open University. He has published extensively on nineteenth century local history and is currently engaged on a major study of the socio-economic structure of Melbourn in the first half of the nineteenth century. He was Chairman of the Open University **Historical Sources and the Social Scientist** from 1978-1982. He is the author of **Landlord and Peasant in Nineteenth Century Britain.**

Stephen Jackson
Lecturer in the Department of Geography, City of Liverpool College of Higher Education.

Paul Laxton
Lecturer in the Department of Geography, University of Liverpool. He is engaged on a long term study of the demographic development of Liverpool c. 1750-1820.

Ronald W. Herlan
Dr Herlan has published several articles in British and American journals on poor relief in seventeenth century London and Bristol. He is an Associate Professor in the Department of History at the State University of New York College at Brockport.

Donald M. McCallum
While reading geography as a mature student at Fitzwilliam College Cambridge his B.A. Dissertation was based upon two Somerset parish registers. At present Donald McCallum is a lecturer at Leicester Polytechnic and his research is concerned with nineteenth century social and geographical mobility and propinquity of kin.

211

Ian G. Doolittle
Ian Doolittle is now a trainee solicitor. He was successively Open Scholar at Lincoln College, Senior Scholar at Merton College and Research Lecturer at Christ Church Oxford. His D.Phil. and subsequent research has been on legal, administrative and political history, but his earlier work concerned the demography of the Colchester area and he published articles on the plague in the **Transactions of the Essex Archaeological Society** (1972) and **Medical History** (1975).

Mary Cook
Introduced to historical demography through the Open University course 'Historical Data and the Social Sciences' Mary Cook spent eighteen months analysing Flintshire Parish Registers for the Cambridge Group for the History of Population and Social Structure. The unpublished results of the analyses are held at the Clwyd County Records Office Harwarden. At present she is teaching in Norfolk.

Roger Finlay
Dr Finlay is assistant librarian in The John Rylands University Library of Manchester. His publications include **Parish Registers: An introduction** (1981) and **Population and Metropolis: The Demography of London 1580-1650** (1981).

Roger Schofield
A founder editor of **Local Population Studies** Dr Schofield has been engaged in historical demographic studies for many years and has also published on the history of literacy. He is a co-director of the Cambridge Group for the History of Population and Social Structure and co-author (with Professor E. A. Wrigley) of **The Population History of England 1541-1871: a reconstruction.**

Derek Turner
Derek Turner was an editor of **Local Population Studies** for many years. He is a former school master and is currently one of Her Majesty's Inspectors of Schools.

Bessie Maltby
Bessie Maltby for forty four years a housewife was one of the earliest volunteers to work for the Cambridge Group for the History of Population and Social Structure and has undertaken aggregative analyses, literacy counts and the Family Reconstitution of the Parish of Easingwold.

Professor E. A. Wrigley
Co-founder and director of the Cambridge Group for the History of Population and Social Structure, Professor Wrigley is now Professor of Population Studies at the London School of Economics. The author of numerous books and articles on historical demography he has recently published (with Dr Roger Schofield) **The Population History of England 1541-1871: a reconstruction.**

Moira Long
After studying history at Somerville College, Oxford she carried out a local parish study for her B.Litt. and published several articles in **The Oxfordshire Victoria County History.** She is currently working in Yorkshire local history and as a part-time tutor for the Workers Educational Association.

W. J. Sheils
Bill Sheils is Senior Archivist at the Borthwick Institute University of York and has published a number of books and articles on aspects of English Reformation History. His interest in population history was aroused through teaching with the Open University (D301) and through contacts with biologists at York University.

Jeremy Millard
Jeremy Millard is a Staff Tutor in the Social Sciences for the Open University based in Nottingham and has made contributions to the course **Historical Data and the Social Scientist.** With a background and research interests in historical geography he has also published articles on adult distance education.

A. H. French et al
This report was prepared by the East London History Group (Population Study Group) Mr. A. H. French, Miss Marybel Moore, Miss Jocelyn Oatley, Mr. M. J. Power, Mrs. D. Summers, Mr. S. C. Tongue.

May F. Pickles
May Pickles is a practicing local historian and has worked extensively on Mid-Wharfedale particularly the seventeenth and eighteenth centuries. She has been an editor of **Local Population Studies** since 1979.